Siegel's
CONSTITUTIONAL
LAW

Essay and Multiple-Choice
Questions and Answers

By

BRIAN N. SIEGEL

J.D., Columbia Law School

Siegel's Series

Published by

Siegel's Constitutional Law, 3rd Edition (1997)
Emanuel Publishing Corp. • 1865 Palmer Avenue • Larchmont, NY 10538

Copyright © 1987, 1997 by

BRIAN N. SIEGEL

ISBN 1-56542-345-3

About the Author

Professor Brian N. Siegel received his *Juris Doctorate* from Columbia Law School, where he was designated a Harlan Fiske Stone Scholar for academic excellence. He is the author of *How to Succeed in Law School* and numerous works pertaining to preparation for the California Bar examination. Professor Siegel has taught as a member of the adjunct faculty at Pepperdine School of Law and Whittier College School of Law, as well as for the UCLA Extension Program.

Acknowledgment

The authors gratefully acknowledge the assistance of the California Committee of Bar Examiners which provided access to questions upon which many of the questions in this book are based.

Introduction

Although your grades are a significant factor in obtaining a summer internship or permanent position at a law firm, no formalized preparation for finals is offered at most law schools. Students, for the most part, are expected to fend for themselves in learning the exam-taking process. Ironically, law school exams ordinarily bear little correspondence to the teaching methods used by professors during the school year. They require you to spend most of your time briefing cases. Although many claim this is "great preparation" for issue-spotting on exams, it really isn't. Because you focus on one principle of law at a time, you don't get practice in relating one issue to another or in developing a picture of the entire course. When exams finally come, you're forced to make an abrupt 180-degree turn. Suddenly, you are asked to recognize, define and discuss a variety of issues buried within a single multi-issue fact pattern. In most schools, you are then asked to select among a number of possible answers, all of which look inviting but only one of which is right.

The comprehensive course outline you've created so diligently and with such pain, means little if you're unable to apply its contents on your final exams. There is a vast difference between reading opinions in which the legal principles are clearly stated, and applying those same principles to hypothetical exams and multiple choice questions.

The purpose of this book is to help you bridge the gap between memorizing a rule of law and **understanding how to use it** in the context of an exam. After an initial overview describing the exam writing process, you will be presented with a large number of hypotheticals which test your ability to write analytical essays and to pick the right answers to multiple-choice questions. **Do them — all of them!** Then review the suggested answers which follow. You'll find that the key to superior grades lies in applying your knowledge through questions and answers, not rote memory.

GOOD LUCK !

TABLE OF CONTENTS

PREPARING EFFECTIVELY FOR ESSAY EXAMINATIONS

ESSAY QUESTIONS

ESSAY ANSWERS

MULTIPLE CHOICE QUESTIONS

MULTIPLE CHOICE ANSWERS

TABLES AND INDEX

PREPARING EFFECTIVELY FOR ESSAY EXAMINATIONS[1]

To achieve superior scores on essay exams, a student must (i) learn and understand "blackletter" principles and rules of law for each subject, and (ii) analyze how those principles of law arise within a test fact pattern. One of the most common misconceptions about law school is that you must memorize each word on every page of your casebooks or outlines to do well on exams. The reality is that you can commit an entire casebook to memory and still do poorly on an exam. Reviewing hundreds of student answers has shown us that most students can recite the rules. The ones who do **best** on exams understand how problems (issues) stem from the rules which they have memorized and how to communicate their analysis of these issues to the grader. The following pages cover what you need to know to achieve superior scores on your law school essay exams.

THE "ERC" PROCESS

To study effectively for law school exams you must be able to **"ERC"** (**E**lementize, **R**ecognize, and **C**onceptualize) each legal principle listed in the table of contents of your casebooks and course outlines. **Elementizing** means reducing the legal theories and rules you learn, down to a concise, straightforward statement of their essential elements. Without a knowledge of these precise elements, it is not possible to anticipate all of the potential issues which can arise under them.

For example, if you are asked, "what is self-defense?", it is **not** sufficient to say, "self-defense is permitted when, if someone is about to hit you, you can prevent him from doing it." This layperson description would leave a grader wondering if you had actually attended law school. An accurate elementization of the self-defense principle would be something like this: "Where one reasonably believes she is in imminent danger of an offensive touching, she may assert whatever force she reasonably believes necessary under the circumstances to prevent the offensive touching from occurring." This formulation correctly shows that there are four separate, distinct elements which must be satisfied for this defense to be successfully asserted: (i) the actor must have a **reasonable belief** that (ii) the touching which he seeks to prevent is **offensive**, (iii) the offensive touching is **imminent**, and

---

1. To illustrate the principles of effective exam preparation, we have used examples from Torts and Constitutional Law. However, these principles apply to all subjects. One of the most difficult tasks faced by law students is learning how to apply principles from one area of the law to another. We leave it to you, the reader, to think of comparable examples for the subject-matter of this book.

(iv) the actor must use no greater force than she ***reasonably believes is necessary under the circumstances*** to prevent the offensive touching from occurring.

Recognizing means perceiving or anticipating which words within a legal principle are likely to be the source of issues, and how those issues are likely to arise within a hypothetical fact pattern. With respect to the self-defense concept, there are four ***potential*** issues. Did the actor reasonably believe that the person against whom the defense is being asserted was about to make an offensive contact upon her? Was the contact imminent? Would the contact have been offensive? Did the actor use only such force as she reasonably believed was necessary to prevent the imminent, offensive touching?

Conceptualizing means imagining situations in which each of the elements of a rule of law have given rise to factual issues. ***Unless a student can illustrate to herself an application of each element of a rule of law, she does not truly understand the legal principles behind the rule!*** In our opinion, the inability to conjure up hypothetical problems involving particular rules of law foretells a likelihood that issues involving those rules will be missed on an exam. It is therefore ***crucial*** to (i) ***recognize*** that issues result from the interaction of facts with the appropriate words defining a rule of law; and ii) develop the ability to ***conceptualize*** fact patterns involving each of the words contained in the rule

For example, an illustration of the "reasonable belief" portion of the self-defense principle in tort law might be the following:

One evening, A and B had an argument at a bar. A screamed at B, "I'm going to get a knife and stab you!" A then ran out of the bar. B, who was armed with a concealed pistol, left the bar about 15 minutes later. As B was walking home, he suddenly heard running footsteps coming up from behind him. B drew his pistol, turned and shot the person advancing toward him (who was only about ten feet away when the shooting occurred). When B walked over to his victim, he recognized that the person he had killed was not A (but was instead another individual who had simply decided to take an evening jog). There would certainly be an issue whether B had a reasonable belief that the person who was running behind him was A. In the subsequent wrongful-death action, the victim's estate would certainly contend that the earlier threat by A was not enough to give B a reasonable belief that the person running behind him was A. B could certainly contend in rebuttal that given the prior altercation at the bar, A's threat, the darkness, and the fact that the incident occurred within a time frame soon after A's threat, his belief that A was about to attack him was "reasonable."

An illustration of how use of the word "imminent" might generate an issue is the following:

X and Y had been feuding for some time. One afternoon, X suddenly attacked Y with a hunting knife. However, Y was able to wrest the knife away From X. At that point X retreated about four feet away from Y and screamed: "You were lucky this time, but next time I'll have a gun and you'll be finished." Y, having good reason to believe that X would subsequently carry out his threats (after all, X had just attempted to kill Y), immediately thrust the knife into X's chest, killing him. While Y certainly had a reasonable belief that X would attempt to kill him the *next time* the two met, Y would probably *not* be able to successfully assert the self-defense privilege since the "imminency" element was absent.

A fact pattern illustrating the actor's right to use only that force which is reasonably necessary under the circumstances might be following:

D rolled up a newspaper and was about to strike E on the shoulder with it. As D pulled back his arm for the purpose of delivering the blow, E drew a knife and plunged it into D's chest. While E had every reason to believe that D was about to deliver an offensive impact on him, E probably could not successfully assert the self-defense privilege because the force he utilized in response was greater than reasonably necessary under the circumstances to prevent the impact. E could simply have deflected D's prospective blow or punched D away. The use of a knife constituted a degree of force by E which was *not* reasonable, given the minor injury which he would have suffered from the newspaper's impact.

"Mental gymnastics" such as these must be played with every element of every rule you learn.

ISSUE-SPOTTING

One of the keys to doing well on an essay examination is issue-spotting. In fact, issue spotting is *the* most important skill you will learn in law school. If you recognize all of the legal issues, you can always find an applicable rule of law (if there is any) by researching the issues. However, if you fail to perceive an issue, you may very well misadvise your client about the likelihood of success or failure. It is important to remember that (1) an issue is a question to be decided by the judge or jury; and (2) a question is "in issue" when it can be disputed or argued about at trial. The bottom line is that if *you don't spot an issue, you can't discuss it*.

The key to issue-spotting is to approach a problem in the same way as an attorney would. Let's assume you're a lawyer and someone enters your office with a legal problem. He will recite the facts to you and give you any documents that may be pertinent. He will then want to know if he can sue (or be sued, if your client seeks to avoid liability). To answer your client's question intelligently, you will have to decide the following: (1) what theories can possibly be asserted by your client; (2) what defense or defenses can possibly be raised to these theories; (3) what issues may arise if these theories and defenses are asserted; (4) what arguments can each side make to persuade the factfinder to resolve the issue in his favor; and (5) finally, what will the *likely* outcome of each issue be. *All the issues which can possibly arise at trial should be discussed in your answer.*

HOW TO DISCUSS AN ISSUE

Keep in mind that *rules of law are the guides to issues* (i.e., an issue arises where there is a question whether the facts do, or do not, satisfy an element of a rule); a rule of law *cannot dispose of an issue* unless the rule can reasonably be *applied to the facts.*

A good way to learn how to discuss an issue is to start with the following mini-hypothetical and the two student responses which follow it.

Mini-Hypothetical

A and B were involved in making a movie which was being filmed at a bar. The script called for A to appear to throw a bottle (which was actually a rubber prop) at B. The fluorescent lighting at the bar had been altered, the subdued blue lights being replaced with rather bright white lights. The cameraperson had stationed herself just to the left of the swinging doors which served as the main entrance to the bar. As the scene was unfolding, C, a regular patron of the bar, unwittingly walked into it. The guard who was stationed immediately outside the bar, had momentarily left his post to visit the restroom. As C pushed the barroom doors inward, the left door panel knocked the camera to the ground with a resounding crash. The first (and only) thing which C saw, however, was A (who was about 5 feet from C) getting ready to throw the bottle at B, who was at the other end of the bar (about 15 feet from A). Without hesitation, C pushed A to the ground and punched him in the face. Plastic surgery was required to restore A's profile to its Hollywood-handsome pre-altercation form.

Discuss A's right against C.

Pertinent Principles of Law:

1. Under the rule defining the prevention-of-crime privilege, if one sees that someone is about to commit what she reasonably believes to be a felony or misdemeanor involving a breach of the peace, she may exercise whatever degree of force is reasonably necessary under the circumstances to prevent that person from committing the crime.

2. Under the defense-of-others privilege, where one reasonably believes that someone is about to cause an offensive contact upon a third party, she may use whatever force is reasonably necessary under the circumstances to prevent the contact. Some jurisdictions, however, limit this privilege to situations in which the actor and the third party are related.

First Student Answer

"Did C commit an assault and battery upon A?

"An assault occurs where the defendant intentionally causes the plaintiff to be reasonably in apprehension of an imminent, offensive touching. The facts state that C punched A to the ground. Thus, a battery would have occurred at this point. We are also told that C punched A in the face. It is reasonable to assume that A saw the punch being thrown at him, and therefore A felt in imminent danger of an offensive touching. Based upon the facts, C is liable for an assault and battery upon A.

"Were C's actions justifiable under the defense-of-others privilege?

"C could successfully assert the defense of others and prevention of crime privileges. When C opened the bar doors, A appeared to be throwing the bottle at B. Although the "bottle" was actually a prop, C had no way of knowing this fact. Also, it was necessary for C to punch A in the face to assure that A could not get back up, retrieve the bottle, and again throw it at B. While the plastic surgery required by A is unfortunate, C could not be successfully charged with assault and battery."

Second Student Answer

"Assault and Battery:

"C committed an assault (causing A to be reasonably in apprehension of an imminent, offensive contact) when A saw C's punch about to hit him, and battery (causing an offensive contact upon A) when he (i) C knocked A to the ground, and (ii) C punched A.

"Defense-of-Others/Prevention-of-Crime Defenses:

"C would undoubtedly assert the privileges of defense-of-others (where defendant reasonably believed the plaintiff was about to make an offensive contact upon a third party, he was entitled to use whatever force was reasonably necessary to prevent the contact); and prevention-of-crime defense (where one reasonably believes another is about to commit a felony or misdemeanor involving a breach of the peace, he may exercise whatever force is reasonably necessary to prevent that person from committing a crime).

"A could contend that C was not reasonable in believing that A was about to cause harm to B because the enhanced lighting at the bar and camera crash should have indicated to C, a regular customer, that a movie was being filmed. However, C could probably successfully contend in rebuttal that his belief was reasonable in light of the facts that (i) he had not seen the camera when he attacked A, and (ii) instantaneous action was required (he did not have time to notice the enhanced lighting around the bar).

"A might also contend that the justification was forfeited because the degree of force used by C was not reasonable, since C did not have to punch A in the face after A had already been pushed to the ground (i.e., the danger to B was no longer present). However, C could argue in rebuttal that it was necessary to knockout A (an individual with apparently violent propensities) while the opportunity existed, rather than risk a drawn-out scuffle in which A might prevail. The facts do not indicate how big A and C were; but assuming C was not significantly larger than A, C's contention will probably be successful. If, however, C was significantly larger than A, the punch may have been excessive (since C could presumably have simply held A down)."

Critique

Let's examine the First Student Answer first. It mistakenly phrases as an "issue" the assault and battery committed by C upon A. While the actions creating these torts must be mentioned in the facts to provide a foundation for a discussion of the applicable privileges, there was no need to discuss them further because they were not the issue the examiners were testing for.

The structure of the initial paragraph of First Student Answer is also incorrect. After an assault is defined in the first sentence, the second sentence abruptly describes the facts necessary to constitute the commission of a battery. The third sentence then sets forth the elements of a battery. The fourth sentence completes the discussion of assault by describing the facts pertaining to that tort. The two-sentence break between the original mention of assault and the facts which constitute this tort is confusing; the facts which call for the application of a rule should be mentioned *immediately* after the rule is stated.

A more serious error, however, occurs in the second paragraph of the First Student Answer. While there is an allusion to the correct principle of law (prevention of crime), the *rule is not defined*. As a consequence, the grader can only guess why the student thinks the facts set forth in the subsequent sentences are significant. A grader reading this answer could not be certain that the student recognized that the issues revolved around the *reasonable belief* and *necessary force* elements of the prevention-of-crime privilege. Superior exam-writing requires that the pertinent facts be *tied* directly and clearly to the operative rule.

The Second Student Answer is very much better than the First Answer. It disposes of C's assault and battery upon A in a few words (yet tells the grader that the writer knows these torts are present). More importantly, the grader can easily see the issues which would arise if the prevention-of crime-privilege were asserted (i.e., "whether C's belief that A was about to commit a crime against B was reasonable" and "whether C used unnecessary force in punching A after A had been knocked to the ground"). Finally, it also utilizes all the facts by indicating how each attorney would assert those facts which are most advantageous to her client.

STRUCTURING YOUR ANSWER

Graders will give high marks to a clearly-written, well-structured answer. Each issue you discuss should follow a specific and consistent structure which a grader can easily follow.

The Second Student Answer above basically utilizes the *I-R-A-A-O format* with respect to each issue. In this format, the *I* stands for the word *Issue*, the *R* for *Rule of law*, the initial *A* for the words *one side's Argument*, the second *A* for *the other party's rebuttal Argument*, and the *O* for your *Opinion as to how the issue would be resolved*. The *I-R-A-A-O* format emphasizes the importance of (1) discussing *both* sides of an issue, and (2) communicating to the grader that where an issue arises, an attorney can only advise her client as to the *probable* decision on that issue.

A somewhat different format for analyzing each issue is the *I-R-A-C format*. The *"I"* stands for *"Issue;"* the *"R"* for *"Rule of law;"* the *"A"* for *"Application of the facts to the rule of law;"* and the *"C"* for *"Conclusion."* I-R-A-C is a legitimate approach to the discussion of a particular issue, within the time constraints imposed by the question. The *I-R-A-C format* must be applied to each issue; it is not the solution to an entire exam answer. If there are six issues in a question, for example, you should offer six separate, independent *I-R-A-C* analyses.

We believe that the *I-R-A-A-O* approach is preferable to the *I-R-A-C* formula. However, either can be used to analyze and organize essay exam answers. Whatever format you choose, however, you should be consistent throughout the exam and remember the following rules:

First, *analyze all of the relevant facts.* Facts have significance in a particular case *only as they come under the applicable rules of law.* The facts presented must be analyzed and examined to see if they do or do not satisfy one element or another of the applicable rules, and the essential facts and rules must be stated and argued in your analysis.

Second, you must communicate to the grader the **precise rule of law** controlling the facts. In their eagerness to commence their arguments, students sometimes fail to state the applicable rule of law first. Remember, the "**R**" in either format stands for "Rule of Law." Defining the rule of law **before** an analysis of the facts is essential in order to allow the grader to follow your reasoning.

Third, it is important to treat **each side of an issue with equal detail.** If a hypothetical describes how an elderly man was killed when he ventured upon the land of a huge power company to obtain a better view of a nuclear reactor, your sympathies might understandably fall on the side of the old man. The grader will nevertheless expect you to see and make every possible argument for the other side. Don't permit your personal viewpoint to affect your answer! A good lawyer never does! When discussing an issue, always state the arguments for each side.

Finally, don't forget to **state your opinion or conclusion** on each issue. Keep in mind, however, that your opinion or conclusion is probably the **least** important part of an exam answer. Why? Because your professor knows that no attorney can tell her client exactly how a judge or jury will decide a particular issue. By definition, an issue is a legal dispute which can go either way. An attorney, therefore, can offer her client only her best opinion about the likelihood of victory or defeat on an issue. Since the decision on any issue lies with the judge or jury, no attorney can ever be absolutely certain of the resolution.

DISCUSS ALL POSSIBLE ISSUES

As we've noted, a student should draw **some** type of conclusion or opinion for each issue raised. Whatever your conclusion on a particular issue, it is essential to anticipate and discuss **all of the issues** which would arise if the question were actually tried in court.

Let's assume that a negligence hypothetical involves issues pertaining to duty, breach of duty, proximate causation and contributory negligence. If the defendant prevails on any one of these issues, he will avoid liability. Nevertheless, even if you feel strongly that the defendant owed no duty to the plaintiff, you **must** go on to discuss all of the other potential issues as well (breach of duty, proximate causation and contributory negligence). If you were to terminate your answer after a discussion of the duty problem only, you'd receive an inferior grade.

Why should you have to discuss every possible potential issue if you are relatively certain that the outcome of a particular issue would be dispositive of the entire case? Because at the commencement of litigation, neither party can be ***absolutely positive*** about which issues he will win at trial. We can state with confidence that every attorney with some degree of experience has won issues he thought he would lose, and has lost issues on which he thought victory was assured. Since one can never be absolutely certain how a factual issue will be resolved by the factfinder, a good attorney (and exam-writer) will consider ***all*** possible issues.

To understand the importance of discussing all of the potential issues, you should reflect on what you will do during the actual practice of law. If you represent the defendant, for example, it is your job to raise every possible defense. If there are five potential defenses, and your pleadings only rely on three of them (because you're sure you will win on all three), and the plaintiff is somehow successful on all three issues, your client may well sue you for malpractice. Your client's contention would be that you should be liable because if you had only raised the two additional issues, you might have prevailed on at least one of them, and therefore liability would have been avoided. It is an attorney's duty to raise ***all*** legitimate issues. A similar philosophy should be followed when taking essay exams.

What exactly do you say when you've resolved the initial issue in favor of the defendant, and discussion of any additional issues would seem to be moot? The answer is simple. You simply begin the discussion of the next potential issue with something like, "Assuming, however, the plaintiff prevailed on the foregoing issue, the next issue would be..." The grader will understand and appreciate what you have done.

The corollary to the importance of raising all potential issues is that you should avoid discussion of obvious non-issues. Raising non-issues is detrimental in three ways: first, you waste a lot of precious time; second, you usually receive absolutely no points for discussing a point which the grader deems extraneous; third, it suggests to the grader that you lack the ability to distinguish the significant from the irrelevant. The best guideline for avoiding the discussion of a non-issue is to ask yourself, "would I, as an attorney, feel comfortable about raising that particular issue or objection in front of a judge"?

DELINEATE THE TRANSITION FROM ONE ISSUE TO THE NEXT

It's a good idea to make it easy for the grader to see the issues which you've found. One way to accomplish this is to cover no more than one issue per paragraph. Another way is to underline each issue statement. Provided time permits, both techniques are recommended. The essay answers in this book contain numerous illustrations of these suggestions.

One frequent student error is to write a two-paragraph answer in which all of the arguments for one side are made in the initial paragraph, and all of the rebuttal arguments by the other side are made in the next paragraph. This is *a bad idea*. It obliges the grader to reconstruct the exam answer in his mind several times to determine whether all possible issues have been discussed by both sides. It will also cause you to state the same rule of law more than once. A better-organized answer presents a given argument by one side and follows that immediately in the same paragraph with the other side's rebuttal to that argument.

UNDERSTANDING THE "CALL" OF A QUESTION

The statements *at the end of* an essay question or of the fact pattern in a multiple-choice question is sometimes referred to as the "call" of the question. It usually asks you to do something specific like "discuss," "discuss the rights of the parties," "what are X's rights?" "advise X," "the best grounds on which to find the statute unconstitutional are:," "D can be convicted of:," "how should the estate be distributed," etc. The call of the question should be read carefully because it tells you exactly what you're expected to do. If a question asks, "what are X's rights against Y?" or "X is liable to Y for:..." you don't have to spend a lot time on Y's rights against Z. You will usually receive absolutely no credit for discussing facts that are not required by the question. On the other hand, if the call of an essay question is simply "discuss" or "discuss the rights of the parties" then *all* foreseeable issues must be covered by your answer.

Students are often led astray by an essay question's call. For example, if you are asked for "X's rights against Y" or to "advise X", you may think you may limit yourself to X's viewpoint with respect to the issues. This is *not correct*! You cannot resolve one party's rights against another party without considering the issues which might arise (and the arguments which the other side would assert) if litigation occurred. In short, although the call of the question may appear to focus on one of the parties to the litigation, a superior answer will cover all the issues and arguments which that person might *encounter* (not just the arguments she would *make*) in attempting to pursue her rights against the other side.

THE IMPORTANCE OF ANALYZING
THE QUESTION CAREFULLY BEFORE WRITING

The overriding *time pressure* of an essay exam is probably a major reason why many students fail to analyze a question carefully before writing. Five minutes into the allocated time for a particular question, you may notice that the person next to you is writing furiously. This thought then flashes through your mind, "Oh, my goodness, he's putting down more words on the paper than I am, and therefore he's bound to get a better grade." It can be stated *unequivocally* that there is no necessary correlation between the number of words on your exam paper and the grade you'll receive. Students who begin their answer after only five minutes of analysis have probably seen only the most obvious issues, and missed many, if not most, of the subtle ones. They are also likely to be less well organized.

Opinions differ as to how much time you should spend analyzing and outlining a question before you actually write the answer. We believe that you should spend at least 12-18 minutes analyzing, organizing, and outlining a one-hour question before writing your answer. This will usually provide sufficient time to analyze and organize the question thoroughly *and* enough time to write a relatively complete answer. Remember that each word of the question must be scrutinized to determine if it (i) suggests an issue under the operative rules of law, or (ii) can be used in making an argument for the resolution of an issue. Since you can't receive points for an issue you don't spot, it is usually wise to read a question *twice* before starting your outline.

WHEN TO MAKE AN ASSUMPTION

The instructions on an exam may tell you to *"assume"* facts which are necessary to the answer. Even where these instructions are *not* specifically given, you may be obliged to make certain assumptions with respect to missing facts in order to write a thorough answer. Assumptions should be made when you, as the attorney for one of the parties described in the question, would be obliged to solicit additional information from your client. On the other hand, assumptions should *never be used to change or alter the question.* Don't ever write something like "if the facts in the question were ..., instead of ..., then ... would result." If you do this, you are wasting time on facts which are extraneous to the problem before you. Professors want you to deal with *their* fact patterns, not your own.

Students sometimes try to "write around" information they think is missing. They assume that their professor has failed to include every piece of data necessary for a thorough answer. This is generally *wrong.* The professor may have omitted some facts deliberately to see if the student *can figure out what to do* under the circumstances. In some instances, the professor may have omitted them inadvertently (even law professors are sometimes human).

The way to deal with the omission of essential information is to describe (i) what fact (or facts) are missing, and (ii) why that information is important. As an example, go back to the "movie shoot" hypothetical we discussed above. In that fact pattern, there was no mention of the relative strength of A and C. This fact could be extremely important. If C weighed 240 pounds and was built like a professional football linebacker, while A tipped the scales at a mere 160 pounds, punching A in the face after he had been pushed to the ground would probably constitute unnecessary force (thereby causing C to forfeit the prevention-of-crime privilege). If the physiques of the parties were reversed, however, C's punch to A's face would probably constitute reasonable behavior. Under the facts, C had to deal the **"knockout"** blow while the opportunity presented itself. The last sentences of the Second Student Answer above show that the student understood these subtleties and correctly stated the essential missing facts and assumptions.

Assumptions should be made in a manner which keeps the other issues open (i.e., necessitates discussion of all other possible issues). Don't assume facts which would virtually dispose of the entire hypothetical in a few sentences. For example, suppose that A called B a "convicted felon" (a statement which is inherently defamatory, *i.e.*, a defamatory statement is one which tends to subject the plaintiff to hatred, contempt or ridicule). If A's statement is true, he has a complete defense to B's action for defamation. If the facts don't tell whether A's statement was true or not, it would **not** be wise to write something like, "We'll assume that A's statement about B is accurate, and therefore B cannot successfully sue A for defamation." So facile an approach would rarely be appreciated by the grader. The proper way to handle this situation would be to state, "if we assume that A's statement about B is not correct, A can not raise the defense of truth." You've communicated to the grader that you recognize the need to assume an essential fact and that you've assumed it in such a way as to enable you to proceed to discuss all other potential issues.

CASE NAMES

A law student is ordinarily **not** expected to recall case names on an exam. The professor knows that you have read several hundred cases for each course, and that you would have to be a memory expert to have all of the names at your fingertips. If you confront a fact pattern which seems similar to a case which you have reviewed (but you cannot recall the name of it), just write something like, "One case held that ..." or "It has been held that ..." In this manner, you have informed the grader that you are relying on a case which contained a fact pattern similar to the question at issue.

The only exception to this rule is in the case of a landmark decision. Landmark opinions are usually those which change or alter established law.[2] These cases are usually easy to identify, because you will probably have spent an entire class period discussing each of them. *Palsgraf v. Long Island Rail Road* is a prime example of a landmark case in Torts. In these special cases, you may be expected to remember the case by name, as well the proposition of law which it stands for. However, this represents a very limited exception to the general rule which counsels against wasting precious time trying to memorize case names.

HOW TO HANDLE TIME PRESSURES

What do you do when there are five minutes left in the exam and you have only written down two-thirds of your answer? One thing **not** to do is write something like, "No time left!" or "Not enough time!" This gets you nothing but the satisfaction of knowing you have communicated your personal frustrations to the grader. Another thing **not** to do is insert the outline you may have made on scrap paper into the exam booklet. Professors rarely will look at these items.

First of all, it is not necessarily a bad thing to be pressed for time. The person who finishes five minutes early has very possibly missed some important issues. The more proficient you become in knowing what is expected of you on an exam, the greater the difficulty you may experience in staying within the time limits. Second, remember that (at least to some extent) you're graded against your classmates' answers and they're under exactly the same time pressure as you. In short, don't panic if you can't write the "perfect" answer in the allotted time. Nobody does!

The best hedge against misuse of time is to **review as many old exams as possible**. These exercises will give you a familiarity with the process of organizing and writing an exam answer, which, in turn, should result in an enhanced ability to stay within the time boundaries. If you nevertheless find that you have about 15 minutes of writing to do and five minutes to do it in, write a paragraph which summarizes the remaining issues or arguments you would discuss if time permitted. As long as you've indicated that you're aware of the remaining legal issues, you'll probably receive some credit for them. Your analytical and argumentative skills will already be apparent to the grader by virtue of the issues that you have previously discussed.

---

2. The only subject to which this does not apply is Constitutional Law, since here virtually every case you study satisfies this definition. Students studying Constitutional Law should try to associate case names with holdings and reproduce them in their exam answers.

WRITE LEGIBLY

Make sure your answer is legible. Students should **not** assume that their professors will be willing to take their papers to the local pharmacist to have them deciphered. Remember, your professor may have 75-150 separate exam answers to grade. If your answer is difficult to read, you will rarely be given the benefit of the doubt. On the other hand, a legible, well-organized paper creates a very positive mental impact upon the grader.

Many schools allow students to type their exams. If you're an adequate typist, you may want to seriously consider typing. Typing has two major advantages. First, it should help assure that your words will be readable (unless, of course, there are numerous typos). Second, it should enable you to put a lot more words onto the paper than if your answer had been handwritten. Most professors prefer a typed answer to a written one.

There are, however, a few disadvantages to typing. For one thing, all the typists are usually in a single room. If the clatter of other typewriters will make it difficult for you to concentrate, typing is probably **not** wise. To offset this problem, some students wear earplugs during the exam. Secondly, typing sometimes makes it difficult to change or add to an earlier portion of your answer. You may have to withdraw your paper from the carriage and insert another. Try typing out a few practice exams before you decide to type your exam. If you do type, be sure to leave at least one blank line between typewritten lines, so that handwritten changes and insertions in your answers can be made easily.

If you decide against typing, your answer will probably be written in a "bluebook" (a booklet of plain, lined, white paper which has a light blue cover and back). It is usually a good idea to write only on the odd numbered pages (i.e., 1, 3, 5, etc.). You may also want to leave a blank line between each written line. Doing these things will usually make the answer easier to read. If you discover that you have left out a word or phrase, you can insert it into the proper place by means of a caret sign ("^"). If you feel that you've omitted an entire issue, you can write it on the facing blank page. A symbol reference can be used to indicate where the additional portion of the answer should be inserted. While it's not ideal to have your answer take on the appearance of a road map, a symbol reference to an adjoining page is much better than trying to squeeze six lines into one, and will help the grader to discover where the same symbol appears in another part of your answer.

THE IMPORTANCE OF REVIEWING PRIOR EXAMS

As we've mentioned, it is **_extremely important to review old exams._** The transition from blackletter law to essay exam can be a difficult experience if the process has not been practiced. Although this book provides a large number of essay and multiple-choice questions, ***don't stop here***! Most law schools have recent tests on file in the library, by course. We strongly suggest that you make a copy of every old exam you can obtain (especially those given by your professors) at the beginning of each semester. The demand for these documents usually increases dramatically as "finals time" draws closer.

The exams for each course should be scrutinized ***throughout the semester***. They should be reviewed as you complete each chapter in your casebook. Generally, the order of exam questions follows the sequence of the materials in your casebook. Thus, the first question on a law school test may involve the initial three chapters of the casebook; the second question may pertain to the fourth and fifth chapters, etc. In any event, ***don't wait*** until the semester is nearly over to begin reviewing old exams.

Keep in mind that no one is born with the ability to analyze questions and write superior answers to law school exams. Like any skill, it is developed and perfected only through application. If you don't take the time to analyze numerous examinations from prior years, this evolutionary process just won't occur. Don't just *think about* the answers to past exam questions; take the time to ***write the answers down***. It's also wise to look back at an answer a day or two after you've written it. You will invariably see (i) ways in which the organization could have been improved, and (ii) arguments you missed.

As you practice spotting issues on past exams, you will see how rules of law become the sources of issues on finals. As we've already noted, if you don't ***understand*** how rules of law translate into issues, you won't be able to achieve superior grades on your exams. Reviewing exams from prior years should also reveal that certain issues tend to be lumped together in the same question. For instance, where a fact pattern involves a false statement made by one person about another, three potential theories of liability are often present — defamation, invasion of privacy (false, public light) and intentional infliction of severe emotional distress. You will need to see if any or all of these apply to the facts.

Finally, one of the best means of evaluating if you understand a course (or a particular area within a subject) is to attempt to create a hypothetical exam for that topic. Your exam should contain as many issues as possible. If you can write an issue-packed exam, you probably know that particular area of law. If you can't, then you probably haven't yet acquired an adequate understanding of how the principles of law in that subject can spawn issues.

AS ALWAYS, A CAVEAT

The suggestions and advice offered in this book represent the product of many years of experience in the field of legal education. We are confident that the techniques and concepts described in these pages will help you prepare for, and succeed, at your exams. Nevertheless, particular professors sometimes have a preference for exam-writing techniques which are not stressed in this work. Some instructors expect at least a nominal reference to the ***prima facie*** elements of all pertinent legal theories (even though one or more of those principles is ***not*** placed into issue). Other professors want their students to emphasize public policy considerations in the arguments they make on a particular issue. Because this book is intended for nationwide consumption, these individualized preferences have ***not*** been stressed. The best way to find out whether your professor has a penchant for a particular writing approach is to ask her to provide you with a model answer to a previous exam. If an item is not available, speak to upperclass students who received a superior grade in that professor's class.

One final point. While the rules of law stated in the answers to the questions in this book have been drawn from commonly used sources (i.e., casebooks, hornbooks, etc.), it is still conceivable that they may be slightly at odds with those taught by your professor. In instances where a conflict exists between our formulation of a legal principle and the one which is taught by your professor, ***follow the latter!*** Since your grades are determined by your professors, their views should always supersede the views contained in this book.

ESSAY EXAM
QUESTIONS AND ANSWERS

ESSAY QUESTIONS

QUESTION 1

City, a municipality of State X, has a permit ordinance that prohibits making speeches in the City owned park without first obtaining a permit from City's police chief. The ordinance authorizes the police chief to establish permit application procedures, and to grant or deny permits based upon the chief's "overall assessment of the good of the community." The ordinance also provides that denial of a permit may be appealed to the city council.

On Tuesday, Tom applied to Dan, City's police chief, for a permit to speak in the city park the following Saturday. Tom gave Dan his name and local address, but Dan denied Tom's application for a permit because Tom refused Dan's request for a summary of what he intended to say in his speech. When Tom told Dan that he intended to make his speech anyway, Dan immediately gave Tom's name and address to the city attorney.

The city attorney did nothing about the matter until Friday, when, without notice to Tom, he made application on behalf of City to a State X court of general jurisdiction for a temporary restraining order preventing Tom from speaking in the city park without a permit. The State X court issued an ex-parte temporary restraining order and an order to show cause, answerable in five days, directed to Tom. The orders were served on Tom in the city park on Saturday as he was about to speak. Despite the temporary restraining order, Tom spoke to about twenty mildly interested persons who were then in the park for various other reasons.

The essence of Tom's speech was that the federal government, "aided and abetted" by City's government, was "leading America to destruction," and that "those who survive will eventually have to fight in the streets of City to regain their liberties." Tom urged the audience to "stockpile weapons" and to "start thinking about forming guerilla units to take back freedom from the government."

Tom was arrested and charged in the State X court which had issued the temporary restraining order with (a) speaking in the city park without a permit, a misdemeanor; (b) contempt of court for violating the temporary restraining order; and (c) violation of the State X criminal advocacy statute prohibiting "advocating insurrection against local, state, or the federal governments," a felony.

Five years ago, the State X Supreme Court construed the criminal advocacy statute as applying only to advocacy that is not protected by the United States Constitution.

A week after Tom's speech, in a case unrelated to the charges against Tom, the State X Supreme Court construed City's permit ordinance as authorizing the City police chief to consider "only the time, place, and manner of the proposed speech, and not its content" in passing upon permit applications.

What rights guaranteed by the United States Constitution should Tom assert in defense to the charges brought against him, and how should the court rule? Discuss.

QUESTION 2

Paul was born in the United States. After voluntarily serving in the Canadian Army for several years, he returned to his home state and became employed as a meter reader by the Water Department of City, a municipal agency. In the performance of his job, Paul enters private residences and commercial buildings in City to read water meters.

No regulations governing the dress or appearance of Water Department employees existed when Paul was hired. Subsequently, City enacted a dress code ordinance which stated: "All City Water Department employees shall wear a uniform supplied by City when engaged in their employment, and no such employee may wear a beard while so engaged." Paul wore a beard when first employed. Although requested by the head of the Water Department to shave off his beard and wear the uniform provided, Paul refused to do either.

Shortly thereafter, a city election occurred. The incumbent Water Department head was replaced. Paul was a registered voter in the same political party as the unsuccessful incumbent, but took no active part in the election campaign. Immediately upon taking office, the newly elected Water Department head, who was a member of a different political party, notified Paul that he was terminated, because he was "registered in the wrong political party and for several other reasons."

After unsuccessfully appealing his dismissal in administrative proceedings with the Water Department and City, Paul filed suit in state court against City, asking for a judgment ordering that his discharge be declared void and that he be reinstated in his job. City's answer alleged that the termination of Paul's employment was proper because (1) Paul had violated City's dress code ordinances for Water Department employees; and (2) a state statute requires that "all state and municipal employees must be citizens of the United States", and a federal statute provides that the United States citizenship of any person who voluntarily serves in the armed forces of a foreign country is deemed surrendered.

What issues under the U.S. Constitution are raised by Paul's suit against City and by City's defenses, and how should each of them be decided? Discuss.

QUESTION 3

The Mayo Christian Church (Church) is located in the city of Mayo, State X. The governing body of Church established the Lawyers Society (Society) as a State X non-profit corporation, to increase the participation of Church in Mayo's community problems. Society is composed exclusively of Church members who are lawyers licensed to practice in State X, all of whom have agreed to work for Society without compensation. Society offers free legal services to residents of Mayo who are "victims of racial or religious discrimination." Society is financially supported by both Church funds and by a grant of funds from Agency, which administers a State X program providing public funds to legal aid organizations.

Soon after its establishment, Society "targeted" certain apparent instances of discrimination in Mayo as appropriate objectives for its services. Society members have directly approached Mayo residents who appeared to be victims of discrimination, explained their legal rights, and then offered them free legal assistance in commencing litigation aimed at redressing the apparent discrimination.

However, Society has begun to have legal problems of its own:

a. An organization called "Mayo Taxpayers for Separation of Church and State" (Taxpayers), consisting of State X taxpayers who are residents of Mayo, has brought an action in federal court in State X against Church, Society and Agency. The complaint challenges the propriety of the use of public funds by a church- sponsored organization and seeks a judgment prohibiting Agency from granting funds to Society.

b. Jay, a lawyer admitted to practice in State X, volunteered to join and work for Society without compensation. He was rejected because he was not a Church member. Jay has brought an action in federal court in State X against Church, Society, and Agency, seeking a judgment requiring Society to admit him to membership. He alleges that his exclusion from membership in Society as an organization supported by public funds constitutes unlawful discrimination in violation of the United States Constitution.

c. The State X Bar Association (Bar), which is responsible for the enforcement of State X law regulating the practice of law, has charged that Society's solicitation practices violate the State X attorneys' professional disciplinary code, which prohibits "direct solicitation" of clients and legal work by lawyers. Bar has instituted an action in State X court against Society and its members, seeking an injunction prohibiting any further "solicitation" activity by Society members.

What issues arising under the United States Constitution are involved in these three cases, and how should each issue be decided? Discuss.

QUESTION 4

Five years ago, City adopted a municipal ordinance prohibiting the placing of "commercial" signs on rooftops within city limits. The stated purpose of the ordinance was "...improving the quality of life within City by emphasizing and protecting aesthetic values." The ordinance also provided that all signs in place on the date of its adoption in violation of its terms, must be removed within five years.

Three years ago, Rugged Cross Church (Church), with its church building situated within City's limits, placed a 20-foot blue neon-lighted sign in the shape of a cross on its church roof, with the message "Join and Support Our Church" in white neon lights inside the blue neon borders of the cross.

After the Church sign was in place, various citizens of City urged that the sign ordinance be amended to include all rooftop signs in City. Other citizens complained to City officials that Church's sign, in particular, was "an eyesore."

Effective two months ago, City amended its sign ordinance by deleting the word "commercial". City then notified Church that its rooftop sign would have to be removed within five years.

Church has brought suit against City in a state trial court of proper jurisdiction, claiming that the amended City sign ordinance is invalid under the United States Constitution, both **(1)** by its terms and general application, and **(2)** as City seeks to apply it to Church.

How should the court rule on each of Church's claims? Discuss.

QUESTION 5

SADS, a national college student organization, decided to conduct a campaign protesting government defense spending. SADS members at a university in City planned to distribute campaign literature within City to motorists stopped at major intersections and to patrons at a shopping center owned by Owen.

For years, community service organizations have distributed literature in City to motorists stopped at intersections. There were several accidents causing serious injuries to persons engaged in such practices. For that reason, the City council had been considering for several months a proposed ordinance that would prohibit pedestrians from approaching motorists stopped at intersections within City. Immediately after the SADS distribution plan was publicly announced, the proposed ordinance was passed out of committee and unanimously enacted by the City council. SADS members have not yet attempted to deliver literature to motorists.

City has a municipal ordinance making it a misdemeanor to trespass on private property, including shopping centers. Owen's shopping center is posted with signs stating that no tenant or visitor may distribute on the premises literature not directly related to the commercial purposes of businesses in the center, and that violators are subject to removal by the center's security guards and prosecution under the anti-trespass ordinance.

SADS has filed two actions in the appropriate federal district court. One action is against City, seeking a declaratory judgment that the recently enacted ordinance violates the rights of SADS members under the United States Constitution. The other action is against Owen, seeking a declaratory judgment that any action by Owen or his employees to stop SADS members from distributing campaign literature at his shopping center would violate the rights of free speech of SADS members under the United States Constitution.

No SADS campaign literature has yet been distributed at Owen's shopping center, and no threat has been made to remove SADS members from the center or to have them prosecuted under the anti-trespassing ordinance if they attempt to distribute their literature on the center premises.

City has filed its answer to the complaint in the first action and that case is set for trial.

Owen has moved to dismiss the second action on the grounds that (a) the action is not ripe, and (b) the complaint fails to state a claim for relief because SADS members have no constitutionally protected right to distribute the campaign literature on private property.

1. What arguments should SADS make in support of its claim against City, and how should the court decide that claim? Discuss.

2. How should the court rule on Owen's motions? Discuss.

QUESTION 6

Acme Brothers (Acme) operates a men's clothing store in a shopping center it owns in City, State X. Acme embarked on an advertising campaign that has been criticized by a feminist coalition as sexist. In its store windows, Acme has life-size posters of a young woman wearing a bikini. The posters' captions portray her as saying things such as, "I like to be treated rough by a man in an Acme suit." The coalition concedes that the posters are not legally obscene.

Members of the feminist coalition in City attempted to picket on the privately owned sidewalk in front of the Acme store to protest these posters. They were told by Acme's private security guards that the shopping center was private property and that the pickets were trespassing. Acme's security guards then physically removed all pickets from the shopping center premises.

The Acme store is part of a sixteen store chain of Acme outlets located in four states. Acme's advertising campaigns are planned in the home office in another state, and are sent to stores such as that in City. The stores have no choice under company policy but to use the advertising.

After removal of the pickets, the city council of City adopted an ordinance that provides in part:

"It shall be unlawful to display for commercial purposes any picture, or to use any other advertising material, that portrays any individual in a demeaning or sexist fashion."

Violation of this section of the ordinance was made a misdemeanor punishable by a fine of up to $500.

The ordinance also provides:

"The right to picket peacefully, with due regard to pedestrian and vehicular traffic and the rights of all other citizens, shall remain inviolate. Such right shall extend to shopping centers and other areas, where the title to sidewalks is privately owned but open to the public for access to retail sales outlets."

Since the adoption of the City ordinance, pickets have appeared in front of the Acme store during business hours. When asked to leave by the Acme store manager, the pickets have shown him a copy of the City ordinance, and have threatened to sue Acme if its security guards attempt to remove them physically.

City has filed a criminal complaint in the appropriate State X court charging that Acme's continuing display of the posters violates the "sexist advertising" section of the ordinance. Acme has also filed suit in a State X court against City, seeking a declaratory judgment that the picketing section of the ordinance is unconstitutional.

What issues arising under the United States Constitution are raised by **(1)** City's prosecution of Acme under the ordinance, and **(2)** Acme's action against City for declaratory relief, and how should each be decided? Discuss.

QUESTION 7

A statute in State A levies an "obscene publication tax" of one dollar a copy "on the publication of each copy of any lewd, lascivious, or obscene material." The publisher must pay the tax within 30 days of publication. If the tax is not paid, State A revenue agents finding such material in State A are authorized to seize and destroy it.

Price is a book publisher in State B. Price published 1,000 copies of a book of questionable taste and sold half of them to independent, "adult bookstores" in State A. Price had received these orders for the books by telephone as a consequence of a promotional flier which he had sent to the purchasers. Price shipped the books by parcel service.

Price has failed to pay any "obscene publication tax" to State A.

1. Is the statute valid? Discuss.

2. May State A revenue agents seize and destroy copies of the books in State A? Discuss.

QUESTION 8

County School Board (Board) cancelled the remedial reading program in County's public schools. At the same time, Board increased funding for drama arts workshops provided for seniors in the public high schools of County. Such increased funding is about 15% of the cost of the remedial reading program.

Racial minorities comprise 10% of the County population and their children comprise 50% of the students enrolled in County's remedial reading program. "AB" is an organization consisting of the parents of these minority students.

Some students are enrolled in the remedial reading program because of learning disabilities or other handicaps adversely affecting reading skills. "CD" is an organization of the parents of these students.

AB objected to the cancellation of the remedial reading program on the ground that the program's termination would disproportionately affect their children adversely. CD objected to the program's termination on the ground that it would effectively end public education for their children.

In recommending termination of the program, Board's director had stated: "This action is a necessary economic measure. We have other programs, such as pre-college math, which are educationally more important. Handicapped students will simply have to be served sometime in the future when we again have sufficient financial resources. We will, even then, have to target the program so that it helps handicapped children, not children of racial minorities who just need to improve their English language skills." Board's actions were based on its director's recommendations.

AB and CD filed suit against Board in federal court, asserting that termination of the remedial reading program violated the constitutional rights of the parents and the children represented by the organizations, and asking that Board be ordered to reinstate the program. While the suit was pending, Congress enacted a federal statute requiring school boards of all state political subdivisions to provide remedial reading courses. In passing this legislation, Congress relied upon findings derived through congressional hearings that adults without reading skills inhibit production, sales and travel in interstate commerce.

Assume that both AB and CD have standing to assert their claims.

1. Is the federal statute constitutional? Discuss.

2. If the court rules that the federal statute is unconstitutional:

A. What issues under the U.S. Constitution should AB raise against the actions of Board? How should they be decided? Discuss.

B. What issues under the U.S. Constitution should CD raise against the actions of Board? How should they be decided? Discuss.

QUESTION 9

Three student groups, each consisting of ten adult students, protested against State X University's decision to cease dormitory construction.

Group A placed advertisements in the local newspapers charging that University's decision resulted from "political pressure exerted by State Senator X, who owns several private apartments that compete with the dormitories." Each member of Group A was convicted of "criminal libel," defined by state law as "publishing any false statements exposing another to public hatred, contempt or ridicule." The convictions were supported by evidence that Group A's statement (1) was false, since Senator X had secretly sold his apartments before he took a position on the issue of the new dormitories, and (2) had severely damaged the Senator's public reputation.

Group B, all carrying "WE WANT DORMS!" signs, paraded along the sidewalk facing the University Administration building. They attracted few spectators and carefully avoided blocking sidewalk traffic, but street traffic was delayed by curious drivers who slowed down as they drove past. Each member of Group B was convicted under a "breach of the peace" statute prohibiting "the congregation of persons upon a public sidewalk under circumstances tending to disrupt public order or tranquility."

Group C was invited to a discussion with University's President in his office. Although subsequently asked to leave, Group C remained in his office as a protest gesture. Each member was convicted under a newly adopted criminal trespass law proscribing "entry upon lands of another after receiving notice prohibiting such entry."

Assume that (1) all of the convictions have been upheld by the highest State X court, and (2) that all constitutional issues were raised and diligently pursued throughout the proceedings.

Should the convictions of the members of Group A, B and C be reversed by the United States Supreme Court? Discuss.

QUESTION 10

D, a State X corporation, maintains a vessel which transports cargo among several states on the Great Lakes. The vessel, equipped with hand-fired coal boilers, emits smoke of a density and duration that exceed the limits imposed by the Smoke Abatement Code of Lakesport, a city in State X. Violations are punishable by a $100 fine, 30 days imprisonment, or both. No such code exists in other ports visited by the vessel. Pursuant to a comprehensive federal statute governing seagoing safety, the Coast Guard has inspected, approved and licensed D's vessels (including boilers and fuel).

D's vessel enters State X's ports for occasional refueling and repairs. Loading and unloading is done at main terminals located in other states. State X has levied its personal property tax on the full value of D's vessel, and no such tax is imposed by the other states visited.

After trials in State X courts, D is convicted of violating Lakeport's Smoke Abatement Code and is found liable for the State X property tax. State X's highest court has affirmed both decisions, and the United States Supreme Court has granted review. What should be the decision of the Supreme Court? Discuss.

QUESTION 11

Doe is the leader of a tenant association in a housing project owned and operated by State X. On May 1, Doe issued a public statement condemning the poor judgment of the housing director in recommending increased rents to the State X agency which oversees these projects. The director then informed Doe that the project "didn't need troublemakers" and that Doe's lease would not be renewed upon its expiration on June 1. Doe challenged the director's decision in the proper State X court, but lost. The court held that applicable State X law did not recognize the retaliatory eviction doctrine, and therefore Doe had no right to be a tenant once the lease expired.

Doe then announced a massive protest rally of 200 tenants to be held on June 2, in a small park, capable of holding approximately 100 persons, adjoining the project. On May 5, the director obtained an *ex parte* order enjoining Doe from "holding any mass rally in the park." Doe did not challenge the order, but went ahead with the June 2 rally.

The rally was conducted peacefully, though the overflow blocked all traffic entering the housing project for about 20 minutes. Doe was subsequently charged with criminal contempt. The court refused to consider Doe's constitutional objections to the injunction, holding that she should have raised such objections by available state procedure prior to the demonstration. Doe was found guilty and sentenced to a jail term.

The U.S. Supreme Court has accepted review of both the original action challenging Doe's eviction and the contempt conviction. What result? Discuss.

QUESTION 12

The legislature of State A recently passed a law requiring drivers of trucks carrying explosives on roads in State A to have "Special Driving Permits." These permits are to be issued only after rigorous physical examinations and driving tests. The State A law also provides that only permits issued by State A are acceptable for truck drivers; permits issued by certain other states, all of which have less stringent requirements, are not acceptable. Under the State A law, permits cannot be issued to persons under 30 or over 60 years of age, because statistical studies have shown that drivers in these categories have higher accident frequencies.

Assume that a federal law prohibits employers from discriminating against employees on the basis of age.

Ned, who is 62 years old, is a driver for Ajax, a truck company engaged in the interstate transportation of dynamite for construction projects in various states, including State A. Ned would normally be assigned to drive dynamite shipments from Ajax's headquarters in State B, into State A, but he cannot obtain a Special Driving Permit from State A. Ned would be able to satisfy both the physical examination and driving test requirements of the State A law, but is barred solely because of his age. Ned has a driver's permit issued by State B qualifying him to drive trucks carrying explosives. As a consequence of the State A law, Ajax has been obliged to revise its normal driver assignment policy to schedule Ned on routes which do not require ingress into State A.

Ajax and Ned have brought suit in the United States District Court in State A against the appropriate State A officials, seeking to have the State A law declared invalid. The defendants have moved to have the case dismissed on the grounds that (1) the plaintiffs lack standing, and (2) State A courts have not yet ruled upon the validity of the new law.

1. How should the court rule on the motion for dismissal? Discuss.

2. Assume the motion for dismissal is denied. What rights arising under the United States Constitution should Ajax and Ned urge in support of their claims that the State A law is invalid, and what result should follow? Discuss.

QUESTION 13

The Pacific State Legislature enacted the "Pacific Home Television Movie Control Act" in response to numerous demands by parents of young children. The Act provides:

1. It is unlawful for any person or enterprise to transmit motion pictures via a cable television system to a home television receiver in the State of Pacific in violation of this Act.

2. No motion picture rated by the National Movie Rating Board as "R" (restricted, to be viewed when accompanied by an adult only), or "X" (adults only), shall be transmitted to any household in Pacific, except between 12:01 a.m. and 4:30 a.m. local time.

3. Any person or enterprise that violates this Act is subject to a fine of not less than $100 nor more than $500 per household in Pacific that subscribes to the violator's transmission system.

4. This Act does not apply to any cable television system owned and operated by a governmental subdivision of Pacific.

Martha, the president of Microsystem (Micro), a company which owns and operates a cable television system in Pacific, has retained you to consider bringing a suit challenging the validity of the Act. She claims that enforcement of the Act by Pacific will bankrupt her company. Both market studies and practical experience in the cable television industry have confirmed that "R" and "X" rated movies are a significant revenue source for Micro in Pacific. Micro shows "R" rated motion pictures starting at 8:00 p.m. and shows "X" rated motion pictures starting at 10:00 p.m. "R" and "X" rated motion pictures were described as "lewd" and "violent" by some legislators as reasons for adoption of the Act. Micro has successfully marketed its cable television motion picture service to over 20,000 subscribers in households in Pacific, most of whom subscribe to Micro's special "R" and "X" channel at an additional charge of $10 per month, per household.

You contemplate filing an action for declaratory relief for Micro as the plaintiff in federal court in Pacific against the Pacific Department of Justice (DJ), which is charged under applicable state law with enforcement of the Act, as the defendant.

What arguments under the United States Constitution should you make against the validity of the Act, what defenses would you expect DJ to assert as to each argument, and how should the federal court decide these contentions? Discuss.

QUESTION 14

Arrow, a retail toy seller, is a State of Hio Corporation with all of its facilities and employees located in Hio. Arrow owns most of its equipment, but leases packaging machines from the U.S. Government. Arrow specializes in mail order sales solicited solely through catalogues mailed throughout the country. Orders are prepaid and are subject to acceptance by Arrow. Toys ordinarily are shipped by return mail, with the purchaser paying mailing costs. However, each year several large orders are delivered in Arrow's own trucks to State of Penn purchasers.

The following taxes have been imposed on Arrow:

(1) The State of Ut imposes a use tax on Ut residents making mail order purchases. Ut law places the burden of collection on the seller, and the failure to collect makes the seller directly liable to Ut.

(2) Penn requires a highway-use license fee of "$20 per truck ordinarily used" in that state. This standard fee applies irrespective of the degree of vehicle use within the state.

(3) Hio imposes an ad valorem property tax based on the value of all equipment owned by Arrow, including the trucks. The property tax does not apply to property leased from any governmental agency. A "leasehold value" tax — applying the same rate to one-half of the value of leased property — is imposed on the lessee in lieu of the property tax. Property leased from Hio, however, is exempted from both the property and leasehold taxes.

Can these taxes and obligations constitutionally be imposed on Arrow? Discuss.

QUESTION 15

U, a large state university with insufficient dormitory space, maintains a housing bureau to assist its students in obtaining off-campus housing. At the request of private homeowners in the area and to save students possible embarrassment, the housing bureau has compiled two different lists. One lists the persons who will rent only to caucasian students. This list is not given to Black students. U is internationally known for its excellent programs for foreign students and has no ascertainable policy of racial or religious discrimination. No federal or state statutes require licenses for, or otherwise regulate, the rental of rooms in private homes.

The N.A.A.C.P. has publicly proclaimed that U's housing policy is morally wrong. It recently sought to publicize this position by picketing the main administration building on U's campus. Campus police informed the fifty picketers that their conduct was prohibited by a university rule forbidding any on-campus activity which disturbed the free flow of traffic or the ability of university officials to carry out their normal functions. Before the campus police acted, a large crowd of opposing students had assembled in the surrounding quadrangle, some with signs supporting U and asserting that the picketers should be concerned with finals (rather than politics). As a consequence of the activities of both groups, some students had difficulty moving around the picketers and their opposition and getting to their next classes on time. After futile efforts to persuade the picketers to leave, state officers (summoned by the campus police) arrested the picketers.

U obtained a restraining order from a state court which enjoined further picketing at U, and, after a full hearing, a permanent injunction which is currently pending on appeal to the highest state court. Meanwhile, the N.A.A.C.P., joined by three black students of U, has sought, in the appropriate U.S. district court, a declaratory judgment and injunction against U's listing of any housing facilities which discriminate against persons based upon race.

As to both proceedings, what result and why?

QUESTION 16

Smith is a permanent resident alien, who has been employed as a temporary science teacher at Centerville High School, a public school. When his term of employment expired, Smith applied to the Centerville School Board for the vacant job of full-time science teacher, but he was not hired. After requesting a public hearing before the Board on the rejection of his application, Smith received the following letter from the School Board, signed by the Board Chairman:

"Dear Mr. Smith:

"The School Board wishes to inform you that it will not grant you a hearing of any kind on your application for full-time employment. The Board has decided to hire another teacher for the position.

"Your recent verbal attacks on our other teachers for teaching what you called 'evolutionary heresy' have been so strong, that we do not believe you could faithfully teach the scientifically-accepted doctrines of evolution in the classroom.

"Further, your continuing insistence that you be allowed to take meditation periods from 10-11 A.M. and 2-3 P.M. each day, although based upon your religious or metaphysical beliefs, so conflicts with the ordinary classroom work schedule from 9:00 A.M. to 3:30 P.M., as to make your employment out of the question.

"Finally, in light of the present high level of unemployment among locally-educated science teachers, the Board would prefer to hire an American citizen who has had teacher training in Centerville State College, rather than a foreigner like yourself who received teacher training elsewhere in the United States."

Assuming the facts recited in the letter from the Board are true and that Smith has a teacher's certificate from the state education department, has the Board deprived Smith of his rights under the United States Constitution? Discuss.

QUESTION 17

Powerco, a private company, generates electric power at a plant in the State of Orange. It transmits that power over its own lines to public utilities in State of Orange, selling the power to these utilities at wholesale prices. The plant in Orange includes several gas-fired generators, and one atomic reactor generator.

The atomic reactor is operated under a permit obtained from the Atomic Energy Commission ("AEC"). The Atomic Energy Act of 1954 authorized the AEC to license the commercial use of atomic reactors, and to regulate the emission of radioactive waste. Section 1(a) of the Act declares as its policy: "The development, use and control of atomic energy shall be directed so as to make the maximum contribution to the general welfare, subject at all times to the paramount objective of contributing to the common defense and security..."

Powerco has been operating its atomic reactor generator for several years. In response to recent public concern about nuclear reactors (precipitated by a minor accident at a nuclear plant in a nearby state), the legislature of Orange has recently enacted two laws:

(1) The State Pollution Control Law ("Pollution Law"), prohibiting any person or firm within the state from emitting radioactive waste in excess of a prescribed level (which is lower than that permitted by the AEC).

(2) The State Power Revenue Law ("Revenue law"), levying an annual license tax of $500,000 on every atomic reactor within the state, and imposing a 2% gross receipts tax upon the proceeds from "all electric power generated within the state."

Powerco's atomic reactor emits relatively minimal amounts of radioactive waste, which are well within the limits established by the AEC. Powerco claims it would be very expensive to comply with the State of Orange emission standards, and has developed substantial evidence in support of its claim.

May Powerco lawfully continue to use the reactor without modification? Must it pay either of the State of Orange taxes? Discuss.

QUESTION 18

A statute of State X concerning the adoption of children states that (1) only agencies licensed by the state may place children for adoption, and (2) the primary duty of such adoption agencies shall be to promote the best interests of the child, including her moral and spiritual well-being. Another section of the statute provides: "The race and religious affiliation of the adoptive parents shall be the same as that of the natural parents, or in the case of illegitimate children, that of the mother."

Husband (H) and Wife (W) applied to Agency, a private, non-profit corporation licensed by State X to place children for adoption, to adopt the next available illegitimate Black child. H is Black, W is White, and both are professed agnostics. Their application was rejected after an investigation by Agency. In a letter to H and W, Agency stated, "Although our investigator found you both highly qualified to be adoptive parents, in other respects we must reject your application because the social problems created by the difference in your ethnic backgrounds and your lack of religious affiliation combine to indicate that the requested adoption would not be in the best interests of the child."

H and W filed suit in the appropriate State X court seeking both a declaratory judgment that the quoted requirements of the statute are unconstitutional, and an order compelling Agency to process and approve their application. The trial court denied relief and the State X Supreme Court affirmed. Assuming all questions are properly preserved, discuss the issues which are likely to arise on review by the United States Supreme Court and how they should be resolved.

QUESTION 19

The President of the United States issued an Executive Order authorizing the F.B.I., without first obtaining a search warrant, to tap telephones of aliens in cases of suspected espionage or subversion by foreign powers.

Congress subsequently passed a bill prohibiting all wiretaps without a warrant, but the President vetoed the bill and Congress was unable to override the veto. Congress then passed a concurrent resolution (which does not require presidential approval) stating that the sense of the Congress is that no warrantless wiretaps should be permitted within the United States. Congress, over the President's veto, passed a statute permitting any federal taxpayer to bring suit in a federal district court to contest the validity of the President's Executive Order. No other statute affects the subject.

An action was later filed in federal district court by Jones, a U.S. citizen and taxpayer. Jones contested the validity of the Executive Order on constitutional grounds and sought to show at the trial that the F.B.I. had, in fact, tapped telephones in the United States without a warrant and that some telephones of U.S. citizens had been tapped. Jones caused an F.B.I. agent to be subpoenaed to testify and produce records regarding the telephone taps in issue, but the President claimed executive privilege and the agent neither appeared nor produced any records.

The federal district and appellate courts ruled against Jones and the Supreme Court has granted review.

What result on all of the constitutional issues? Discuss.

QUESTION 20

Suburban Primary School ("Suburban") is a public school supported entirely by local property taxes and federal grants. The Parent Teachers Association ("PTA") is an unincorporated association consisting of parents of some of the students at Suburban. PTA decided to institute an extra-curricular program for the school's students, in which PTA would sponsor four courses, each to be held once a week, after regular hours. Certain PTA members would voluntarily serve as teachers for the courses. After such classes, participating students would be allowed to take the "late" school bus home. The Suburban principal has agreed to let the PTA use the school premises and bus for the program.

The PTA determined that because of possible behavior problems, none of the courses would be co-educational.

Each parent was to register his child, in person, at 8:45 a.m. on the opening day of the program. Classes were to be filled on a "first-come, first-served" basis. Before the program began, it was described in a pamphlet given to each child attending Suburban to take home. The available courses were described as:

1. Embroidery — 8 girls, 5th and 6th grades, $3.00;

2. Creative Crafts — 10 boys, 2nd grade, $4.00;

3. Baseball Practice — 10 boys, 5th and 6th grades, $2.00;

4. Bible Studies — 12 girls, no fee.

Mother (M), who is not a PTA member, did not arrive at school on the prescribed day until 9:15 a.m. because of a flat tire on her car. M attempted to enroll her son Harold ("H"), a second-grader at Suburban, in Creative Crafts, but was told that the course was filled. She also tried to enroll her daughter Alice ("A"), a sixth-grader at Suburban, in Baseball Practice, but was refused (although several vacancies were left).

M has sued the PTA in the appropriate U.S. district court to compel enrollment of H in Creative Crafts, and of A in Baseball Practice. Two other parents who are not members of PTA, but who are taxpayers residing in the school district with children attending Suburban, have sued to enjoin continuation of the entire program. Both suits rely exclusively on rights guaranteed to the plaintiffs under the United States Constitution.

Assume that all proper defendants have been joined in both actions.

What constitutional issues are raised by the suits, and how should they be decided? Discuss.

QUESTION 21

Three years ago, the United States completed construction of a dam upon a large river, creating a navigable lake in State X. Regulatory control of the lake as a fishery was granted by the United States to State X, "subject to all constitutional provisions."

One year ago, at its own expense, State X stocked the lake with an imported fish species, the "river salmon," which grew to spectacular size due to unique physical and chemical properties of the lake. On weekends and holidays, sportspersons from all over the United States came to the lake to catch the large fish as trophies.

Six months ago, realizing the lake was rapidly being depleted of "river salmon," State X enacted the following statute (the "Act"):

"Sec. 1: A special license shall be required to fish for river salmon in this state. The license fee for residents shall be $10 and the license fee for non-residents shall be $100.

"Sec. 2: No river salmon shall be transported out of State X.

"Sec. 3: No one shall fish for river salmon in this state unless such person is accompanied by a guide licensed by this state for that purpose, and only residents of this state are eligible to apply for, or to hold, such guide licenses."

Guy had been a State X resident and held a license to guide upon the lake for the purpose of fishing for "river salmon." On most weekends and holidays, Guy would guide a small boatload of persons desiring to fish on the lake. Two years ago, Guy moved his domicile from State X to adjoining State Y. Solely because he had become a non-resident, Guy's annual application for renewal of his license was recently refused.

Guy commenced a suit in State X contending that the entire State X statute is unconstitutional. He has been unsuccessful in the state courts and his case is now before the United States Supreme Court for decision on the merits. Assume Guy has preserved all constitutional claims.

(1) Does Guy have standing to assert claims of the unconstitutionality of Sections 1 and 2 of the State X statute? Discuss.

(2) Assuming that Guy has standing, what claims of unconstitutionality might Guy reasonably assert with respect to the entire Act, and how should they be resolved? Discuss.

QUESTION 22

State X requires that every person teaching in public or private schools be certified by the state. Legislatively established grounds for denial of certification include the following:

"1. Knowing membership in any Fascist, Nazi or Communist party, or any other organization that advocates or teaches the propriety of overthrowing the government by force or violence;

"2. Failure to provide the certification committee with complete answers to questions seeking legally relevant information."

John Doe sought certification in order to take a job with a private secondary school. In checking his references, state investigators were told that Doe was a member of the American Nazi party. Doe was informed of this charge, and the state scheduled a hearing on the matter.

Doe attended the hearing, but stated at the outset that he would not answer any questions concerning his alleged membership in the Nazi Party. Doe claimed that to compel answers to such questions constituted a denial of his "right of privacy as guaranteed by the Fifth Amendment." He did not offer any further explanation of his refusal, nor was he asked to do so. The committee then announced that Doe's application was denied.

Doe has now brought suit in federal court attacking the constitutionality of the committee's action. What result? Discuss.

QUESTION 23

The County Board of Education (Board) seeks your advice as Board's legal counsel regarding two current problems:

1. The public high school in the County District has scheduled graduation ceremonies for a Saturday morning, as has been the custom for all schools in the District. This year's senior class valedictorian, Val, holds religious beliefs that prevent her from attending the graduation ceremony because Saturday is the Sabbath day observed by her religion. Val has demanded that the Board reschedule the graduation so she can attend and deliver the traditional valedictory address.

2. Board has had a policy of permitting community groups to use the high school auditorium for evening and weekend meetings at a modest rental fee. Now NFO, a local organization which advocates racial and religious discrimination, has applied for use of the auditorium for a major recruiting meeting on April 20. Persons and groups opposed to what they characterize as the "extremist" views of NFO are demanding that Board reject the application "out of hand, without giving it serious consideration." The local police chief also opposes the application on the basis of "hard intelligence" that some militant "anti-fascists" plan to remove NFO members from the school auditorium by physical force if the meeting takes place.

Both Val and NFO have each delivered letters to the Board invoking "rights under the U.S. Constitution" in support of their respective demands and applications.

What issues arising under the U.S. Constitution are presented by:

1. Val's demand? Discuss.

2. NFO's application? Discuss.

ESSAY ANSWERS

ANSWER TO QUESTION 1

(a) *The misdemeanor charge:*

Tom ("T") could initially contend that the misdemeanor charge should be dismissed because it was based upon a statute which was overly broad (i.e., the entity charged with enforcing the law had virtually total discretion in determining whether or not it should be applied to a particular situation). Such broad enactments cannot serve as the basis for governmental action; *Lovell v. Griffin*, 303 U.S. 444 (1938). Since the statutory standard to be utilized in granting or refusing licenses is highly subjective in nature (i.e., the "overall community good"), T would argue that it was constitutionally defective. While it would be difficult for City to argue that the test for determining if licenses should be granted is adequate, it could assert that where the defendant should have anticipated a constitutionally curative construction, an overly broad enactment may serve as the basis for governmental action; *Shuttlesworth v. Birmingham*, 394 U.S. 147 (1969). Since the State X Supreme Court had made a proper narrowing interpretation of the criminal advocacy statute five years earlier, T should have foreseen that a constitutionally proper interpretation of the misdemeanor statute would also be rendered upon judicial review. *See* ELO Ch.14-IV(E)(2)-(3).

T could respond, however, that he could *not* foresee a constitutionally curative interpretation of the licensing ordinance because it appeared to be plain on its face (i.e., it would have been very difficult to anticipate that the requirement for speaking would be almost completely repudiated and the factors of time, place and manner of speech substituted in lieu thereof).

Alternatively, T could argue that, even if a proper narrowing interpretation could have been anticipated, a law which is unconstitutionally applied (i.e., the permit was rejected for T's failure to disclose the content; not time, place or manner considerations) cannot serve as the basis for a criminal conviction where there is no adequate opportunity for review. T would assert that this standard was satisfied because (1) there was no provision for independent review by a judicial body (any appeal was to be heard by the city council, presumably the same entity which enacted the law), and (2) the facts are unclear as to how often the city council met (if it was not until after T's projected speaking date, no timely appeal to that body could possibly be taken). Although City could rebut that T waived any potential constitutional defect in the prescribed review by neglecting to contest the police chief's denial of T's permit request before the city council, this procedure requiring appeal to a legislative branch of local government is probably inadequate. In summary, the prosecution of T for violation of the licensing ordinance will probably **not** be successful. *See* ELO Ch.14-IV(E)(5).

(b) *The contempt of court decree:*

Ex-parte orders are ordinarily not appropriate unless there is a need to act immediately and there is no opportunity to give the opposing party notice. Since the attorney for City was apparently aware of T's prospective speech on Tuesday (the facts indicate that Dan "immediately" gave the City attorney T's name and address), T probably should have been given an opportunity to contest the injunction. While even an improper court order must ordinarily be obeyed, where an ex-parte injunction is deliberately sought and served in such a manner as to preclude effective judicial review (here, City's attorney served the order upon T just as he was beginning to speak), it may be attackable in a subsequent proceeding; *Walker v. Birmingham*, 388 U.S. 307 (1967). *See* ELO Ch.14-IV(E)(5)(D).

(c) *The felony charge:*

Although the First Amendment (applicable to the states via the Fourteenth Amendment), protects the advocacy of ideas, speech made for the purpose of inciting immediate unlawful conduct and which is likely to incite such action may be proscribed; *Brandenburg v. Ohio*, 395 U.S. 444 (1969). T could contend that the felony charges must be dismissed because (1) the statute in question is too vague (i.e., a person of ordinary intelligence could not determine what constitutes "advocating insurrection"); and (2) alternatively, the above cited standard is not satisfied in this instance because (i) while he advocated that the listeners "stockpile weapons," he never suggested doing so illegally (in most states, various types of firearms can be purchased in a lawful manner), (ii) even if his words could be construed as urging illegal conduct, the conduct would not be imminent (i.e., it would take time to aggregate these weapons), and (iii) it was unlikely that the listeners would respond to T's speech, since they were (a) in the park for "various other reasons," and (b) only "mildly interested" in T's speech. Finally, T's comment to "begin thinking about forming guerilla units" obviously does not contemplate immediate unlawful conduct (it merely suggests "thinking"). *See* ELO Ch.14-II(F).

While City could respond to T's vagueness assertion by pointing out that the statute had received a constitutionally curative interpretation, there appears to be no successful rebuttal to T's argument that the *Brandenburg* test is not met. Thus, the felony charge should be dismissed.

ANSWER TO QUESTION 2

Since City ("C") did not put into issue the "wrong party" statement of the newly-elected department head, this assertion is presumably not in question.

Can C exclude Paul ("P") because he is purportedly not a U.S. Citizen?

P could attack this ground for dismissal in three ways. He would contend (1) that the U.S. statute is unconstitutional; and (2), that the state statute requiring municipal employees to be U.S. citizens is unconstitutional; and (3) that the state statute forbidding beards and requiring uniforms is also unconstitutional.

Is the U.S. statute constitutional?

(If not, then P was technically still a citizen and the state statute requiring municipal employees to be citizens would be satisfied.)

P would probably initially contend that the federal statute is unconstitutional because he did not consent to forfeit his citizenship; *Afroyim v. Rusk*, 387 U.S. 253 (1967). While C might argue in rebuttal that a citizen is presumed to know the law, and therefore P voluntarily forfeited his citizenship, P should prevail on this point since there are no facts which indicate P knowingly consented to a loss of U.S. citizenship.

Is the state statute requiring municipal employees to be U.S. citizens constitutional?

Assuming, however, that the federal statute was valid, P would argue that the state statute requiring municipal employees to be U.S. citizens is invalid. Aliens are ordinarily regarded as a "suspect" classification, unless involved in a "basic" or "political" governmental function. Reading water meters would probably not be regarded as such since this task is not critical to the effective functioning of local government. Thus, C will have to show that a compelling interest is served by restricting meter readers to U.S. citizens, and that there is no less burdensome means of accomplishing that objective. C could contend that there is a compelling interest in having only U.S. citizens work as meter readers because persons would be reluctant to let someone into their homes and businesses if he could not speak English clearly. However, a less burdensome means of satisfying the state's concern would be to require each applicant for this position to pass a fluency test which demonstrates his ability to respond to customers' questions. Thus, P probably could *not* be constitutionally discharged on the basis that he was *not* a U.S. citizen. *See* ELO Ch.10-VI(C).

Is the state statute forbidding beards and requiring uniforms constitutional?

First, it is assumed that the "no beard" and uniform requirements have been enforced against all employees, so P cannot contend that the statute is being applied unequally (thereby violating his equal protection rights).

The constitutionality of legislation pertaining to the health, safety and welfare of a state's citizens is ordinarily judged by the rational relationship test (i.e., as long as there is a rational relationship between a legitimate state interest and the statute's attempt to further that interest, the legislation is constitutional). While P could argue that a beard and lack of a uniform bear no relationship to one's capability for meter reading, C could probably successfully contend in rebuttal that customers are more likely to permit meter readers into their homes and stores if they are (1) clean shaven, and (2) have an identifying characteristic (i.e., a specifically designated uniform). *See* ELO Ch.10-II(A)-(B).

P might next argue that the right to dress and groom as one desires is a fundamental right (similar to the rights of privacy found within the penumbra of the Bill of Rights). However, C could probably successfully contend in rebuttal that due process rights of privacy have not been extended to grooming and dress requirements at work (i.e., they have been limited to an individual's home or body); *Kelly v. Johnson*, 425 U.S. 238 (1976). *See* ELO Ch.9-IV(P).

P might finally contend that since the "no beard" and uniform requirements were not promulgated until **after** his employment with C had commenced, the state's action constituted an impairment of an existing contractual relationship; Article I, Section 10, of the U.S. Constitution. However, C could probably successfully argue in rebuttal that (1) there was no agreement that measures reasonably necessary to make performance of the job more efficient would not be undertaken; and (2) in any event, the beard and uniform requirements are an inconsequential modification of the employment arrangement (i.e., P has not been asked to accept major modifications, such as reduced compensation or reassignment to a different geographical area). *See* ELO Ch.11-III(B), (E) & (F).

Also note that P is apparently **not** contending that his beard has religious significance. Thus, no "freedom of exercise" assertion appears to be violated.

Since there was an independent, constitutional basis for P's dismissal, his lawsuit against C probably would **not** be successful.

ANSWER TO QUESTION 3

(a) *Mayo Taxpayers ("Taxpayers") v. Church, Society and Agency*

Do taxpayers have standing? The defendants' initial contention would be that Taxpayers lack standing to pursue this lawsuit. However, since the State X spending program whereby Agency provides funds to legal aid organizations was created through a state (as opposed to a federal) statute, the criterion for standing is simply: "does the state action involve measurable expenditures?" Since the amounts expended on the legal aid program are easily calculable, Taxpayers would appear to have standing. *See* ELO Ch.16-III(B)(3)(c).

Is there state action? The Establishment Clause (applicable to the states via the 14th Amendment) pertains only to governmental action.

The Taxpayers could contend that there is significant governmental involvement in the program since it is funded by a state agency; *Norwood v. Harrison*, 413 U.S. 455 (1973). While the defendants could argue in rebuttal that mere governmental funding should not constitute state participation (the facts are silent as to the extent of the funding provided to Society by Agency), since Society is allegedly performing an unconstitutional activity, state action would probably be found. *See* ELO Ch.12-III(E)(3).

Does the legislation violate the Establishment Clause? Pursuant to the Establishment Clause, legislation which impacts upon religion is invalid unless (1) it has a secular purpose, (2) its primary effect is neither to advance nor to inhibit religion, and (3) it does not produce excessive entanglement between religion and the state. The program arguably has a secular purpose because it assists the victims of discrimination in vindicating their legal rights. It does not appear to advance or inhibit religion, since preventing discrimination against someone for racial or religious reasons appears to be neutral in its impact. (Although taxpayers might contend that assisting the victims of religious discrimination promotes religion, this contention should fail because protecting the right to practice religion is a neutral governmental function.) However, Taxpayers would probably be successful in asserting that the plan produces excessive government entanglement because state officials would have to constantly monitor Society to make certain that preference was not given to cases affecting Church members. Thus, the legislation is unconstitutional. *See* ELO Ch.15-II(A)(2) & (H).

(b) *Jay v. Church, Society and Agency*

Does Jay have standing? To have standing in federal court, the plaintiff must ordinarily demonstrate a direct and immediate personal injury resulting from the allegedly unconstitutional action. The defendants could contend that since Society members work gratuitously, there is no significant injury to Jay (they are only refusing to let him work without pay). While Jay could argue in rebuttal that participation in Society might enhance his professional reputation and possibly lead to referrals, these gains are extremely speculative so the defendants should prevail. *See* ELO Ch.16-III(C)(2) & (4).

Assuming, however, that there was standing and state action (discussed above), there seems to be little doubt that Society's refusal of admittance to Jay would violate both the Equal Protection Clause of the 14th Amendment (there is no rational relationship between practicing law for a particular entity and not being a member of a specific religious sect) and the Establishment Clause (an arrangement whereby only members of a particular religious sect can obtain a particular governmental position). *See* ELO Ch.10-II(G)(1) and Ch.15-II(A)(2)(b).

(c) *Bar v. Society*

Does Bar have standing? An association has standing to assert the rights of its members where (1) one or more of its members would have standing, (2) the interest asserted is pertinent to the association's purpose, and (3) the claim asserted and relief requested do not require that individual members participate in the suit. Since (1) Bar is presumably concerned with practices which would diminish its credibility and public esteem, and (2) these requisites would seem to be satisfied in this instance, Bar would probably have standing. *See* ELO Ch.16-III(C)(3)(d).

Does the State X disciplinary code violate the First Amendment? While "legitimate" commercial speech has been held to be within the First Amendment, Bar could contend in rebuttal that in-person solicitations (which raise the potential of overreaching and the initiation of frivolous litigation) can be restricted. However, Society can probably successfully argue in rebuttal that since it was offering its services gratuitously, the application of this situation to Bar's code violates Society's First Amendment rights; *In re Primus*, 436 U.S. 886 (1982). *See* ELO Ch.14-VIII(C)(2)(b).

ANSWER TO QUESTION 4

Church will probably raise the following contentions with respect to its assertion that the amended statute is invalid.

Is the statute a valid exercise of the police power?

Church ("C") will initially contend that pursuant to the Tenth Amendment, the state is allowed to legislate for the health, welfare and safety of its citizens. Since the acknowledged purpose of the ordinance was primarily aesthetic in nature (i.e., to enhance the appearance of City), the applicable standard is **not** satisfied. However, City could argue in rebuttal that (1) improving the physical outlook of an area is a valid general welfare purpose; and (2) another possible purpose of the law might have been to diminish visual distractions, and thereby reduce vehicular accidents; *Railway Express Agency v. New York*, 336 U.S. 106 (1949). Thus, the law is probably valid. *See* ELO Ch.11-II(B)(7).

Does the statute violate C's First Amendment rights of freedom of speech?

C could next contend that the statute violates its First Amendment rights of freedom of speech (applicable to the states via the Fourteenth Amendment) because the sign law prohibits C from communicating its message to the public. C could argue that a private means of communication to the public (rooftop billboards) may not be foreclosed entirely; *Metromedia, Inc. v. San Diego*, 453 U.S. 490 (1981); *Schad v. Mount Ephraim*, 452 U.S. 61 (1981). In the former case, a law prohibiting billboards from containing commercial messages was deemed to violate the plaintiffs First Amendment rights. However, City could distinguish the above cited cases because the Supreme Court found that they involved situations where there were no ample, alternative channels for communication of the information in question. In contrast, C still has numerous means of soliciting new members and financial support (i.e., newspaper advertisements, flyers distributed on sidewalks, etc.). Although this is a close question, City would probably prevail (unless C can demonstrate that it would be prohibitively expensive for it to advertise in any other manner). *See* ELO Ch.14-IV(M)(3).

Does the ordinance constitute an unconstitutional taking?

C could contend that (1) requiring it to dismantle the sign constitutes a governmental "taking" under the Fourteenth Amendment; and (2) since the ordinance does not provide for compensation, it is unconstitutional. However, City could argue in rebuttal that no "taking" has occurred, since C did not have any reasonable "investment backed expectations" that the sign would be extant forever; *Penn Central Transportation Co. v. New York City*, 438 U.S. 104 (1978); and (2) in any event, the five-year phaseout period (probably) fairly correlates to the useful life of the sign. Again, City should prevail. *See* ELO Ch.11-II(B).

Does the ordinance violate C's First Amendment rights to freedom of religion?

Legislation (1) which does not have a secular purpose (i.e., was aimed at inhibiting the practice of a particular religion), or (2) whose primary effect is to inhibit religion, is unconstitutional under the Establishment Clause of the First Amendment. C could argue that because City responded to the complaints of individuals who wanted C's sign removed, the City's action was done with the basic purpose and primary effect of impeding C's religious views. However, City could probably successfully contend in rebuttal that (1) there is no indication that the persons complaining about C's sign (nor the members of City's council who enacted the ordinance) were motivated by anti-religious feelings toward C, and (2) the ordinance had, at most, only an incidental affect upon C's ability to function. As noticed above, C can still attract new members and solicit financial support by any and all other means. The ordinance probably did *not* violate C's First Amendment rights to freedom of religion. *See* ELO C.15-II(A)(2).

Does the ordinance violate C's equal protection rights?

Finally, C might argue that the ordinance violates its equal protection rights, since it is irrational and arbitrary to prohibit only rooftop signs. If the City's concern is the distraction of drivers and aesthetics, it should also preclude other highly visible forms of advertising (i.e., billboards, signs painted onto the sides of buildings, etc.). However, it is well established that a legislative body can elect to deal with one aspect of a problem at a time; *Williamson v. Lee Optical Co.*, 348 U.S. 483 (1955). Thus, City would prevail on this issue. *See* ELO Ch.10-II(C).

Summary:

Since all of C's arguments would probably be unsuccessful, the ordinance is valid.

ANSWER TO QUESTION 5

1. *Arguments of SADS against City ("C"):*

SADS would initially contend that an association has standing to assert the rights of its members where (1) one or more of its members would have standing, (2) the interest sought to be protected is pertinent to the association's purpose, and (3) neither the claim nor the relief requested require that individual members participate in the suit. Since (1) the rights of SADS members to convey their message are proscribed by the C ordinance, (2) the extent of government spending on defense is an issue about which college students are appropriately concerned, and (3) it is unnecessary that any particular individual member of SADS participate in the suit, the requisites of "organizational" standing appear to be satisfied. *See* ELO Ch.16-III(C)(3)(d).

SADS should next be able to successfully claim that this is not an appropriate situation for federal court abstention since (1) the statute, being clear on its face, would not be susceptible to a constitutionally curative interpretation by a state court, and (2) the case involves a First Amendment (applicable to the states via the Fourteenth Amendment) question. *See* ELO Ch.16-VI(A)(4)(e).

Substantively, SADS could claim that the streets are a traditional public forum, and speech cannot be completely proscribed in such an arena. Since the ordinance limits use of a part of the public streets for speech, it is arguably unconstitutional. C could contend in rebuttal, however, that public safety constitutes a sufficiently significant state interest (especially where there have already been several accidents resulting in serious injuries as a consequence of the means of communication sought to be utilized by SADS). Additionally, only a complete ban on this type of activity could accomplish the governmental objectives sought to be achieved; it would be too difficult for C to legislate or supervise a more limited ban.

Whether SADS's contention will be successful or not probably depends upon whether other means of distribution of their message are readily available. Assuming SADS may still hold rallies in parks, distribute literature on sidewalks and hold marches in the streets during low traffic density periods, the total closure of distribution to momentarily stopped motor vehicles is probably constitutionally permissible. *See* ELO Ch.14-IV(M)(2)(d).

SADS could alternatively contend that the statute is violative of its equal protection rights, since its enactment was hastened when the council learned of SADS' distribution plan. Where a statute appears to be speech-neutral upon its face, but was enacted with the intention of discouraging speech with a particular content, its enforcement violates the First Amendment. However, C could probably successfully contend in rebuttal that the ordinance was being considered prior to SADS' decision to protest, and that it was the possibility of additional injuries (rather than the message sought to be conveyed by SADS) which prompted the council's action. *See* ELO Ch.14-IV(M)(2)(a).

2. *Owens' ("O") motions*

(a) *Ripeness:* Article III, Section 2, of the U.S. Constitution limits federal court jurisdiction to actual "cases or controversies." O could therefore contend that SADS's action is not ripe (i.e., there is no real and immediate danger to SADS members), since (1) no SADS member has actually attempted to publicize their message at O's shopping center, and (2) O has not tried to remove SADS members or have them prosecuted under the anti-trespass ordinance. However, SADS could successfully argue in rebuttal that its members should not have to be exposed to (1) physical harm (i.e., there is always the possibility that a protestor could be injured while being removed from the shopping center), or (2) criminal sanctions (i.e., if O desired to file a complaint against those persons distributing literature on his property, they would presumably be prosecuted by the authorities) to vindicate their First Amendment right of free speech. So SADS'action is probably ripe. *See* ELO Ch.16-V(A)-(C).

(b) *SADS' right to distribute campaign literature on private property:* In *Hudgens v. National Labor Relations Board*, 424 U.S. 507 (1976), the Supreme Court ruled that there is no First Amendment right to access upon a private shopping center, unless the area could be considered to be engaged in a public function (i.e., the shopping center was in effect, a company owned town). Since the facts fail to indicate that SADS has no other feasible means of communicating its message to residents of C other than by use of the shopping center, SADS has no constitutionally protected right to distribute its literature at the shopping center.

In *Pruneyard Shopping Center v. Robins*, 447 U.S. 74 (1980), the Supreme Court held that where a *state constitution* had been interpreted by the highest court of that jurisdiction to permit reasonable access to a privately-owned shopping center to disseminate information of public concern, the property owner's due process and First Amendment rights were not violated. Assuming, however, there has been no similar interpretation of this state's constitution or corresponding legislative enactment, SADS would have no constitutional right to protest upon O's property. *See* ELO Ch.14-IV(N)(3).

ANSWER TO QUESTION 6

The criminal prosecution of ACME ("A"):

Since a city is a subdivision of a state, the ordinance must be analyzed as "state" action. A would contend that the statute is unconstitutional upon each of the following, independent grounds.

Overbreadth: It should initially be noted that, although the statute is limited to commercial and advertising materials, it is nevertheless entitled to constitutional protection; *Virginia Pharmacy Bd. v. Virginia Consumer Council*, 425 U.S. 748 (1976).

A statute is overly broad where it can be interpreted as circumscribing constitutionally protected conduct or speech. While obscene literature may be constitutionally restricted, the facts stipulate that the allegedly "demeaning" and "sexist" pictures are not obscene. Although City presumably has an interest in not having its citizens view individuals portrayed in a "demeaning" or "sexist" fashion (these portrayals arguably engender degrading and sexist conduct), it is unlikely that this relatively vague objective would overcome A's First Amendment free speech rights (applicable to the states via the Fourteenth Amendment). In summary, the statute is overly broad. *See* ELO Ch.14-III(A).

Vagueness: A statute is unconstitutionally vague when a person of ordinary intelligence would, even though aware of the law, not know if his conduct was illegal. A would contend that the words "demeaning," "sexist" and "advertising material" are too vague. Given that two people can look at the same picture (e.g., a beauty contest participant dressed in a skimpy bathing suit) and have dramatically different views of the portrayal (one might think it demeaning and sexist, and another might feel there is absolutely nothing wrong with the portrayal), A should prevail on this argument as well. *See* ELO Ch.14-III(B).

Unreasonable interference with interstate commerce: Where a local statute impacts upon interstate commerce, it will be adjudged unconstitutional if the interference with interstate commerce outweighs the local objective of the legislation. A could contend that City's ordinance places an unreasonable burden upon A's interstate activities, since A would be required to create separate advertising for City (in contradistinction to the other three states in which it does business). This process would necessarily detail a greater financial expenditure to be borne by A. However, this argument is unlikely to be successful, since the cost of creating different advertising for City would probably be relatively minimal. *See* ELO Ch.4-IV(A).

Equal protection: Finally, A would probably also assert that the City ordinance violates its equal protection rights, since similar displays for non-commercial purposes are not proscribed. However, general welfare legislation like the type in question must only satisfy a legitimate state objective (in this instance, it is probably aimed at preventing the debasement of City citizens). Legislation need not address every possible evil within the area covered by a law. Thus, City should prevail on this contention. *See* ELO Ch.10-II(A) & (C).

Summary:

In summary, since the statute is probably overly broad and vague, it cannot serve as the basis for a criminal prosecution of A. Thus, City's prosecution of A should fail.

A's declaratory judgment action:

There does not appear to be much question that the statute is valid (i.e., it serves a legitimate constitutional purpose by assuring and promoting citizens' First Amendment rights).

Ripeness: City might initially contend that since A has not attempted to remove any of the pickets, the case is not ripe. However, A could probably successfully argue in rebuttal that (1) injury to its business is presently occurring (the pickets are on A's land, and presumably discouraging at least some persons from entering A's premises), and (2) A should not have to risk criminal and civil liability (i.e., by physically ejecting the pickets) to determine if the pickets' actions are lawful. *See* ELO Ch.16-V(C).

Vagueness: The statute apparently fails to define the terms "shopping center" and "retail sales outlet." Is a "shopping center" two or more stores with common private parking facilities, or does it include any physically connected series of retail store outlets under a common landlord? Is a "retail sales outlet" a place which sells only to the ultimate consumer, or does it also include a business which sometimes acts as a distributor (i.e., some sales are made to the public, while larger volume transactions are entered into with other retail entities)? City could contend in rebuttal that (1) a shopping center is a series of business establishments with common, private parking facilities; and (2) *any* sales to an ultimate consumer would make a business establishment a "retail sales outlet" for purposes of the ordinance. This is a close question, but City would probably prevail. *See* ELO Ch.14-III(B).

Deprivation of property/First Amendment:

Pursuant to the 14th Amendment, a state may not deprive persons of "property" without due process of law. A could contend that the picketing ordinance is unconstitutional because it permits the public to use private property without compensation to the landowner (i.e., authorizing the picketing constitutes a "taking" of a portion of A's property interest in its business premises). A could also argue that his First Amendment rights are violated by the ordinance, since persons going to the shopping center might presume that the picketers had been authorized by the owner of the shopping center (and their views shared by the owner). However, similar contentions were rejected in *Pruneyard Shopping Center v. Robins*, 447 U.S. 74 (1980). Thus, City would prevail on these issues. *See* ELO Ch.14-V(N)(3)(d).

Equal protection:

A might also contend that its equal protection rights are violated by the picketing ordinance, since only shopping centers are covered by the statute (leaving all other types of commercial and business establishments unaffected). Again, however, assuming the legislation has a constitutional purpose (which it does), it is not necessary that all of the potential problems in the field be cured in a single instance. Thus, City would prevail in this instance too. *See* ELO Ch.10-II(C).

In summary, it appears that the picketing statute is constitutional.

ANSWER TO QUESTION 7

1. *Is the statute valid?*

There are several ways in which Price ("P") could attack the State A statute.

Due Process: P could initially contend that the State A statute violates his substantive due process rights (contained in the Fourteenth Amendment) by purporting to tax the publisher of prohibited material, whether or not (1) he has any physical presence in State A, or (2) the literature is ever distributed in State A (i.e., read literally, anyone publishing such materials, anywhere, is libel for the tax, whether or not (a) the written matter is ever distributed within State A, or (b) the publisher knew, or had reason to believe, that the written matter would ever be distributed in State A). Thus, there is no sufficient nexus between the levying authority and the activity sought to be taxed. While State A could assert in rebuttal that a reasonable construction of the legislation would be that it applied only to materials which were actually delivered to buyers within State A, P would still have insufficient contacts (merely responding to telephone orders initiated through literature mailed to potential buyers) with State A to satisfy due process. *See* ELO Ch.9-IV(A) and Ch.12-III(E).

Vagueness: P could alternatively assert that the due process clause of the Fourteenth Amendment is violated because the statute is unconstitutionally vague (i.e., a person of ordinary intelligence and aware of the statute would be uncertain as to whether her conduct is proscribed by the legislation). This contention would be predicated upon the assertion that whether material is "lewd" or "lascivious" is highly subjective. Since an unconstitutionally vague statute cannot serve as the basis of governmental action, the legislation is invalid. State A could respond in rebuttal that (1) the words in question are adequately defined in most dictionaries, and are therefore sufficiently certain, and (2) *if the material in this instance was obscene* (the facts are silent as to this aspect), the words in question should be read as being equivalent to "obscene" (a term which has been defined by the U.S. Supreme Court). Nevertheless, the terminology in question would probably be deemed unconstitutionally vague, and therefore the statute would be invalid. *See* ELO Ch.14-III(B).

First Amendment: P could alternatively assert that although printing entities are not immune from taxes of general application, the statute in question is a disguised regulatory measure which unconstitutionally infringes upon P's First Amendment rights (applicable to the states via the Fourteenth Amendment). This is arguably demonstrated by the facts that (1) the statute is directly related to the content of the printed matter in question (i.e., it applies to only lewd, lascivious or obscene literature), and (2) the $1 fee applies to each publication, (regardless of the number of pages or the price charged for the material). While obscene matter may be constitutionally regulated, merely "lewd" and "lascivious" materials may not be. Although State A could contend in rebuttal that the levy is a mere "privilege" tax upon the right to undertake a specific activity (the sale of "lewd", "lascivious" or "obscene" matter within that jurisdiction), the content-related nature of the legislation would probably result in a finding in favor of P on this issue also. *See* ELO Ch.14-IV(J)(3)(b) and VII(E)(1)(b).

2. *May State A revenue agents seize and destroy copies of P's books?*

Procedural Due Process: Under the due process clause of the Fourteenth Amendment, a state may not significantly affect property rights of an individual without a prior, adequately noticed hearing. Since the destruction of the items would constitute an irreparable deprivation of property, P and the vendors of the books would contend that their procedural due process rights were violated by the lack of any provision in the State A law for a hearing as to whether the materials were within the statute's purview. Unless State A could persuade the court that an intervening (i.e., between seizure and actual destruction of the books) hearing was implicit in the legislation, P and the vendors would probably be successful in their assertion of this theory. *See* ELO Ch.9-V(K)(1).

Prior Restraint: P and the vendors of the books could alternatively contend that the statute constitutes an invalid prior restraint, since it authorizes "large scale" seizures of materials without prior judicial determination that the items fall within the scope of the statute; *A Quantity of Books v. Kansas*, 378 U.S. 205 (1964). As a consequence, publishers would be reluctant to print questionable materials (i.e., if the items could be seized and destroyed, potential vendees might be hesitant to purchase them). While State A could contend that, unless the seizure of the materials was immediate, it would be impossible to determine the appropriate amount of tax to be levied, this argument would probably fail. The (1) evidence could be preserved by purchase of a single copy of the material by the governmental authority, and (2) precise amount of books printed could probably be determined from invoices and order forms transferred amongst P and the book purchasers. *See* ELO Ch.14-XI(C)(2).

Thus, State A revenue agents may ***not*** lawfully seize and destroy copies of the books in State A.

ANSWER TO QUESTION 8

1. *Is the federal statute constitutional?*

Under Article I, Section 8 (Clause 3), of the U.S. Constitution, Congress has the right to legislate with respect to any activity which has an appreciable effect, even though indirect, on interstate commerce. Congressional findings as to the impact of an activity upon interstate commerce are ordinarily given great deference. Since people with reading difficulties would (1) be limited in the types of economic activities in which they could participate (i.e., participation in occupations which required significant reading skills or use of equipment would be precluded), (2) purchase fewer types of items (i.e., computers, sophisticated equipment and machinery), and (3) travel less (i.e., such persons might be unable to read signs or menus), the legislation appears to be within Congress' power (i.e., the interstate commerce provision and the "necessary and proper" clause attendant thereto). *See* ELO Ch.4-IV(A) & (H)(2)(b)(iii).

Board might contend that this legislation violates the Tenth Amendment, since it encroaches upon an area (i.e., education) which has traditionally been a local function, and therefore cannot be regulated by the federal government; ***National League of Cities v. Usery***, 426 U.S. 833 (1976). However, because ***Garcia v. San Antonio Metropolitan Transit Authority***; 105 S. Ct. 105 (1985), overruled *Usery*, this argument should be unsuccessful. *See* ELO Ch.40V(C)-(F).

Thus the federal statute was probably constitutional.

2a. *Assuming the federal statute is unconstitutional, what issues should the AB group raise against Board?*

The AB group would raise equal protection and due process objections to Board's action.

In determining whether a law which is neutral on its face (as the present legislation, which discontinues *all* remedial reading programs) has a discriminatory purpose, a court may consider any pertinent data (including the statements made by Board's director). If purposeful discrimination could be shown, County's actions would have to satisfy the strict scrutiny standard (i.e., a compelling state interest is furthered by the governmental conduct, and there is no less burdensome means of satisfying that objective). Since the termination of the program has a disproportionately adverse racial impact (while racial minorities comprise 10% of County's population, they constitute 50% of the students enrolled in the program), Board would have the burden of proving that its actions were *not* racially motivated.

Board could argue that (1) its action was dictated by financial necessity, and (2) the effect of the program's termination also impacts upon nonminority students. In rebuttal, the AB group could contend that Board's purposeful discrimination is proven by the facts that (1) there were *increased* monies available for the drama arts workshops (however, the total of this amount was only 15% of the funds which had been available for the remedial reading program), and (2) the director indicated handicapped students would receive preference over minority students if adequate funding subsequently became available (although this could be defended by the fact that the latter group would completely fail to learn to read if their regular studies were not supplemented by the remedial program). Without data about Board's financial situation, it is impossible to determine if terminating the program was "a necessary economic measure" or racially inspired. Assuming, the court found that it was *not* racially motivated, then County would only have to show that the program's termination had a reasonable relationship to a constitutional purpose to sustain its action. County's showing that monetary pressures compelled cessation of the remedial reading program establishes this relationship. *See* ELO Ch.10-III(C).

The AB group could alternatively contend that the program's termination violated their substantive due process rights. Under the Fourteenth Amendment, one cannot be deprived of fundamental "liberties" (i.e., rights recognized as essential to the orderly pursuit of happiness). The right to possess reasonably adequate reading skills is arguably "fundamental", since a failure to read proficiently inevitably results in lower paying jobs and an overall diminished ability to enjoy life. While the Supreme Court has held that there is no fundamental right to an equally financed education (i.e., all school districts within a particular county do not have to expend an equal dollar amount per child; *San Antonio School District v. Rodriguez*), 411 U.S.1 (1973), it has never held that a school district can offer less than an adequate education. *See* ELO Ch.10-X(A)(4) and Ch.9-IV(A)(4)(b).

Again, more facts are necessary to determine if children of the AB group would be literate without the program. If not, continuation of the program is probably a fundamental right, and therefore, the strict scrutiny test would be apply (i.e., Board would have to show that discontinuing the remedial reading program was virtually the only means of meeting its budgetary crisis). However, if the AB group would receive an adequate education without the program, Board's action would only have to have a reasonable relationship to a constitutional purpose. This would seem to be present in this case, since any good faith decision with respect to how a limited amount of education money is apportioned would be reasonable.

2b. *Assuming the federal statute is unconstitutional, what issues would the CD group raise against Board?*

The CD group would also raise the substantive due process argument that reading skills are a "fundamental" right, and therefore cessation of the program is subject to a strict scrutiny analysis. The facts indicate that, given their innate learning disabilities, this group would not acquire adequate reading skills without the program. Since it is unlikely that Board could show that other programs are more important than minimal reading proficiency, it is highly doubtful that (1) cancellation of the program served a compelling state interest, and (2) there was no less burdensome means available to Board of satisfying its financial constraints. In summary, the substantive due process argument of the CD group should be successful. *See* ELO Ch.9-IV(A)(4)(b).

Alternatively, the CD group would contend that their equal protection rights were violated. There is no case law supporting the proposition that educationally handicapped students are a "suspect" or "quasi-suspect" group. Since (1) there has probably been no history of purposeful unequal treatment with respect to educationally handicapped persons, and (2) their handicaps are (presumably) not unalterable, it appears to be doubtful that the CD group would be classified as "suspect" or "quasi-suspect." Since the program's cessation would probably meet the rational relationship test, CD's equal protection argument should be unsuccessful. *See* ELO Ch.10-II(A) & (D).

ANSWER TO QUESTION 9

Jurisdiction of the U.S. Supreme Court:

Review of state court decisions by the Supreme Court is limited to federal questions (i.e., those arising under the Constitution, a federal statute, or a U.S. treaty). Assuming Groups A, B and C have each contended that the statutes in question were violative of their First Amendment rights (applicable to the states via the Fourteenth Amendment), this requirement is fulfilled. Review by appeal is permitted when a state statute is upheld against an assertion of invalidity under the Constitution. Thus, the Supreme Court may properly review these decisions. *See* ELO Ch.2-II(A)(1).

Convictions of Group A:

Where a public figure is the subject of an allegedly defamatory statement, prosecution cannot successfully occur unless the defendant acted with actual malice; *Garrison v. Louisiana*, 379 U.S. 64 (1964). Group A might initially contend that the statute is overly broad on its face (and therefore cannot constitute a basis for valid governmental action), since it purports to punish conduct which is constitutionally permissible (i.e., actual malice is not required by the statute). State X, however, will argue in rebuttal that, unless a statute gives the enforcing entity virtually unlimited discretion in deciding whether the law is applicable or not (i.e., the law is not substantially overbroad), it may serve as the basis of governmental action if it is constitutionally **applied**. Given the relatively precise standard of "hatred, contempt and ridicule", the statute is probably **not** substantially overbroad. Thus, Group A could be prosecuted under the statute (if it is constitutionally applied). *See* ELO Ch.14-III(A) & IV(E)(2).

Actual malice is present where the defendant (1) knew her statements were false, or (2) should have seriously doubted their accuracy. Group A would have contended that (1) Senator X, being a state legislator, qualifies as a public official, and (2) since Senator X had "secretly" sold the apartments, the statements involved cannot be said to have been made with actual malice. However, State X could have argued in rebuttal that (1) the defamatory portion of the advertisement was the assertion that he had unduly influenced University officials in their decision to cease dormitory construction (rather than the statement that he owned private apartment houses which competed with the dormitories), and (2) it is unclear as to how Group A determined that Senator X had pressured State X University officials. If Group A premised its advertisements upon mere rumor, their statements could be deemed to have been made recklessly (and therefore the actual malice standard would be satisfied).

The prosecution could have alternatively contended that *Dun & Bradstreet v. Greenmoss Builders, Inc.*, 105 S. Ct. 2939 (1985), overruled earlier decisions and held that where a defamation pertains to matters of "private" (as opposed to "public") concern, state libel law applies (which often requires only that the statements in question have been false). Since the matter involved was private in nature (i.e., the Senator had influenced University officials to cease dormitory construction for his personal financial gain), prosecution under the state law was appropriate. However, a decision about whether to undertake dormitory construction would probably be viewed as a matter of "public" concern. Thus, even if the constitutional protection of an "actual malice" standard extends only to speech pertaining to matters of "public" concern, State X would still be obliged to show that Group A's communications satisfied this standard. *See* ELO Ch.14-VI(D).

Convictions of Group B

Vagueness: A statute is unconstitutionally vague where persons of ordinary intelligence could not determine if contemplated conduct was, or was not, prohibited. Group B could have contended that the phrase, "circumstances tending to disrupt public order or tranquility" is too vague, since it is unclear as to whether (1) the physical act of "congregating" must be the source of the public disruption, or (2) the message disseminated by those congregating may be the basis of prosecution. Additionally, the determination of what constitutes a "disruption" of the "public order or tranquility" is highly subjective in nature (i.e., would the stopping of vehicle drivers to shout their approval or disapproval of the message being publicized fall within this standard?). If a statute fails for vagueness, it cannot serve as the basis for governmental action. While State X probably argued in rebuttal that the "disruption" of "public order or tranquility" is sufficiently definite (i.e., where, as a consequence of a defendant's conduct, a possibility of violence or physical injury existed), Group B would probably prevail upon this contention. *See* ELO Ch.14-III(B).

Overbreadth: Group B could have alternatively contended that the statute was overly broad on its face (i.e., the entity charged with enforcing the law had virtually complete discretion in determining whether it should be applied to a particular situation). The determination of when the "public order or tranquility" has been "disrupted" is highly subjective in nature. Therefore, the enactment cannot serve as the basis for governmental action; *Lovell v. Griffin*, 303 U.S. 444 (1938). State X could have argued in rebuttal, however, that the determination of what constitutes "disruption" of the "public order or tranquility" constitutes an adequate limitation upon its conduct to avoid application of the facially overbreadth doctrine. Although a close question, State X properly prevailed on this issue. *See* ELO Ch.14-III(A) & IV(E)(2).

Group B could next have argued that the statute is unconstitutional as applied. While "fighting words" (communicative words or conduct which, by their very utterance or occurrence, have a tendency to incite an immediate breach of the peace) may be the subject of a criminal prosecution, there is no indication that violence was threatened in any manner (the facts state only that traffic was delayed by curious drivers who slowed down to view the picketing).

Thus, even if the State X statute survives attacks for vagueness, and facial overbreadth, it would probably still be deemed unconstitutional as applied. Therefore, the Group B convictions should be reversed. *See* ELO Ch.14-III(A)(5)(d).

Public Forum: State X could have also contended that the area within one block of the administration building (while generally open to the public) is not a public forum; *Cox v. Louisiana*, 377 U.S. 288 (1965). Therefore, speech may be completely prohibited in that area. However, since the statute does not purport to preclude all demonstrations (but merely disruptive ones) from the locale in question, Group B's conduct probably could ***not*** be criminally sanctioned. *See* ELO Ch.14-IV(M)(2)(d).

Group C

Due Process: Group C probably contended that its due process rights were violated since the statute failed to adequately advise them that their conduct was prohibited (i.e., the legislation only punishes encroachment upon the lands of another ***after receiving notice prohibiting such entry***). The law does not purport to cover a refusal to leave land upon which the defendant had previously been invited. While State X could have argued in rebuttal that a reasonable interpretation of the trespass statute would be that deliberately refusing to egress from land after receiving notice to leave was within the purvey of the statute, Group C should have prevailed on this issue. Thus, the convictions of Group C should also be reversed. *See* ELO Ch.9-V(K).

ANSWER TO QUESTION 10

D's Conviction for Violating the Lakeport Smoke Abatement Code ("LSAC")

Dormant Commerce Clause: Pursuant to the Tenth Amendment, a state (and its subdivisions) is empowered to enact legislation for the health, safety and general welfare of its populace. However, where local legislation places an undue burden upon interstate commerce (i.e., the burden imposed outweighs the merits and purposes of the law), the local regulation will be invalidated; *Southern Pacific Co. v. Arizona*, 325 U.S. 761 (1945). D might contend that the LSAC would require expensive alterations (the facts are silent as to this point), with the consequence that compliance with the law would make it impossible for D to maintain its business of transporting cargo among several states. However, since the (1) LSAC does not appear to be in conflict with the laws of any other state to which D's vessel travels, and (2) facts fail to indicate that a significant number of other ships are not in compliance with the LSAC, it is unlikely that mere enhanced expense would result in a finding that an undue burden upon interstate commerce had occurred. *See* ELO Ch.6-I(H)(2).

Pre-emption: There would appear to be little doubt that the Congressional Act is valid, since there is a constitutional basis for the law (seagoing safety) pursuant to both (1) the commerce clause, and (2) Congress' right to legislate with respect to navigable waterways; *United States v. Appalachian Electric Power Co.*, 311 U.S. 377 (1940).

D could contend that where Congress has enacted legislation with the intent that it occupy that field completely, local regulations pertaining to that area (even though not actually in conflict with the federal law) are deemed to be superseded. In the absence of a clear declaration of Congressional intent, the Supreme Court may consider the following factors in deciding if the federal law was intended as exclusive legislation in that area: (1) whether the subject matter of the local enactment has traditionally been considered within a state's police power; (2) the completeness of the federal regulatory scheme; (3) whether the area covered by the federal law is one for which national, rather than local, regulation is more appropriate; and (4) the similarity between the federal and local enactments. Since there apparently is no legislative history which specifically indicates that the federal legislation was intended to be the exclusive body of law pertaining to vessel construction and operation, the intent of Congress must be determined from the other factors cited above. D could contend that the LSAC should be deemed to be superseded because of the "comprehensiveness" of the federal statute and the need to have legislative consistency where instrumentalities of interstate commerce are involved.

However, Lakeport officials could contend in rebuttal that (1) a similar municipal smoke abatement ordinance was sustained against a supersession attack in *Huron Portland Cement Co. v. City of Detroit*, 362 U.S. 440 (1960); (2) matters involving the public health or safety of citizens have traditionally been left to local government; and (3) the subject matter of the federal law was vessel safety (not emissions).

Assuming D's vessel can be made to comply with the LSAC without violating federal requirements pertaining to boilers and fuel, it probably would ***not*** be deemed to be superseded by the federal legislation. *See* ELO Ch.6-III(C).

Validity of the State X Personal Tax: Consistent with due process, a taxpayer's domiciliary state may ordinarily tax the full value of an instrumentality of interstate commerce. Nevertheless, where the property involved has been "habitually employed" in another jurisdiction, the commerce clause requires apportionment of the value of such property to the extent that it has acquired a taxable situs in another state (whether or not other states are actually taxing the item); *Central Railroad v. Pennsylvania*, 370 U.S. 607 (1972).

Since the (1) vessel in question only "enters State X's ports for occasional refueling and repairs", and (2) loading and unloading of transport is done at terminals in other states, D can probably prove that its vessel has acquired a taxable situs in several other jurisdictions. Thus, as a consequence of the commerce clause, D should not be liable for an amount of tax which exceeds the proportion of time which the vessel is located within State X relative to all time spent in other ports.

It might be mentioned that the "homeport doctrine" (pursuant to which a vessel sailing on international waters may be taxed only by the country in which its "homeport" is located) would ***not*** be applicable since (1) the facts indicate that D's vessel travels only on the Great Lakes, and (2) this relatively arcane doctrine probably would not be followed today. *See* ELO Ch.4-IV(B)(3).

ANSWER TO QUESTION 11

1. *Lease Non-Renewal*

State X might next assert that review by the U.S. Supreme Court is inappropriate because there is an adequate, independent state ground for the decision (i.e., under State X law, a tenant has no right to obtain an extension of her lease, even though the landlord's refusal to renew the agreement is based on the fact that the tenant has engaged in lawful activities). However, D could probably successfully argue in rebuttal that the essence of her case is that her First Amendment and due process rights have been violated by the director's decision. Therefore, a right of action exists under federal law, and so review by the U.S. Supreme Court is appropriate. *See* ELO Ch.2-II(D)(2).

Substantive Issues:

State action: Since the housing project was owned and operated by State X, there would be little question that official actions by the director with respect to operation of the facility would be attributed to State X. *See* ELO Ch.12-I(A).

Procedural Due Process: Although there is no case which stands squarely for the proposition that there is a Fourteenth Amendment property right to public housing, D's situation could be analogized to public employment. A "property" right to continued public employment may be found where there is some clear practice or understanding that the employee (in this instance, the lessee) will be terminated only for cause; *Arnett v. Kennedy*, 416 U.S. 134 (1974). If leases at the housing project are ordinarily renewed automatically, D could contend that she had a justifiable expectation of continued occupancy at the project. Therefore, she was constitutionally entitled to some type of adversarial hearing prior to the director's refusal to extend her leasehold interest. While State X could argue in rebuttal that the renewal of outstanding leases is merely done as a matter of convenience (and therefore should not have created an expectation of automatic continuation of one's lease), D should prevail on this issue. Therefore, D would have a constitutional right to reinstatement of her leasehold interest. *See* ELO Ch.9-V(K)(1).

First Amendment: D could alternatively contend that the director's action violated her First Amendment rights of free speech and association (applicable to the states via the Fourteenth Amendment), since one may not be deprived of public employment for speaking out on issues of general importance; *Pickering v. Board of Education*, 391 U.S. 563 (1968). Similarly, speech about a subject of great interest to lessees at a housing project (i.e., rental rates) cannot be the basis for terminating a tenant's occupancy. State X would argue in rebuttal that a public employee's (in this instance, a public lessee) First Amendment rights must balance against efficient performance of the governmental function being performed; *Connick v. Myers*, 461 U.S. 138 (1983). Since D's statements constitute nothing more than a personal attack against the director for his recommendations pertaining to operation of the housing project, D's First Amendment rights were outweighed by the harmful effects of her criticism.

Even if D's statements were incorrect (i.e., the director had not exercised "poor judgment" in recommending increased rents), her statement was more in the nature of an opinion about a matter of legitimate concern to residents of the housing project, than factual criticism about the director. Thus, D should prevail on this question too. *See* ELO Ch.14-X(C)(7).

Equal Protection: Finally, D could assert that her equal protection rights (embodied in the Fourteenth Amendment) were violated since, as a consequence of the refusal to renew her lease, D has been singled out for different, adverse treatment than that imposed upon other residents of the housing project. This contention should also prevail. *See* ELO Ch.10-I(B)(3).

2. *Contempt of Court Conviction*

Exhaustion of State X remedies: State X would initially contend that review by the U.S. Supreme Court is inappropriate, since D apparently failed to appeal her case to the highest court in State X in which a decision on her matter could be rendered. Assuming D was aware of the injunction and the order was appealable to an appellate court, this assertion by State X should be successful. For purposes of analysis, however, it will be assumed that the contempt conviction was not subject to review by a higher State X court. *See* ELO Ch.2-II(B)(2).

A court order, even one that has been incorrectly issued, must be obeyed unless (1) judicial review of the injunction was deliberately made impracticable by the prosecuting entity, or (2) it is patently invalid on its face; *Walker v. Birmingham*, 388 U.S. 307 (1967). Since the injunction was issued on May 5 and presumably served upon D soon afterwards, D could *not* successfully contend that judicial appeal was impracticable. However, if there is no State X statute pertaining to public demonstrations, D could argue that the injunction was "patently invalid," since (1) it is well established that a public forum (such as a park) cannot be completely foreclosed to speech-related activity; and (2) while public forums are subject to reasonable regulations pertaining to time, place and manner, the injunction in question completely precluded D's rally in the park (rather than simply limiting it to the appropriate number of persons). Nevertheless, given the strong presumption of validity with respect to court orders, State X should prevail on this question. Therefore, the contempt of court conviction would probably be upheld, assuming D's incarceration did not exceed six months; *Baldwin v. New York*, 399 U.S. 66 (1970) (where a prison term of more than six months is imposed, a defendant is entitled to a jury trial). *See* ELO Ch.14-IV(E)(5)(d).

If, however, the injunction was patently invalid on its face, D could probably successfully contend that the director's *ex parte* order constituted a deprivation of her Fourteenth Amendment due process rights. Since a significant right is affected by the injunction (D's First Amendment right of speech and association), she was entitled to notice and an opportunity to be heard prior to issuance of the court order. Because the injunction was obtained almost one full month prior to the pre-determined speaking date, the "emergency" situation which must exist to justify an *ex parte* order was not present in this instance. *See* ELO Ch.9-V(K).

Additionally, the injunction is probably invalid upon (1) due process (i.e., vagueness), and (2) First Amendment grounds, respectively, since (1) a reasonably intelligent person might have difficulty understanding what constitutes a "mass rally" (20, 50, 100 or 200 persons?), and (2) the order sought to preclude the rally entirely, rather than place a reasonable limitation (i.e., 100 persons) on the number of individuals who could attend (without causing any interference with the normal traffic flow). *See* ELO Ch.14-III(B) & IV(M)(2)(d).

ANSWER TO QUESTION 12

The Motion for Dismissal:

Abstention:

A U.S. District Court may abstain from hearing a case which challenges the constitutionality of an ambiguous non-federal statute if the alleged defect might be cured by a narrowing interpretation by a state court. While State A might contend that abstention is appropriate in this instance because no state court has yet construed the statute in question, Ajax and Ned ("Plaintiffs") could probably successfully argue in rebuttal that a curative construction is unlikely since both the (1) 30-60 year parameters, and (2) specific testing requirements, leave virtually no room for a constitutionally valid interpretation. *See* ELO Ch.5-IV(D)(1).

Standing:

Article III of the Constitution requires that to have standing in federal court, a plaintiff must show a direct and immediate personal injury which is traceable to the challenged action; *Simon v. Eastern Kentucky Welfare Rights Organization*, 426 U.S. 26 (1976). State X might contend that Ned has suffered no injury since he has not been terminated from his employment, nor is there any indication that he is receiving less compensation than he received prior to the State A enactment. Ajax arguably lacks standing because it apparently has other drivers who are capable of obtaining the "Special Driving Permits." Assuming, however, (1) Ned's re-assignment (a) to other routes ultimately results in lessened compensation (of any amount) for him, or, (b) is disadvantageous for any other reason (i.e., the substituted routes are more physically demanding because they are longer and/or more dangerous); and (2) altering driving assignments to comply with State A law could result in some drivers deciding to leave Ajax's employ, the Plaintiffs probably have standing. *See* ELO Ch.16-III(A)(5).

The State A Statute:

Pursuant to the Tenth Amendment, a state may ordinarily enact legislation which is aimed at promoting the health, safety or welfare of its citizenry. Since the legislation in question is obviously aimed at decreasing the possibility of accidents involving explosive-carrying trucks, it would be constitutionally valid (unless it contravenes some federal interest). *See* ELO Ch.6-I(I)(2).

Supremacy Clause:

Where a state statute conflicts with the language of, or purposes sought to be achieved by, a federal statute, the former enactment will be invalid under the Supremacy Clause. Plaintiffs will contend that the State A statute is inconsistent with the purposes sought to be achieved by the federal law because it would induce age discrimination (i.e., to avoid being obliged to juggle schedules to circumvent State A, employers would (a) hire drivers within State A's age parameters, and (b) be more likely to terminate employees who could not travel within State A). However, State A could argue in rebuttal that (1) Plaintiffs' argument is premised on speculative secondary effects of its law, and (2) it is unlikely that Congress intended to pre-empt state legislation which was based upon *bona fide* occupational qualifications (statistical studies support the State A's age restrictions). Unless there is clear legislative history that Congress intended to totally preclude age as a consideration for employment, Plaintiffs probably would *not* succeed on this argument. *See* ELO Ch.6-III(B) & (C).

Equal Protection Clause:

Since the elderly have not historically been subjected to purposeful unequal treatment or relegated to a position of political powerlessness, the strict scrutiny standard would probably not apply; *Massachusetts Board of Retirement v. Murgia*, 427 U.S. 307 (1976).

Plaintiffs might nevertheless contend that the rational relationship test (i.e., there must be a rational relationship between the classification drawn by the statute and the governmental object sought) is not satisfied. This is because (1) the physical examination and driving test measure more accurately one's ability to drive safely than strict biological age; and (2) persons with perfect driving records could be excluded as a consequence of the statute, while others with negative driving histories might nevertheless qualify for a Special Driving Permit ("SDP"). However, since the classification (1) need only be rational (i.e., maybe drivers over 60 are more prone to heart attacks), and (2) is supported by empirical data, State A would probably prevail on this issue as well. *See* ELO Ch.10-II(F)(2)(a).

Dormant Interstate Commerce Clause:

State legislation which unduly burdens interstate commerce (i.e., the interference with interstate commerce outweighs the interest sought to be protected by the law) is invalid; *Bibb v. Navajo Freight Lines, Inc.*, 359 U.S. 520 (1959). Plaintiffs could contend that the State A statute imposes a substantial burden upon interstate commerce, since interstate trucking companies will now be obliged (probably at substantial inconvenience and expense) to avoid State A or be compelled to hire additional employees who can acquire a SDP. State A, however, could argue in rebuttal that it has a strong interest in the legislation (i.e., the desire to avoid catastrophic explosions which have a potential for causing great loss of lives and property). Assuming State A could show that most truck companies have drivers within their employ who qualify for a SDP (and therefore the statute merely results in the inconvenience of having to alter job assignments), it would again prevail. *See* ELO Ch.6-I(H)(4)(a).

Due Process:

Where a state statute conclusively presumes that certain facts exist which result in an adverse classification, the Supreme Court held at one time that the denial of an opportunity to challenge that presumption could violate an individual's Fourteenth Amendment's due process right to demonstrate that the fact presumed is not true in his case. *Vlandis v. Kline*, 412 U.S. 441 (1973). Thus, under *Vlandis*, Plaintiffs could have argued that the presumption that persons over 60 were more prone to accidents than others was invalid (especially since Ned was capable of satisfying the physical examination and driving test requirements of State A). However, today the *Vlandis* rule allowing due process scrutiny of irrebuttable presumptions applies only where, even apart from the existence of the presumption, there is reason to give heightened scrutiny to the classification. *Weinberger v. Salfi*, 422 U.S. 749 (1975). Since as discussed above age-based classifications don't get heightened Equal Protection scrutiny, probably heightened due process scrutiny of the irrebuttable presumption won't be applied either. *See* ELO Ch.10-X(G)(1)-(4).

Even if the court were to scrutinize the irrebuttable presumption, State A could probably successfully contend that (1) there is no "property" interest in private employment, and (2) statistical studies (which were presumably methodologically sound) have established that drivers over 60 have a higher incidence of accidents than those under 60.

In summary, it is unlikely that Plaintiffs would be able to invalidate the State A statute.

ANSWER TO QUESTION 13

There are several contentions which Micro ("M") could assert to invalidate the Act.

There is little question that the Act represents a valid exercise of Pacific's Tenth Amendment right to enact laws for the general welfare of its citizenry. The Act arguably promotes and protects the morality of Pacific's citizens.

Impairment of Contracts:

Pursuant to Article I, Section 10 of the U.S. Constitution, a state may not enact a law which substantially changes outstanding contract rights. The facts fail to indicate whether M's outstanding contracts with its subscribers stated that "R" rated pictures would begin at 8:00 P.M. and "X" rated movies would commence at 10:00 P.M. If they did, M could contend that the Act results in a substantial impairment of those agreements. The DJ could argue in rebuttal that merely changing the times (rather than completely precluding the showing of such pictures) does not result in a "substantial" impairment of the Micro-subscriber contracts. However, since most persons cannot practically watch movies through the latest hours of the night, M would probably prevail with respect to this contention. *See* ELO Ch.11-III(A) & (C).

Cruel and Unusual Punishment:

Under the Eighth Amendment (applicable to the states via the Fourteenth Amendment), a sentence which is grossly disproportionate in relation to the offense committed, is unconstitutional (and therefore invalid). Since (1) the Act provides that violators may be assessed a fine of $100.00 to $500.00 *per household*, and (2) there are 20,000 subscribers, the transmission of a non-complying movie into a single home could result in a fine of between two and ten million dollars. While the DJ might argue in rebuttal that a reasonable construction of the language is that the fines would apply only to those households that actually watched the illegal movie, this contention appears to be inconsistent with the plain meaning of the Act. M would probably prevail on this argument also. *See* ELO Ch.9-V(K)(3)(b).

Privacy:

M could also contend that the statute in question violates the due process right of privacy embodied in the Fourteenth Amendment. M would argue that the Act unconstitutionally regulates what people may view in the privacy of their own homes; *Stanley v. Georgia*, 394 U.S. 557 (1969). The DJ could assert in rebuttal, however, that *Stanley* is distinguishable because (1) the Act does not totally preclude the transmission of "X and R" movies to subscribers' homes, and (2) children could unwittingly "stumble upon" the offensive movies (which would, in effect, violate their right of privacy); *FCC v. Pacifica Foundation*, 438 U.S. 728 (1978). Nevertheless, M would probably prevail upon this issue too, since (1) the time parameters set forth in the Act make it virtually impossible for most persons to practicably see "X" or "R" rated movies; and (2) there is little likelihood of a child inadvertently viewing the restricted movies since (a) television programs are ordinarily under parental supervision in the late evening hours, and (b) television listings are usually more readily accessible than radio listings. *See* ELO Ch.9-III(O)(2)(c), (S)(1)(c) and Ch.14-VII(C) & (D).

First Amendment:

M might next contend that its First Amendment rights were violated because the Act, in effect, precludes speech which is constitutionally protected (i.e., there is no indication that the "R" or "X" movies are obscene); *Schad v. Mount Ephraim*, 452 U.S. 61 (1981). The DJ could argue in rebuttal, however, that the Act is a time and place regulation, and therefore is valid if it (1) serves a substantial interest (i.e., protecting the morals of minors), and (2) does not unreasonably limit alternative avenues of communication (i.e., persons who want to view the films can simply stay up later); *Young v. American Mini Theatres*, 427 U.S. 50 (1976). The DJ could also cite *FCC v. Pacifica Foundation*, 438 U.S. 726 (1978), for the proposition that the First Amendment affords less than complete protection with respect to speech which may be overheard by children and lacks "social value." Since the broadcasting in question involves violent and sex-oriented scenes, the Act is arguably valid.

However, M could initially respond that the *Young* decision (which, in effect, limited adult movies to certain areas within a city) is distinguishable. The legislation in that instance was primarily concerned with the secondary effects of "adult" movies (crime, neighborhood deterioration, diminished property values, etc.), rather than the content of the speech. M would also argue that there is a significant difference between merely making it inconvenient for persons to view a particular material and making it virtually impossible for them to do so (as the Act does by permitting the movies to be shown only during the very latest hours of the night). Finally, M would argue that *FCC v. Pacifica Foundation* is distinguishable because (1) the language at issue there was probably more severe than would be contained in an "R" rated movie, and (2) radios (which are accessible to almost all teenagers) are less subject to parental supervision than television shows viewable only after 8:00 P.M. (well after when most parents have returned home from work). *See* ELO Ch.14-IV(L)(5).

Again, M should prevail.

Equal Protection:

M might also argue that its Fourteenth Amendment equal protection rights were violated by the fact that, while private companies were regulated by the Act, governmental subdivisions were not. However, it is well established that a legislature may "take one step at a time to remedy only part of a broader problem;" *Williamson v. Lee Optical Co.*, 348 U.S. 483 (1955). The legislature could have reasonably believed that governmental subdivisions, being more amenable to the will of their constituents, would be less likely to transmit questionable subject matter. *See* ELO Ch.10-II(C).

Thus, this contention by M would probably be unsuccessful.

Vagueness:

M could conceivably contend that the Act is unconstitutionally vague (and therefore violates its due process right to be adequately informed of conduct which is illegal), since it is unclear (1) what constitutes an "enterprise," and (2) whether a corporation is a "person" within the meaning of the Act. However, the DJ could probably successfully contend in rebuttal that (1) the Act was obviously aimed at precluding the transmittal pictures in question by *any* private entity, and (2) corporations are ordinarily deemed to be included within the word "person" or "enterprise" when used in a statute which obviously affects business concerns. Thus, the DJ would prevail on this issue. *See* ELO Ch.14-III(B).

Summary:

Since the Act is probably unconstitutional upon First Amendment, privacy (due process), impairment of contract, and Eighth Amendment (cruel and unusual punishment) grounds, it should be invalidated by a federal court.

ANSWER TO QUESTION 14

(1) *The Ut Use Tax:*

It is assumed that Ut ordinarily charges a sales tax on toy purchases made in that state. If it did not, the use tax would probably constitute an impermissible discrimination against interstate commerce (i.e., local merchants would have a significant advantage over out-of-state vendors, since sales by the latter group would be burdened with a tax which had not been imposed on the former group). It should also be mentioned that the Ut *use* tax could not exceed the difference between the Ut sales tax and the sales tax assessed by the State of Hio. *See* ELO Ch.6-II(E).

Arrow ("A") could, however, contend that the Ut use tax violates its equal protection rights, since it applies only to mail order sales (i.e., those persons who sell goods to Ut residents in a non-mail manner are exempted from the tax). A would assert that there is no rational basis for this distinction. However, Ut could probably successfully argue in rebuttal that (1) a state may deal with a problem (i.e., equalizing the taxation rate of in-state sales with those purchases made out-of-state, so that consumers are not encouraged to buy items in other jurisdictions) one step at a time; and (2) possibly, it is easier to identify mail order sellers than other types of out-of-state vendors. *See* ELO Ch.10-II(C).

A might also assert that the tax violates the privileges and immunities clause of Article IV of the U.S. Constitution. This clause prohibits discrimination against non-residents with respect to "basic" rights, unless the law in question is substantially related to an important governmental purpose. However, use taxes are a recognized means of preventing in-state businesses (which are ordinarily required to assess a sales tax) from being disadvantaged by lower sales tax rates in other jurisdictions. Additionally, there is probably no "basic" right by an out-of- state seller to insist upon complete equality with respect to the imposition of a use tax. *See* ELO Ch.7-IV(B)(1)-(3).

Thus, the Ut use tax is probably valid.

(2) *Collection of the Ut Use Tax:*

Under the due process clause of the Fourteenth Amendment, a taxpayer must have sufficient contacts with the taxing state for the latter to be able to constitutionally require the former to pay taxes to it. It is well established that the solicitation of sales by mail does not satisfy the requirement of sufficient contacts enabling the imposition of a duty on an interstate seller to collect a use tax on sales to local residents; *National Bellas Hess, Inc. v. Illinois Department of Revenue*, 386 U.S. 753 (1967). Thus, A does **not** have to collect the Ut use tax. *See* ELO Ch.6-II(F)(1)(a).

(3) *The Penn Highway Use License Fee:*

A could assert that this tax is unconstitutional on due process grounds, since (1) it is too vague (i.e., a person of ordinary intelligence would be unable to determine if contemplated conduct was illegal) because the meaning of "regularly" is unclear, and (2) the tax (a flat amount) bears no relationship to the amount of actual highway use.

As to the latter contention, Penn could probably successfully argue that the relatively nominal $20.00 fee is valid as long as the funds raised by the tax are utilized in a highway-related manner; *Capitol Greyhound Lines v. Brice*, 339 U.S. 542 (1950). Penn could have concluded that attempting to apportion the use tax amongst *all* actual users of its highways would simply be too cumbersome (and perhaps even impossible to do with sufficient certainty).

As to A's vagueness argument, Penn could contend the validity of its fee would be determined by the particular circumstances to which it was applied (i.e., at a hearing, A could contend that the (a) number of times its trucks traveled on Penn highways, and (b) amount of mileage traveled by their vehicles in Penn, did not constitute "regular" usage). Since it is unclear exactly how much A's trucks used Penn roads (i.e., the facts state only that "several large orders" were delivered to Penn each year in A's trucks), it is difficult to assess whether the tax could be validly applied against A's vehicles. However, assuming its trucks made at least limited use of Penn highways (i.e., four times per year, for an aggregate total of at least 100 miles), the Penn highway use tax would probably be sustained. *See* ELO Ch.14-III(B).

(4) *Ad Valorem Tax:*

A state may ordinarily impose an *ad valorem* tax against personal property. Where instrumentalities of interstate commerce are concerned, the state in which the taxpayer is domiciled can ordinarily make this assessment against 100% of the taxpayer's property, unless the items have acquired a taxable situs elsewhere. In the latter event, due process requires that the assessment be reduced to the extent that the instrumentality was "habitually employed" in other jurisdictions. However, since A's trucks travel into Penn on an irregular basis (i.e., only whenever large orders must be delivered), A is probably *not* entitled to any type of apportionment. *See* ELO Ch.6-II(D).

Additionally, an equal protection argument would probably not be successful (i.e., it is irrational to tax property owned by a taxpayer at one rate, and that which is leased by her at a lower rate), since property which is merely being leased (and therefore must be returned to the owner at the end of the term) has less value to the taxpayer than that which the latter (as the owner) can sell at any time.

(5) *The Leasehold Tax:*

The fact that A's utilization of federal property is being taxed does not necessarily lead to the conclusion that the tax is unconstitutional under the Supremacy Clause; *Detroit v. Murray Corp.*, 355 U.S. 489 (1958). A could argue, however, that the 50% of leasehold value tax imposes an undue burden upon the U.S. Government's ability to lease surplus property, and therefore violates the Supremacy Clause (especially in light of the fact that property leased from the state is not taxed at all, giving the state a significant advantage over the federal government). A should prevail on this contention, so the leasehold tax is probably unenforceable.

A could also contend that the tax is violative of its equal protection rights because lessees of the state government have arbitrarily been exempted from the tax. Hio could argue in rebuttal that favoring itself is not irrational, since (1) the state has numerous public functions to perform (all of which require money), and (2) without such an advantage, it's used equipment (which presumably is often leased) might have to be sold for scrap at only a small fraction of its value. However, since Hio has numerous means at its disposal for raising the funds necessary to effectively perform its functions, this argument should fail. Thus, the leasehold tax is probably unconstitutional on equal protection grounds also.

ANSWER TO QUESTION 15

(1) *The injunction against picketing:*

The defendants in the state court action probably contended that the injunction violated their First Amendment rights (applicable to the states via the Fourteenth Amendment). Regulations pertaining to traditional public forums (such as streets) can ordinarily regulate only time, place and manner. Since the injunction totally precludes picketing, it is arguably invalid. However, U could have argued in rebuttal that, even assuming streets within a college campus constitute a traditional public forum, activities which disrupt the educational functions of the college (i.e., the ability of students to traverse the campus to arrive at their next class in a timely manner) may be foreclosed entirely; *Grayned v. City of Rockford*, 408 U.S. 104 (1972). Nevertheless, the total ban upon picketing by the N.A.A.C.P. is probably too broad in nature. The picketing can presumably be limited to a visible, yet non-critical area of the campus, where the message sought to be conveyed by the protestors can still be communicated. Thus, the injunction will probably be overturned, subject to a new order which permits the picketing to be carried out in a manner which does not interfere with U's ability to function.

Alternatively, U might argue that given the antagonistic response of other students to the demonstrators, the ban was necessary to preclude a breach of the peace; *Feiner v. New York*, 340 U.S. 315 (1951). However, the speech in this instance was merely offensive to the listener's viewpoint; *Cox v. Louisiana*, 377 U.S. 288 (1965). Given the facts that (1) no physical violence appeared to be threatened as a consequence of the picketing (the opposing group of students merely heckled the protesters), and (2) potential violence could be suppressed by having an adequate number of police on hand, the injunction could *not* be validated on this basis. *See* ELO Ch.14-IV(M)(5)(b).

(2) *The action for a declaratory judgment and injunction in federal court*

Abstention: A U.S. District Court may abstain from hearing a case which challenges the constitutionality of an ambiguous non-federal statute or rule, if the alleged defect might be cured by a narrowing state court interpretation. U might contend that abstention is appropriate because no state court has ruled on the validity of the U policy in question. However, the plaintiffs could probably assert in rebuttal that this doctrine is inapplicable because (1) no state court action is pending, and (2) the action of the U housing board is not susceptible to a curative interpretation (either it does, or does not, violate the Fourteenth Amendment's equal protection rights of Black students). It is unlikely that the federal court will abstain.

Standing: To have standing in federal court, an individual must show a direct and immediate personal injury which is traceable to the challenged action; *Simon v. Eastern Kentucky Welfare Rights Organization*, 426 U.S. 26 (1976). U could contend that (1) there is nothing to indicate that the three U students who joined the lawsuit have ever attempted to procure housing through the bureau, or (2) they would have actually attempted to secure a room from one of the persons who had indicated that only caucasians would be accepted. Without additional facts indicating that the three students had at least solicited the directory of available rentals from the housing bureau, it is unlikely they would have standing.

U could argue that the N.A.A.C.P. has no standing to assert the rights of students at U who had not been given the "Whites only" list. However, a third party may assert another's rights where it would be highly burdensome for the latter to do so. The N.A.A.C.P. could respond that it would be difficult for Blacks at U to commence an action since they might fear reprisals from students, professors, or homeowners who were sympathetic with U's present housing policy. The antagonistic response to the picketing which occurred at U strengthens this argument. Given the strong national interest is eradicating racial discrimination, the N.A.A.C.P. would probably be deemed to have standing.

U might alternatively contend that, in any event, no injury was suffered by those Blacks who were not shown the "Whites only" list. Since the homeowners on that directory would presumably have refused to rent to Blacks, Blacks have not been "injured" by being precluded from going through the futile action of being rejected by these lessors. Plaintiffs could argue in rebuttal, however, that confronted with the unavoidable embarrassment of being compelled to reject an individual simply because of race, many "Whites only" homeowners would overcome their prejudices and rent to Blacks. In any event, an actual injury does occur by the fact that facilities are foreclosed to Blacks simply because of their race; *Brown v. Board of Education*, 347 U.S. 483 (1954). Thus, Plaintiffs should prevail on this argument too. *See* ELO Ch.16-III(C)(4)(c).

State Action: U could next contend that simply by honoring the wishes of local homeowners to be omitted from the list tendered to Blacks, the state is not discriminating against this group. U would argue that if it refused to comply with the wishes of the homeowners in question, the homeowners would disallow the listing of their names. However, Plaintiffs could probably respond that there is sufficient state involvement because (1) the housing bureau facilitates discrimination by allowing the "Whites only" landlords to avoid the embarrassment of refusing to rent to Blacks; and (2) there is a symbiotic relationship in that (a) the homeowners involved are helping U make certain that there is adequate housing for its students, in return for which (b) the homeowners are permitted to avoid the distasteful experience of having to reject Black lessees. Since it is at least possible that (1) a number of the "Whites only" landlords would eventually agree to accept Blacks, and (2) some landlords would be financially obliged to accept Black lessees if a "Whites only" list was **not** made available to students, state action probably exists. *See* ELO Ch.12-III(D).

Equal Protection: Classifications based upon race must satisfy the strict scrutiny standard (i.e., there must be a compelling state interest served by the legislation or policy involved, and no less restrictive means of accomplishing that objective). U could conceivably argue that (1) there is a compelling interest because campus housing is inadequate, and (2) there are no less restrictive means available (i.e., racially prejudiced landlords would otherwise refuse to make their homes available for additional housing). However, the plaintiffs could probably successfully contend in rebuttal that (1) it is unclear whether there would be insufficient housing accommodations if U refused to permit landlords to opt for a "Whites only" directory, and (2) additional housing could be built by the state if the "Whites only" landlords actually withdrew their names from the off-campus housing list. *See* ELO Ch.10-III(A)(1).

In summary, the U housing bureau can probably be enjoined from having a "Whites only" listing of additional housing.

ANSWER TO QUESTION 16

Refusal to grant hearing:

Smith ("S") might initially contend that, under the due process clause of the Fourteenth Amendment, he was entitled to a hearing with respect to the rejection of his application. However, in the absence of circumstances which, under applicable state law, would create a legitimate expectation of continued public employment, a governmental worker has no right to a pre-termination hearing; *Perry v. Sinderman*, 408 U.S. 593 (1972); *Bishop v. Wood*, 426 U.S. 341 (1976). Unless the Centerville School District ("District") had an established policy of giving hiring priority to existing temporary teachers whenever a full-time position became vacant, S would have no reason to anticipate being rehired (and therefore would *not* be entitled to a hearing pertaining to rejection of his application). *See* ELO Ch.9-V(E)(2).

Refusal to hire:

Even if S was not entitled to a hearing on his application to become the full-time science teacher, the refusal of District to hire him could *not* be predicated on a non-constitutional basis. If it was, S would be entitled to an order requiring that his application be re-considered. However, if any constitutionally valid basis for rejection of S's application exists, the fact that it was partially premised upon unconstitutional grounds would be insignificant.

First Amendment:

S could contend that refusal to accept his application for the full-time position violated his First Amendment right of free speech (applicable to the states via the Fourteenth Amendment). One may not be deprived of public employment for speaking out on issues of general importance; *Pickering v. Board of Education*, 391 U.S. 563 (1963). S would argue that his contention that other teachers were incorrectly instructing their students with respect to evolution constituted a matter of public concern. District could respond, however, that (1) a public employee's First Amendment rights must always be balanced against efficient performance of the particular governmental function involved, and (2) constantly accusing other teachers of misinforming their students would lower morale and engender dissension amongst the staff at the high school. It is unclear from the facts whether S had, despite his personal beliefs, previously taught his science class in accordance with the Board's viewpoint on the question of evolution. If he had, his "verbal attacks" would probably have to be highly offensive (rather than merely persistent and unpopular) to be the basis for not hiring him. *See* ELO Ch.14-X(C)(7)(a)(iii).

Free Exercise:

Assuming S could assert that his meditation periods were an integral part of his religious (rather than merely metaphysical) beliefs, three factors would be balanced in determining whether S's actions were protected by the Free Exercise clause of the First Amendment: (1) the severity which the burden imposes upon the plaintiff's exercise of his religious practices, (2) the importance of the governmental interest sought to be achieved by the statute, and (3) whether the state could accomplish the objective by means which would lessen the imposition upon the plaintiff's religious practices. It is unclear (1) how many periods of science must be taught each day, and (2) how difficult it would be for Board to schedule the science classes around S's "meditation hours". Assume, since the facts do not state otherwise, that S was able to both teach his science course and meditate at the required times during the previous academic year. If S's meditation periods could be integrated into the high school's overall schedule without a serious disruption to other classes, S would probably prevail on this question. *See* ELO Ch.15-III(A)(3).

Equal Protection:

While legislation pertaining to legal aliens is usually analyzed under the strict scrutiny standard, mere "rationality" is required where public school teachers are involved; *Ambach v. Norwick*, 441 U.S. 68 (1979). In *Ambach*, legal aliens who had shown an unwillingness to acquire U.S. citizenship were barred from becoming teachers in public schools. This classification was deemed rational in accomplishing the state's goal of fostering (1) respect for governmental processes, and (2) a sense of social responsibility, into its pupils. However, the Board's concern in this instance seems to be with the quality of S's previous training, rather than with his status as a legal alien.

If the Board's concern is the quality of S's training, S could contend that the Board's action is irrational because there is no legitimate reason to believe that teacher training at Centerville State College is superior to training received at other institutions. Although the Board could contend there is nothing unreasonable about giving preference to an institution whose training is known to be acceptable, S would probably prevail on this issue. *See* ELO Ch.10-VI(C)(4).

Dormant Commerce Clause:

Assuming, as indicated in the Board's letter to S, the Board gave preference to another person because she earned her graduate degree from Centerville State College, S could also contend that such action violated the Commerce Clause. He would argue that giving priority to persons from one's own state would, as a practical matter, impede migration into that jurisdiction; *Edwards v. California*, 314 U.S. 160 (1941). While the Board again would argue that there is a substantial state interest in hiring persons (1) from an established academic institution, and (2) who are familiar with local customs, S would probably prevail on this theory. *See* ELO Ch.6-I(I).

Finally, note that S could **not** successfully contend that giving employment preference to graduates of a local college is violative of the privileges and immunities clause of Article IV of the Constitution. This provision can be asserted only by citizens (as opposed to aliens) of the United States.

Summary:

If the Board prevailed on **any** of the foregoing issues, rejection of S's application for full-time employment would be constitutional (i.e., there would be a valid, independent ground for not hiring S). If S prevailed on all of the foregoing issues, the Board could be obliged to reconsider S's application.

ANSWER TO QUESTION 17

Federal Authority:

State Orange ("O") might initially argue that the federal statute was unconstitutional, since Powerco's business operations occurred solely within O. Therefore, the interstate commerce clause was not a proper basis for the law. However, Powerco ("P") could contend in rebuttal that the Act was constitutional under **both** (1) the interstate commerce clause, since the activity itself (the regulation of nuclear reactors) has, in the aggregate, an appreciable affect upon interstate commerce (i.e., the greater the amount of energy produced at nuclear plants within a state, the less likely it would be that citizens of that state would be obliged to purchase energy from sources in another jurisdiction); and (2) the war power clauses (Article I, Section 8, clauses 11, 12, 13 and 14), since atomic reactors under appropriate supervision, can be utilized for military and national defense purposes. Thus, the federal legislation is valid.

It is well established that, pursuant to valid legislation, Congress may delegate its authority to a commission. While the guidelines conferred upon the AEC in this instance are somewhat broad (i.e., the AEC is authorized to "license" the commercial uses of nuclear reactors and "regulate the emission of radioactive waste"), Congress' grant of power to the AEC would probably be sustained; *Lichter v. United States*, 334 U.S. 742 (1948).

Pre-emption:

O could contend that there was no "conflict" with the AEC's emission levels because its standards were more stringent than those promulgated by the federal entity (i.e., the Pollution Law encompassed the federal emission standard within it). Thus, the Pollution Law is *not* invalid under the Supremacy Clause. However, P could make two arguments in rebuttal.

First, P would assert that the Act was intended to pre-empt the entire area of atomic energy, and therefore *any* state legislation within its sphere was unconstitutional under the Supremacy Clause. In determining if this was Congress' intent, several factors would be considered: (1) any language in the federal enactment which indicates such a purpose, (2) whether the subject matter of the local enactment has traditionally been dealt with under the states' police powers, (3) the completeness of the federal regulatory scheme, and (4) whether the area is one for which national, rather than local, regulation is more appropriate. P would argue that given (1) the broad policy language in the first clause of the Act (referring to the (a) general welfare, and (b) common defense and security), (2) the broad grant of legislative authority to the AEC (presumably, so that additional ordinances could be promulgated expeditiously and on a continuing basis), and (3) the importance of developing a coherent nuclear energy policy, the Act was intended to pre-empt the entire field of atomic energy. While O could respond that (1) Congress could have, if it had desired to do so, easily exempted the area of nuclear power from state regulation by the simple expedient of clear language to that effect, and (2) the states have traditionally legislated in the area of environmental pollution, P would probably prevail on this issue. Thus, the portion of the Pollution Law pertaining to emission standards is probably invalid.

Alternatively, P could contend that, even if Congress did not intend to pre-empt the entire area, the emission provisions of the Pollution Law would frustrate the particular purposes sought to be achieved by the Act (i.e., the development of energy resources); *Perez v. Campbell*, 402 U.S. 637 (1971). P can apparently show that it would **not** be economically feasible to comply with O's emission standards. Again, P's argument would probably be successful.

Thus, the emission standards contained in the Pollution Law are probably unconstitutional under the Supremacy Clause. *See* ELO Ch.6-III(C).

The O License Tax:

P could attack the License Tax on both Supremacy Clause and due process grounds.

Because the AEC has been specifically authorized to "license" the commercial use of atomic reactors, O would probably be pre-empted from introducing new requirements into this area. *See* ELO CH.6-III(C)(5).

Licensing fees must be proportional to the services which are provided by the taxing authority; *Complete Auto Transit, Inc. v. Brady*, 430 U.S. 274 (1977). Since O cannot impose additional licensing requirements on atomic reactors, the annual license tax bears no relationship to services provided by O with respect to the activity in question. The tax was apparently passed in response to concerns of the citizenry with respect to the dangers of accidental radiation emissions (rather than to reimburse O for governmental expenses associated with protecting and maintaining P as a business entity). Thus, O's tax is, in effect, a taking (making it impossible for P to do business) without due process of law, and is therefore invalid.

The Gross Receipts Tax:

Gross receipt taxes are ordinarily upheld, provided that (1) they bear some relationship to the services provided by the state, and (2) the taxpayer is not obliged to pay for the same services received from the state more than once (these are both due process considerations). Assuming (1) the license fee was invalid, and (2) no income tax is assessed against entities such as P, the tax is probably valid. Since a number of governmental instrumentalities are constantly available to P (i.e., police protection, fire department, etc.), O would be entitled to assess a tax which is fairly related to these services.

ANSWER TO QUESTION 18

Agency would probably raise the following issues before the U.S. Supreme Court.

State Action:

Agency would initially argue that no governmental action is involved, since it is a private corporation. The fact that it is licensed and extensively regulated by State X does not transform Agency's decision into state action; *Moose Lodge No. 107 v. Irvis*, 407 U.S. 163 (1972). H and W could argue in rebuttal, however, that (1) adoption should be viewed as a "public" function, and therefore the conduct of the entity undertaking that function is properly viewed as state action; *Terry v. Adams*; 345 U.S. 461 (1953); or (2) there is significant state involvement, since State X has legislatively mandated most of the standards which Agency must apply in deciding if potential parents should be permitted to adopt children. While H and W's first contention should fail because adoption has *not* traditionally been the exclusive province of the state, their second argument should be successful. Thus, the state action requisite is probably satisfied. *See* ELO Ch.12-II & III(B).

H and W's agnosticism:

H and W could assert that their lack of religious affiliation cannot constitutionally be considered in determining if they should be permitted to adopt. A state regulation violates the Establishment Clause of the First Amendment (applicable to the states via the Fourteenth Amendment), unless (1) it has a secular purpose, (2) its primary effect doesn't advance or inhibit religion, *and* (3) it produces no excessive entanglement between religion and the state. H and W could assert that there can be little question that the effect of the law would be to generally promote religion, since non-religious persons in State X would be precluded from adopting children. Since State X appears to have no satisfactory response to this assertion, H and W probably have a constitutional right to have their lack of religious affiliation excluded from the determination of whether they should be permitted to adopt. *See* ELO Ch.15-II(A)(2).

The difference in H and W's ethnic (i.e., racial) backgrounds:

H and W could contend that rejection of their application as a consequence of their different ethnic backgrounds violates their (1) due process, *and* (2) equal protection rights.

Due Process:

As to the due process assertion, H and W would argue that the right to adopt children, like the rights to procreate (*Skinner v. Oklahoma*, 316 U.S. 535 (1942)) and marry (*Loving v. Virginia*, 388 U.S. 1 (1967)) is fundamental. Therefore, it can be precluded only by compliance with the strict scrutiny standard (i.e., there is a compelling reason for the classification and there is no less burdensome means of accomplishing the governmental objective). While State X certainly has an interest in attempting to insure the well being of a prospective adoptee, completely excluding a mixed couple from adoption is arguably inappropriate. Assuming applicants were otherwise qualified, a less burdensome means of accomplishing this objective would be to permit the adoption, but require adopting parents to show (at a specified, subsequent point in time) that a sense of unity had developed between them and the adopted child. *See* ELO Ch.9-IV(N)(1).

Procedural Due Process:

Where important interests involving an individual are affected by groupings which are arguably overinclusive, her procedural due process rights are violated in the absence of some reasonable opportunity to rebut the presumption implicit the classification. In *Stanley v. Illinois*, 405 U.S. 645 (1972), a state law provided that the natural father of an illegitimate child automatically lost custody of the child upon the death of the child's natural mother. The Supreme Court held that the father had a right to a hearing upon the question of whether he was a suitable parent. A law or policy which absolutely (1) requires an adoptee's new parents to be of the same racial affiliation as her natural mother, or (2) precludes parents from adopting solely because of their diverse racial backgrounds, is arguably defective because the parents desiring to adopt have no opportunity to rebut the implicit presumption that they are not qualified. Since Agency has already declared that H and W would (except for their differing ethnic backgrounds) be qualified to adopt a child, a hearing on their fitness is unnecessary. Thus, Agency should be ordered to permit H and W to adopt.

Equal Protection:

H and W's equal protection argument would be predicated upon the assertion that where classifications involving a married couple are made on the basis of their different ethnic backgrounds, it is subject to strict scrutiny; *Palmore v. Sidoti*, 104 S. Ct. 1879 (1984). In *Palmore*, the Supreme Court invalidated the transfer of custody of a child back to her father solely because her mother had wed a Black man. The Court acknowledged that the child would probably suffer some "social stigmatization" from her peers, but held that succumbing to these prejudices was not a valid means of satisfying the state's concern (i.e., the child's best interests). Since custody of a child cannot be altered merely because her parents are racially diverse, similar reasoning would dictate that adoption procedures also **cannot** be predicated exclusively on this factor. *See* ELO Ch.10-III(E)(6)(c)(ii).

Requirement that the race and religious affiliation of the adopting parents be the same as the natural mother's:

Although Agency did not state that its rejection of H and W was premised on the State X requirement that adoptive parents be of the same racial and religious persuasion as the illegitimate child's mother (Agency asserted that the racial diversity of the parents was a sufficient reason for denying their application), H and W would probably seek to have this requirement declared unconstitutional so that it not be utilized against them when their application was reconsidered.

Read literally, the statute would seem to indicate that if the natural mother had no religious affiliation, her child would simply not be adoptable (i.e., under such circumstances, how could the religious affiliation of the natural mother and adopting parents be the same?). It will be assumed, however, that State X would argue in rebuttal that where the natural parent had no religious affiliation, the requirement of similar theological beliefs would in effect be inapplicable.

The requirement of a religious affiliation is also probably violative of the Establishment Clause (it would oblige a natural mother to join a religious group to prevent her child from being unadoptable). Additionally, it would probably contravene the equal protection clause of the Fourteenth Amendment because excluding parents from adopting an illegitimate child because their religious views (if any) were different from those of the natural mother would arguably be irrational. In many instances, a child is given up for adoption prior to receiving any type of religious instruction from her mother. In any event, a child may not have formed any significant religious attachment prior to the time she was given up for adoption. Thus, the State X rule forbidding adoption unless the religious affiliation of the natural mother and the couple seeking to adopt is the same, violates the equal protection rights of the prospective parents.

For basically the same reasons discussed above (under the heading of **Equal Protection**), the requirement that the adopting parents be of the same race as the natural mother also violates equal protection rights.

ANSWER TO QUESTION 19

Standing:

The President ("P") could initially contest Jones' standing.

Jones ("J") would argue that Congress has specifically permitted tax-payers to contest the validity of the P's Executive Order permitting warrantless wiretaps. Pursuant to Article III of the Constitution, the existence of federal courts (other than the U.S. Supreme Court) is left to the discretion of Congress. Since Congress has the power to create federal courts, this authority would presumably embody the right to determine what groups of persons can assert a particular cause of action within the federal judicial system.

However, P could contend in rebuttal that the Constitution provides that federal courts are competent to hear only "cases and controversies," Article III, Section 2. Congressional acts cannot, of course, override the Constitution. Thus, persons contesting executive orders must still show that an imminent and direct injury will occur as a consequence of the challenged activity. P would therefore assert that J lacks standing since (1) J is not an alien, and so he would ***not*** be covered by the Executive Order in question, and (2) even if J occasionally had telephone discussions with aliens (and therefore might coincidentally be overheard during an allegedly illegal wiretap), he would still be obliged to show that the telephones of the particular aliens with whom he spoke had been tapped (i.e., those aliens were perceived by the F.B.I. as being persons suspected of espionage or subversion).

A taxpayer (who has suffered no direct harm) ordinarily has no right to challenge governmental actions of federal officials, even if no one would otherwise have standing; *Schlesinger v. Reservists Committee*, 418 U.S. 208 (1974). (Our situation does not, of course, deal with a federal expenditure which allegedly infringes upon a constitutional guarantee; *Flast v. Cohen*, 392 U.S. 83 (1968).) *See* ELO Ch.16-III(B)(2).

It would therefore appear that J lacks standing to contest the Executive Order in question. However, additional issues will be discussed in the event that this conclusion is erroneous.

Presidential Authority:

J could contend that the Fourth Amendment protects persons from unreasonable searches and seizures. As a consequence, wiretaps (which constitute a search) are invalid unless issued by a ***judicial*** officer upon probable cause. Since the Executive Order permits a wiretap to be installed (1) in the case of "suspected" espionage or subversion, and (2) without the authorization of a judicial order, it is unconstitutional.

P could argue in rebuttal that his action was proper because implicit in the power of the presidency is the right to undertake emergency measures which are necessary to protect the country from hostile forces. Since the aliens in question are allegedly contemplating acts of espionage and subversion (activities which could presumably result in loss of life), the Executive Order should be sustained. However, since the (1) facts fail to indicate that any violent acts (i.e., explosions, fires, etc.) are imminent, and (2) P is not responding to a current "crisis" situation precipitated by a foreign government (*Dames & Moore v. Regan*, 453 U.S. 654 (1981)), it is unlikely that P would be successful. Thus, the Executive Order is probably invalid. *See* ELO Ch.8-I(B)(3).

Due Process:

Even assuming a national emergency did exist, the Fifth Amendment due process rights of aliens have arguably been violated by P's action, since the Executive Order extends to the entire class of aliens (without any type of judicial finding that the persons whose phones have been tapped intended to engage in espionage). While P might contend that F.B.I.'s determination as to those persons who represented a threat to the national security was an adequate limiting standard, this contention would probably fail. Thus, the directive's overbreadth and lack of any independent review of the actions undertaken by the executive branch would probably cause the Executive Order to be deemed unconstitutional.

Additionally, the term "subversive" is arguably too vague (i.e., a person of ordinary intelligence and who had knowledge of the Executive Order could not determine if contemplated conduct was proscribed) to serve as the basis for governmental action. This term has been deemed to be unconstitutionally vague in the context of a loyalty oath requirement; *Baggett v. Bullitt*, 377 U.S. 360 (1964). While the P could argue in rebuttal that "subversive" should be interpreted as being equivalent to "illegal activities which threaten the national government," J would probably prevail on this issue. Thus, the Executive Order is probably illegal on due process grounds also. *See* ELO Ch.14-III(B).

Executive Privilege:

An executive privilege protecting the disclosure of presidential communications has been recognized by the Supreme Court; *United States v. Nixon*, 418 U.S. 683 (1974). However, in the context of criminal cases, these communications are only presumptively privileged. Thus, J would contend that P's communications are subject to an *in camera* review by the trial judge for the purpose of determining if they were sufficiently related to the performance of executive activities (i.e., to protect the country from illegal conduct by foreign agents). P could argue, in rebuttal, however, that *U.S. v. Nixon* dealt with a criminal proceeding. Where a lesser proceeding (i.e., a mere civil case) is involved, the executive privilege should be absolute. However, J would probably prevail on this issue. Thus, the judge would be permitted to make an *in camera* review of the materials in question. If the materials do *not* relate to matters of national security, J would be permitted to obtain them. *See* ELO Ch.8-IV(D)(3)(b) & (c).

ANSWER TO QUESTION 20

1. *Mother's ("M's") lawsuit*

State Action: The PTA could initially contend that no state action is involved because it is a private organization, consisting of non-school officials or employees. Thus, their activities are not subject to constitutional limitations. However, M could argue in rebuttal that where a governmental entity is significantly involved with the allegedly unconstitutional activity, the state action requirement is satisfied. Such involvement would probably be found in this instance since: (1) the PTA subjects were taught on school premises, (2) the children returned home on the "late" school bus, and (3) information pertaining to the courses was distributed through the school. *See* ELO Ch.12-III(E)(4).

Standing: The PTA could next assert that M lacks standing (i.e., she has suffered no direct, immediate injury because it is her daughter, not M, who has been denied admission to the baseball practices). However, M could probably contend in rebuttal that (1) she is "injured" in the sense that M will be precluded from the enjoyment of watching her child engage in this activity, and (2) standing is often found to exist when there is a special relationship between the claimant and the party who has directly suffered the alleged harm. Since matters affecting a child's development invariably affect her mother (at least to some degree), standing would probably be deemed to exist. *See* ELO Ch.16-III(C)(2).

Equal Protection: M could contend that Alice's ("A's") Fourteenth Amendment equal protection rights were violated by the PTA's exclusion of girls from baseball practice. Where a gender based classification is utilized by the state, an intermediate level of scrutiny is ordinarily applied (i.e., an "important" or "significant" governmental interest must be involved, and the legislation must be substantially related to the achievement of that objective); *Craig v. Boren*, 429 U.S. 190 (1976). M could argue that the PTA's claim that there might be possible "behavior problems" if baseball practice were coeducational is too inadequate to constitute a "substantial state" interest. Since boys and girls interact in regular classes, there is no reason to believe that they couldn't co-exist during baseball practice.

The PTA would, however, probably contend that they were also concerned about the (1) possibility of physical injury to girls (i.e., sliding into bases often involves substantial bodily contact), and (2) potential litigation which might ensue. Thus, there is a substantial governmental interest, and no other means of satisfying this concern. Nevertheless, M could probably successfully argue in rebuttal that the (1) minimal amount of contact in a baseball game among children of that age does not present a significant risk of physical injury to girls; and (2) governmental interest can be met by requiring all participants in the activity to sign "consent" forms; and (3) in any event, there is no showing that girls are more prone to baseball injuries than boys. Although a close question, M would probably prevail. *See* ELO Ch.10-V(C)(3).

Due Process: M could also conceivably argue that children have a fundamental right to engage in athletic activities in elementary school. Such activities build physical strength and character. Since baseball practice is the only "sports" activity offered by the PTA, M's daughter's Fourteenth Amendment due process rights are violated by the PTA's refusal to let her participate. However, there is no case law recognizing a "liberty" or "property" interest to engage in elementary school sports. Since these activities are probably not essential to becoming a well adjusted individual or leading a productive life, it is unlikely that substantive due process would be extended to this area. Thus, M would ***not*** be successful with respect to this contention.

However, since M's equal protection argument should prevail, she probably could obtain a declaratory judgment requiring A's participation in baseball practice.

Procedural Due Process: It will be assumed that M can show that, if her car had not gotten a flat tire, she would have arrived at the school in sufficient time to register H for Creative Crafts (i.e., the other parents were not queued up to register their children in advance of the time that M would have arrived, even had the flat tire been avoided). Without such a showing, M would be unable to prove a causal relationship between the alleged constitutional infringement and the "harm" which she suffered, and would therefore lack standing.

M could contend that the exclusion of H from the Creative Crafts class violated her procedural due process rights, since participation in that activity should not be dependent upon so fortuitous an event as arrival at the school at a particular time. However, enrolling in a Creative Crafts class is probably ***not*** a sufficiently important interest for procedural due process rights to attach (i.e., elementary school students could presumably become productive, successful adults without special training in this activity). Additionally, even if there was a "right" to notification prior to exclusion from the class, enrolling applicants on a "first come, first served" basis would probably constitute a fair methodology for selecting a limited number of potential enrollees. Thus, any applicable procedural due process concerns are satisfied. *See* ELO Ch.9-V(A)(2).

2. *Claims of the other two parents ("P's")*

Standing: The facts fail to indicate that the children of P's were (1) interested in joining any of the PTA's classes, or (2) in any manner, excluded from doing so. Unless a taxpayer is personally injured, he ordinarily has no standing to contest particular governmental conduct; except where it can be shown that a spending measure has exceeded a specific constitutional limitation. Since the after-school classes are apparently self-supporting, this standard does not appear to be satisfied. Thus, P's probably would **not** have standing to raise their claims in federal court. *See* ELO Ch.16-III(C)(2).

Equal Protection: Assuming, however, P's were deemed to have standing (i.e., their children were denied admission to one or more of the PTA activities because of gender), they could assert basically the same arguments made by M with respect to baseball practice. However, in the other situations (Embroidery, Creative Crafts and Bible Studies), the PTA's rebuttal contentions would be weaker since these activities do not embody the risk of physical injury which is inherent in a sporting event.

Establishment Clause: P's could also assert that the existence of the Bible Studies class violates the Establishment Clause of the First Amendment (applicable to the states via the Fourteenth Amendment), since it (1) does not have a secular purpose (i.e., the Bible is the major sourcebook of many religions), (2) its primary effect is to further religion (i.e., persons who read the Bible would arguably acquire a greater religious orientation), and (3) would result in excessive entanglement between church and state (i.e., classes are held on school grounds and teachers might encourage their pupils to adopt a particular religious view). However, the PTA could argue in rebuttal that academic study of the Bible merely acquaints students with a renowned piece of literature, it does not indoctrinate them with a particular religious belief; *Abington School District v. Schempp*, 374 U.S. 203 (1974). Additionally, since school facilities are being made available for other types of PTA activities, precluding Bible Study would arguably violate the establishment clause by deliberately impeding religion; *Widmar v. Vincent*, 454 U.S. 263 (1981). Finally, because the PTA programs (1) are voluntary, (2) are taught by non-school personnel, and (3) occur after school, there is no indirect coercion of non-observing individuals; *Engel v. Vitale*, 370 U.S. 421 (1962). In summary, it is unlikely that a violation of the Establishment Clause would be found. *See* ELO Ch.15-II(B)(1)(d).

ANSWER TO QUESTION 21

1. *Does Guy ("G") have standing with respect to Sections 1 and 2 of the Act?*

To have standing in federal court, a plaintiff must ordinarily show that he has been injured (or is threatened with injury) as a consequence of the allegedly unconstitutional conduct. The facts do not state whether G (1) ever fished for "river salmon" himself, or (2) merely guided others. If G actually fished in the lake and carried his catch out of State X, he would probably have standing to challenge Sections 1 and 2 of the Act. Even if he did not, G could assert that, as a guide, he has a close financial association with non-residents who would be affected by Sections 1 and 2 of the Act; *Craig v. Boren*, 429 U.S. 190 (1976). The standing requirement is probably satisfied. *See* ELO Ch.16-III(C).

2. *Are the various provisions of Act unconstitutional?*

Invalid Delegation of Congressional Power: G might initially argue as follows: (1) the lake in question is a navigable waterway; (2) navigable water bodies are within the admiralty and maritime power of Congress; *Oklahoma v. Guy F. Atkinson Co.*, 313 U.S. 508 (1941); (3) Congress may not delegate this authority to the states; and (4) therefore, any State X regulations pertaining to the lake are unconstitutional. However, State X could contend in rebuttal that its authority to pass the Act was not dependent upon federal legislation. Under the Tenth Amendment, State X retained the right to enact legislation pertaining to the lake (provided no conflict existed between the Act and federal statutes). Thus, the Act probably could *not* be invalidated on the ground that it was passed pursuant to an unconstitutional delegation of Congressional authority.

Privileges and Immunities Clause of Article IV: Under the privileges and immunities clause of Article IV, Section 2, states may not discriminate against citizens of other jurisdictions with respect to "essential" activities, unless the classification is substantially related to an important state interest; *Hicklin v. Orbeck*, 437 U.S. 518 (1978). G could assert that the Act discriminates against U.S. citizens who are not residents of State X because they (1) must pay a higher license fee, (2) cannot carry lake salmon back to their own states, (3) must be accompanied by a licensed State X guide, and (4) cannot obtain licenses to become guides. State X could argue in rebuttal, however, that (1) recreational fishing is not an "essential" or "basic" activity; *Baldwin v. Fish & Game Commission*, 436 U.S. 371 (1971); and, in any event, (2) substantial state interests are involved: (a) (presumably) Section 1 merely equalizes the overall and long term expense to State X of maintaining the lake (which was previously paid for via taxation of State X citizens), (b) Section 2 preserves state resources, and (c) Section 3 was dictated by the desire for water safety (i.e.,

State X residents would ordinarily be more familiar with the lake and local customs pertaining to boating safety than individuals from outside of the jurisdiction).

It is unclear from the facts whether G derived his primary income as a fishing guide at the lake. If relatively significant income was earned by G as a guide, Section 3 of the Act would probably violate the privileges and immunities clause of Article IV, since an essential activity (i.e., earning a living) would be involved; *Hicklin*, 437 U.S. 518 (1978). Sections 1 and 2, however, would probably not be invalid, since the licensing fee and non-exportation provisions do not affect out-of-state residents with respect to an "essential" or "basic" activity. *See* ELO Ch.7-IV(B)(3).

Commerce Clause: State laws which facially discriminate against commerce with another state are invalid, unless the first state can demonstrate that (1) an overriding local interest is achieved by the legislation, and (2) there is no non-discriminatory means of accomplishing that objective; *Hughes v. Oklahoma*, 441 U.S. 322 (1979). Since there is a better means of impeding the depletion of lake salmon (i.e., limiting the amount of fish which a person may extract from the lake over a specified period of time), Section 2 of the Act is probably invalid under the commerce clause; *Sporhase v. Nebraska*, 458 U.S. 941 (1982). *See* ELO Ch.6-I(J)(3)(b).

Equal Protection: The equal protection clause of the Fourteenth Amendment requires that classifications be reasonably related to a legitimate state purpose. As described above (under the discussion with respect to the privileges and immunities clause of Article IV), State X could advance justifications for each provision of the Act. However, limiting lake guides to citizens of State X is arguably irrational, since out-of-state residents (like G) could be, or become, equally familiar with the lake and the necessary safety procedures. Thus, limiting lake guides to State X citizens is probably invalid. *See* ELO Ch.10-I(B)(7)(a).

Procedural Due Process: G might have conceivably contended that the fishing guide license was a "property" right, and therefore renewal could not be refused without a neutral hearing. However, there is no "right" to obtain governmental benefits. Thus, in the absence of some legitimate expectation under applicable state law that the license would automatically be renewed, State X's refusal to re-issue G's license did **not** violate procedural due process; *Bishop v. Wood*, 426 U.S. 341 (1976). *See* ELO Ch.9-V(G).

Summary: Based upon the discussion above, only Section 1 of the Act appears to be valid.

ANSWER TO QUESTION 22

Abstention:

A U.S. District Court may abstain from hearing a case where the plaintiff is challenging the constitutionality of an ambiguous non-federal statute, if the alleged defect might be cured by a narrowing interpretation by a state court. State X might contend that abstention is appropriate in this instance (i.e., any attacks which Doe ("D") could make against the law might be cured by a state court's interpretation of the legislation). However, since (1) D is presently being prejudiced by his inability to obtain a teaching certification, and (2) a First Amendment right (applicable to the states via the Fourteenth Amendment) is allegedly at issue, it is unlikely that a federal court would abstain in this instance.

(a) *Section 1*

Bill of Attainder:

A bill of attainder (a legislative act which punishes named individuals or an ascertainable group without trial) is unconstitutional. D could assert that the State X certification law is essentially a bill of attainder, since it non-judicially punishes members of the Nazi Party by precluding them from becoming teachers; *United States v. Brown*, 381 U.S. 437 (1965). However, State X would contend in rebuttal that the prejudice suffered by the complainant must have been intended as a punishment by the legislature; *Nixon v. Administrator of General Services*, 433 U.S. 425 (1977). Since the statute in question was arguably only a means of assuring that impressionable, young students would not be influenced to break the law (rather than a means of penalizing members of an organization), the initial clause is *not* a bill of attainder. Since State X has a legitimate interest in assuring that teachers advocate respect for the law, it should prevail on this issue. *See* ELO Ch.11-V(C)(1).

Overbreadth:

D could next contend that Section 1 of the statute is facially overbroad, and therefore cannot serve as the basis for governmental action. This contention would be premised upon the facts that (1) the statute precludes persons from being teachers even though they may not presently be members of a prohibited organization; *Schware v. Board of Examiners of New Mexico*, 353 U.S. 232 (1957), and (2) there is no requirement that refusal of certification be based on the applicant's specific intention of furthering the illegal goals of the organization; *Elfbrandt v. Russell*, 384 U.S. 11 (1966).

State X could contend in rebuttal, however, a statute is not facially invalid, unless its overbreadth is substantial; *Broadrick v. Oklahoma*, 413 U.S. 601 (1973). Since the determination of the standards to be applied in deciding who may become a teacher are not totally discretionary with the licensing body, it is unlikely that the statute would be deemed to be facially overbroad; *Arnett v. Kennedy*, 416 U.S. 134 (1974). *See* ELO Ch.14-III(A).

Overbreadth As Applied:

Requiring disclosure that a person is a member of a particular group violates his First Amendment right of association, unless the information demanded serves a substantial governmental interest and is closely tailored to satisfy that concern; *Buckley v. Valeo*, 424 U.S. 1 (1976). D could contend that since the certifying committee did not inquire as to whether he (1) was presently a member of the Nazi Party, and, if so, (2) whether he had the specific intent to further the illegal aims of that organization, the certification process as applied to him was unconstitutional; *Law Students Research Council v. Wadmond*, 401 U.S. 154 (1971). However, the committee could contend in rebuttal that they were not obliged to undertake an obviously futile act. Since D had announced that he would not answer any questions pertaining to his membership in the Nazi Party, the committee probably was not compelled to proceed further.

Fifth Amendment:

A potential employee cannot be obliged to forego the privilege against self-incrimination as a precondition to public employment; *Spivack v. Klein*, 385 U.S. 511 (1967). Thus, D could contend that his refusal to answer questions about his membership in the Nazi Party could not be a basis for denying him certification. However, State X could argue in rebuttal that (1) D never claimed that he was asserting the Fifth Amendment to avoid self-incrimination (rather, he alluded to a "right of privacy"); (2) merely being a member of the Nazi Party would probably not constitute a crime (i.e., advocating the propriety of overthrowing the government by force or violence is not criminal, since there is no urging of *immediate*, lawless action; *Brandenburg v. Ohio*, 395 U.S. 444 (1969)), and so the Fifth Amendment right against self-incrimination is *not* applicable; and (3) the Fifth Amendment privilege could not properly be asserted by D until a question which might expose him to criminal culpability was actually asked (i.e., D announced his refusal to answer any questions at the commencement of the hearing). Since D probably lacked both an actual or objective good faith basis for asserting the Fifth Amendment, his refusal to answer any questions pertaining to his membership in the Nazi Party was incorrect. As described above, questions pertaining to membership in an organization which advocates the violent overthrow of the government are considered appropriate in determining fitness for employment in significant governmental positions; *Konigsberg v. State Bar of California, II*, 366 U.S. 36 (1961). *See* ELO Ch.14-X(C)(2).

(b) *Section 2*

Overbreadth:

D could also contend that Section 2 of the statute is overly broad in that it permits denial of certification, even though the applicant may have been privileged to refuse to respond to the inquiry. However, a court would probably rule that the right to assert constitutional privileges (without prejudice) is implicit in the statute.

Additionally, D could assert that the term "relevant" is vague (and therefore violates his due process rights), since the party making the inquiry has no guidelines to determine how the term should be applied. However, State X could again probably successfully contend in rebuttal that "relevant" would be construed as meaning information which was directly related to the applicant's fitness to teach in public or private schools. *See* ELO Ch.14-III(A) & (B).

Summary:

A federal court would probably direct that a re-hearing be held upon D's teaching certification, with the further directions that (1) Section 1 be construed and applied in accordance with the *Schware* and *Law Students Civil Rights Research Council* cases, (2) present, knowing membership in the Nazi Party with the specific intention to further its illegal goals is a legitimate subject of inquiry (and would be a valid basis for denying certification to D), *and* (3) D's assertion of the Fifth Amendment may be based only upon a good faith belief that his response would subject him to criminal culpability.

ANSWER TO QUESTION 23

1. *Val's ("V's") demand:*

V could contend that scheduling the graduation ceremonies on a Saturday morning violates the Establishment and Exercise Clauses of the First Amendment (applicable to the states via the Fourteenth Amendment).

A three-part test is employed to determine if a law which allegedly impacts on religion is constitutional (i.e., does it have a secular purpose, was its primary effect to benefit or diminish religion, would it result in excessive entanglement between religion and a governmental entity?); *Lemon v. Kurtzman*, 403 U.S. 602 (1971). The District's selection of Saturday would seem to satisfy this test: there is a secular purpose (to choose a time and day when many parents and students probably would *not* be at work), its primary effect does not benefit or diminish religion (any persons who observe Saturday as their Sabbath would merely have to bypass a particular, non-essential ceremony), and, it would not produce entanglement between religion and government. Thus, V's Establishment Clause argument should fail. *See* ELO Ch.15-II(A)(2).

V could alternatively contend that the District's rule violates the Free Exercise Clause of the First Amendment. In determining if a law runs afoul of this provision, three factors are weighed: (1) the severity of the burden upon the plaintiff's performance of her religious duties, (2) the importance of the governmental interest sought, and (3) the availability of alternative means of accomplishing the governmental objective. V could argue that (1) the convenience of persons attending a graduation ceremony is not a significant governmental interest, and (2) an alternative means of satisfying this concern would be to hold graduation exercises on a weekday evening or on a Sunday. However, District will probably prevail because the impact upon V's ability to practice her religion is *not* severely diminished by the Saturday graduation. By abstaining from the graduation exercises, V would be sacrificing only the intangible honor of making the valedictorian speech (an omission which would not have any significant, detrimental affect upon her life). *See* ELO Ch.15-III(E)(1).

In summary, V's demand should fail.

2. *N.F.O.'s application:*

Board could initially contend that high school auditoriums are *not* traditional public forums, and therefore N.F.O. has no right to require the Board to make these facilities available to it. However, N.F.O. could argue in rebuttal that where a governmental agency has opened up a non-traditional forum to the public for a particular type of activity (i.e., meetings of community organizations), it must make that forum available to similar types of entities on identical terms; *Southeastern Productions, Ltd. v. Con-*

rad, 420 U.S. 546 (1975). Since Board has chosen to open the auditorium for rent to community groups in general, N.F.O. ***cannot*** legally be refused access to that facility merely because the Board disapproves of the principles which the organization espouses. *See* ELO Ch.14-IV(M)(4)(a)(ii).

Board might next contend that it could nevertheless refuse N.F.O.'s application because of the hard intelligence information that the police have received (i.e., that a militant anti-fascist group plans to expel N.F.O. members by force). Under the "fighting words" doctrine, where a speaker's words are likely to make the persons to whom they are addressed commit an act of immediate violence, they are ***not*** protected by the First Amendment. However, N.F.O. could assert in rebuttal that while its message might be offensive to the racial and religious groups against which it advocates discrimination, advocacy cannot be proscribed simply because it stirs the listeners to anger. The police can intervene to stop constitutionally protected speech only if they are, in fact, physically incapable of preventing imminent violence. Since the anti-N.F.O. group might not actually materialize at the auditorium and the police are (presumably) capable of being present in sufficient force to dissuade those who desire to physically harm N.F.O. members, Board cannot legally refuse the N.F.O.'s application upon this ground. *See* ELO Ch.14-IV(H)(2).

Finally, if it were illegal for private parties to engage in religious or racial discrimination in this jurisdiction, Board might contend that it is entitled to prohibit speech aimed at inciting such conduct. However, under the *Brandenburg v. Ohio*, 395 U.S. 444 (1969), test, the speech in question must be likely to incite "imminent" lawless conduct. There is no indication that those attending the N.F.O. meeting for the purpose of joining that group would immediately engage in such illegal conduct. Rather, it is more probable that these persons would discriminate against others on the basis of religion and race at a subsequent time (in their business or social affairs). Additionally, the gathering in question is merely a recruitment meeting, and N.F.O.'s views might not even be aired at the meeting. *See* ELO Ch.14-II(F)(1)(b)(i).

In summary, the Board would probably be legally obliged to grant N.F.O.'s application.

MULTIPLE CHOICE
QUESTIONS AND ANSWERS

MULTIPLE CHOICE QUESTIONS

1. Under a recent federal statute, the U.S. government was to clean up heavily used water areas (including the beach in Santa Monica, California). Kevin (who is a U.S. citizen living in Los Angeles) believes that the Secretary of the Interior is not performing his duties under this statute in an adequate manner. He sues the Secretary of the Interior, alleging that he occasionally (six to eight times per year) swims at Santa Monica Beach, intends to continue to do so, and that his enjoyment of this activity is diminished by the Secretary's failure to enforce the statute in an adequate manner.

Based upon the foregoing, if the Secretary of the Interior contends that Kevin lacks standing, it is most likely that:

(A) Kevin will prevail, since any U.S. citizen can sue federal government officials for a failure by the latter to perform their duties.

(B) Kevin will prevail, since he has suffered a direct and immediate injury.

(C) Kevin will not prevail, since U.S. citizenship is not, *per se*, a basis for standing against a federal government official.

(D) Kevin will not prevail, since he has suffered no direct economic loss as a consequence of the Secretary's failure to perform his duties.

2. The State of Utopia recently passed legislation which states that if administrative school personnel believe that a child may have psy-chological problems, that child is to be tested by a school psychologist who works at a public school and is licensed by Utopia. If those tests are positive, the child promptly receives remedial counseling by a licensed school psychologist located at one of the public schools.

Where a psychological problem is detected at a religious school, a licensed school psychologist comes to the institution and tests the child there. If the results are positive, the child is obliged to come for counseling at a psychologist's office at the nearest public school. The statute also provides for reimbursement of any travel expenses incurred by the child in this situation.

Believing that his tax dollars were being utilized to sustain religious institutions, Ralph, a Utopia citizen and state taxpayer, brought an action in federal court. He contends that application of the statute to students at religious schools violates the Establishment Clause.

Based upon the foregoing, it is most likely that:

(A) Ralph will prevail, since services (the initial testing) are being provided by *public* employees at religious institutions.

(B) Ralph will prevail, since monies are being expended in assisting students at religious schools for travel to and back from the counseling sites.

(C) Ralph will not prevail, since state required testing may be administered at a religious institution.

(D) Ralph will not prevail, since the testing is presumably impersonal in nature, and children are then simply reimbursed for a function required by Utopia.

3. The Sikkum religion has, as one of its tenets, the principle that its members should be prepared to defend themselves at all times. As a consequence, members of this religious group are taught to conceal weapons such as handguns, knives and brass knuckles on their persons.

The State of Utopia recently enacted legislation which makes it illegal, except in the case of persons who typically carry substantial amounts of money or jewelry due to their occupations, to carry a concealed weapon of any type. The term "weapon" is defined in the statute to cover the items referred to above. The legislative history of this law indicates that the legislators were concerned with the expanded tendency of private citizens to arm themselves.

A member of the Sikkum religious group who ordinarily carries one or more of the items described above challenges this statute as being violative of the Establishment Clause.

Based upon the foregoing, it is most likely that:

(A) The law is unconstitutional, if concealed weapons are a *major* tenet of the Sikkum religion.

(B) The law is unconstitutional, since it is violative of a tenet of the Sikkum religion.

(C) The law is constitutional, since it is merely a generally applicable criminal prohibition.

(D) The law is constitutional, if, upon an objective balancing of the governmental and religious interests involved, the former exceeds the latter.

4. The Great Bobco Company ("Bobco") operates a garbage disposal facility in Claremont County, Utopia. When the facility was initially commenced, the land around it was barren. However, in the last fifteen years, a number of residential homes and shopping centers have "grown up" around the facility. Although the facility is operated in accordance with applicable law, it nevertheless generates unpleasantly smelling fumes. This situation has commenced to disturb the nearby residents. They recently persuaded the Utopia legislature to pass a law which requires (1) Bobco to install equipment which will diminish the unpleasant smell, and (2) the facility's closure within a maximum period of time of five years. The equipment will cost Bobco about $75,000 over the succeeding five years to install and maintain. Bobco ordinarily earns per-annum profits of $250,000 to $300,000 from the facility. After the five-year period, Bobco can use the land for any other lawful commercial (or residential) purpose.

Based upon the foregoing, if Bobco contends that the law constitutes an unconstitutional "taking" under the Fifth Amendment, it is most likely that:

(A) It will prevail, since the legislation eventually deprives Bobco of the ability to operate a garbage disposal on land which it owns.

(B) It will prevail, since the facility was there prior to the time that the surrounding land became residential in character.

(C) It will not prevail, since the purported "taking" substantially advances a legitimate government interest.

(D) It will not prevail, since there is a rational relation between the state interest and the regulation.

5. A federal law makes it a crime for any U.S. citizen, not specifically authorized by the President, to negotiate or otherwise communicate with a foreign government for the purpose of influencing the foreign government with respect to a dispute involving the United States. The STRONGEST constitutional grounds for sustaining the validity of this law is that:

(A) Congress may legislate to preserve the monopoly of the national government over the conduct of United States foreign affairs.

(B) The President's inherent power to negotiate for the United States with foreign countries authorizes the President, even in the absence of statutory authorization, to punish citizens who engage in such negotiations without permission.

(C) The law deals with foreign relations, and therefore is not governed by the First Amendment.

(D) Federal criminal laws dealing with international affairs need not be as specific as those dealing with domestic affairs.

6. In Utopia, robbery with "a weapon" was a crime punishable by a fine and 6-10 years in state prison. (A "weapon" was defined as any device capable of causing serious bodily injury.) This offense was called "Aggravated Robbery." As this type of crime increased, the Utopia legislature passed a new statute called "Armed Robbery," which involved robbing someone with a firearm. The jail sentence for this crime was 10-15 years (but no fine was applicable). Dellum robbed James at gunpoint just prior to passage of the Armed Robbery statute. However, when Dellum was *arrested*, the Armed Robbery statute had recently been passed. He was charged and convicted of Armed Robbery (rather than Aggravated Robbery), and sentenced to 12 years in prison.

Based upon the foregoing, if Dellum asserts that the sentence is unconstitutional, it is most likely that:

(A) Dellum will prevail, since punishment was enhanced *after* the illegal act had occurred.

(B) Dellum will prevail, if he had actual knowledge that Aggravated Robbery carried only a 6-10 year sentence.

(C) Dellum will not prevail, since he was not arrested and charged until *after* the new criminal statute had taken effect.

(D) Dellum will not prevail, since Armed Robbery is an entirely different (i.e., narrower) offense than Aggravated Robbery.

7. Recent studies available to Congress indicate that there is a close correlation between smoking and lung cancer. Although this has been known for some time, the medical evidence is now more corroborative of this conclusion. Anti-smoker's groups successfully lobbied Con-

gress to pass a law which precludes smoking advertisements from computer Internet, television and radio and in regularly printed literature (magazines, newspapers and brochures). In fact, other than "word of mouth" or distributing flyers, it is now virtually impossible to advertise cigarettes. However, no similar legislation has been passed with respect to cigars. While the evidence is not quite as strong that cigars cause lung cancer, there is arguably sufficient data to indicate this result. Several tobacco companies have recently commenced an action in U.S. District Court, claiming that the statute violates their First Amendment rights and the Equal Protection Clause.

Based upon the foregoing, it is most likely that:

(A) The statute is unconstitutional, based upon Equal Protection grounds.

(B) The statute is unconstitutional, based upon the First Amendment.

(C) The statute is constitutional, since it directly advances a substantial governmental interest.

(D) The statute is constitutional, since, in light of the recent medical studies, advertising cigarettes without clearly describing the likelihood of lung cancer is misleading.

8. The U.S. Congress recently passed a law which states that, two years from the date of passage of the bill, professionals (doctors, lawyers, dentists, etc.) may not utilize salaries paid to receptionists as business related deductions. A receptionist is defined as an employee whose primary function is to answer tele-

phonic or "in person" inquiries, or who spends at least 50% of her time performing such an activity. The APA (American Physicians Association) brought an action in federal court asserting that this law was discriminatory and a deprivation of due process.

Based upon the foregoing, it is most likely that:

(A) The APA lacks standing, since the law applies to all professionals.

(B) The APA lacks standing, since taxpayer standing is lacking (i.e., none of the members could successfully sue).

(C) The APA has standing, since the act discriminates against professionals, while not ending this deduction for all other businesses.

(D) The APA has standing, since most individual members of the organization have suffered a direct injury.

Questions 9-10 are based upon the following fact situation:

Kristin, Harriet, and Jenny live in the State of Euphoria. They also live in the same neighborhood, and are the very best of friends. They are all seven years old, but each attends a different school. Kristin attends St. Mary's Parochial School, a private school which offers religious instruction; Harriet attends The Sedgewick School for Girls, a private, girls-only school, that offers elementary and secondary education (but which also denies admission to anyone of Hispanic origin); and Jenny attends the local public school. All of the public schools in the State of Euphoria have been desegregated. A Euphoria law provides for the free distribution of computers to students in ***all*** public and private schools. Accordingly, Euphoria provides free computers to St. Mary's, The Sedgewick School, and the public school. Euphoria accredits all state elementary schools, and certifies all teachers.

Jenny's parents, who are avowed liberals and atheists, object to Euphoria's providing of free computers to St. Mary's and The Sedgewick School for Girls.

9. The ***strongest*** constitutional argument that Jenny's parents could make ***against*** Euphoria's distribution of computers to The Sedgewick School for Girls is probably that:

   (A) Euphoria may not, in any way, aid private schools.

   (B) The U.S. Constitution forbids private discrimination, of any kind.

   (C) Euphoria is promoting segregation by the distribution of computers to students attending The Sedgewick School for Girls.

   (D) The distribution of computers by Euphoria promotes no significant educational function.

10. The ***strongest*** argument that Jenny's parents could make ***in favor of*** the constitutionality of the free distribution of computers to students at St. Mary's Parochial School is probably that:

   (A) State promoted instruction at private schools is constitutionally permissible.

   (B) Euphoria's distribution of computers is secular in nature, and

does not engender church/state entanglement.

   (C) Similar treatment of students at public and private religious schools is required by the Free Exercise Clause.

   (D) Private religious schools fulfill an important state educational function.

11. Doe is prosecuted for giving his 14-year-old daughter a glass of wine in violation of a state statute prohibiting any person from serving an alcoholic beverage to a minor. Doe defends on the ground that the state statute as applied in his case unconstitutionally interferes with the free exercise of his religion. In determining the constitutionality of the state statute as applied in this instance, the court may ***not*** properly:

   (A) Require the state to bear the burden of persuading the court that the statute is unconstitutional as applied to Doe.

   (B) Determine the reasonableness of Doe's religious beliefs.

   (C) Ascertain whether Doe's religious beliefs require him to serve wine to his child.

   (D) Decide whether Doe is sincere in his religious beliefs (that is, whether he really believes them).

12. A federal law requires United States Civil Service employees to ordinarily retire at age 75. However, the statute also states that civil service employees of the armed forces must retire at age 65. Prentis, a 65-year old civil service employee of the Department of the Army, seeks a declaratory judgment that would

forbid his mandatory retirement until age 75.

The STRONGEST argument that Prentis can make to invalidate the requirement that he retire at age 65 is that the law:

(A) Denies him a privilege or immunity of national citizenship.

(B) Deprives him of a property right without just compensation.

(C) Is not within the scope of any of the enumerated powers of Congress in Article I, Section 8.

(D) Invidiously discriminates against him on the basis of age in violation of the Fifth Amendment.

13. Pfeifer Madison, a wealthy eccentric living in the State of Ukiah, is an "anti-tax" person. He formed a new political party called Americans Against Taxes. Pfeifer told his followers that, if he is elected, he will do everything in his power to severely minimize state taxes. To run for office in Ukiah, however, Pfeifer must file a petition containing 20% of the registered voters' signatures before he can be placed on the ballot. Pfeifer and his campaign supporters worked diligently to obtain enough signatures to put his name on the ballot. But, they were unsuccessful. (They obtained only 12%.) Thus, Pfeifer failed to get onto the Ukiah state ballot as an independent candidate for Governor.

Pfeifer then retained Ukiah's largest law firm to commence a suit against the appropriate state officials in U.S. District Court. This firm sought an injunction against the signature requirement on the

ground that it was unconstitutional, and therefore invalid.

The *strongest* argument for the Ukiah's statute's unconstitutionality is probably that:

(A) The statute was intended to keep candidates who lacked strong voter support off of the ballot.

(B) Relatively few independent candidates have, in fact, ever succeeded in obtaining the requisite number of signatures.

(C) There is probably a less burdensome means of accomplishing the statute's purpose.

(D) The voters' signature requirement is an unreasonable means of insuring that a potential candidate has adequate popular support.

14. The State of Euphoria is located close to the border between the United States and Mexico. Within the past several years, Euphoria has experienced increasing problems with illegal immigration. Unattended yard items and license plates are constantly stolen. This has resulted in anti-illegal immigrant protests. Members of the Euphoria legislature have proposed laws which prohibit the state from providing medical and educational services to illegal immigrants, as well as English literacy requirements for voting in local, state and federal elections.

Several minority rights groups decide to challenge their constitutionality. (Assume these entities have standing.)

The ***strongest*** basis for finding the English literacy voting law unconstitutional is probably the:

(A) Equal Protection Clause of the Fourteenth Amendment.

(B) Due Process Clause of the Fourteenth Amendment.

(C) Power of Congress to exclusively determine the manner of holding elections for U.S. Senators and Representatives (Article I, Section 4).

(D) Constitutional provision that U.S. Representatives be chosen by the people of the several states.

15. Polly Pitman is a citizen of the State of Macon. She has been lobbying her local assemblyman, Roy Hodges, to pass a law authorizing the construction of a new highway to run directly through the small rural town in which Polly owns a small business. This road would connect up two already existing state highways. This development would presumably result in more business for Polly. Also, Polly's husband, Bob, owns the "Pitman Construction Company." Roy, in fact, ultimately secured legislation which authorized funds for the new state highway. Shortly thereafter, Macon retained the Pitman Construction Company to assist with building the new road. However, when news of this legislation became widely known, the Macon legislators were criticized for failing to allocate funds to improve its existing highways. As a consequence, the legislature repealed the statute authorizing the new state highway and repealed the contract with the Pitman Construction Company. Bob Pitman commenced an action to

compel Macon to adhere to the agreement.

Based upon the foregoing, it is most likely that the cancellation of the contract with the Pitman Construction Company is:

(A) Invalid, under the Contracts Clause.

(B) Invalid, if Bob had relied upon the original statute in a substantial manner.

(C) Valid, since a state legislature may rescind its own laws.

(D) Valid, since pursuant to the Eleventh Amendment, a state is not liable to individuals.

16. Recently, Congress enacted a statute which appropriated $30 million to study the effect of AIDS upon the families of persons suffering from that disease, and to determine if costs could be saved by having members of those families render medical-type assistance to the infected person. Pursuant to this legislation, the Secretary of Health and Human Services was required to "distribute all of the appropriated funds within one year" from the date upon which the statute was passed.

A short time later, however, the need for a balanced budget again came to the political forefront. To demonstrate that he was doing his part, the President ordered the members of his cabinet to effectuate an "across-the-board" 20% reduction in their departmental expenditures. Based upon various reports that a cure for AIDS was imminent, the President (via an executive order) instructed the Secretary of Health and Human Services to spend only 50% of the monies allocated for this particular program. Numerous AIDS groups now contend that this action by the President is unconstitutional.

Based upon the foregoing, the Secretary of Health and Human Services may constitutionally expend which of the following amounts for the AIDS program described above:

(A) $15 million, if the President reasonably determined that this program had ceased to be of significant importance to the general welfare.

(B) $15 million, since the President may exercise control over the actions of his subordinates by executive order.

(C) $24 million, since a more drastic cut would contravene the Equal Protection Clause, as compared to the beneficiaries of other programs.

(D) $30 million, since the President cannot impair a valid federal statute imposing a duty to spend appropriated monies.

Questions 17-19 are based on the following fact situation:

As part of a comprehensive federal aid-to-education program, Congress included the following provisions as conditions for state receipt of federal funds: (1) Whenever textbooks are reimbursed by the federal government, they must be used in classes which include no religious instruction and must be made available on the same terms to students in all public and private schools accredited by the state educational authority; (2) Salary supplements can be paid to teachers in public and private schools, up to ten percent of existing salary schedules, where present compensation is less than the average salary for persons of comparable training and experience, provided that no such supplement is paid to any teacher who instructs in religious subjects; (3) construction grants can be made toward the cost of physical structures at private colleges and universities, provided that no part of the grant is used for buildings in which instruction in religious subject matters is offered.

17. Federal taxpayer Allen challenges the provision that allows the distribution of free textbooks to students in a private school where religious instruction is included in the curriculum. On the question of the adequacy of Allen's standing to raise the constitutional question, the most likely result is that standing will be:

(A) Sustained, because any congressional spending authorization can be challenged by a federal taxpayer.

(B) Sustained, because the challenge to the exercise of the congressional spending power is based on a claimed violation of a specific constitutional limitation.

(C) Denied, because there is an insufficient nexus between the taxpayer and the challenged expenditures.

(D) Denied, because, in the case of private schools, no state action is involved.

18. Federal taxpayer Bates also challenges the salary supplements for teachers in private schools where religious instruction is included in the curriculum. On the substantive constitutional issue, the most likely result is that the salary supplements will be:

(A) Sustained, because the statute provides that no supplements will be made to teachers who are engaged in any religious instruction.

(B) Sustained, because to distinguish between private and public school teachers would violate the religious freedom clause of the First Amendment.

(C) Held unconstitutional, because some religions would benefit disproportionately.

(D) Held unconstitutional, because policing the restriction would amount to an excessive entanglement with religion.

19. Federal taxpayer Bates also challenges the construction grants to church-operated, private colleges and universities. The most likely result is that the construction grants will be:

(A) Sustained, because aid to one aspect of an institution of higher education not shown to be pervasively sectarian does not necessarily free it to spend its other resources for religious purposes.

(B) Sustained, because the construction of buildings does not aid religion in a way forbidden by the Establishment Clause of the First Amendment.

(C) Held unconstitutional, because any financial aid to a church-operated school strengthens the religious purposes of that institution.

(D) Held unconstitutional, because the grants involve an excessive entanglement with religion.

20. State X accredits both public and private schools, licenses their teachers, and supplies textbooks on secular subjects to all such schools. Country Schoolhouse, a private school that offers elementary and secondary education in State X, denies admission to all non-Caucasians. In a suit to enjoin as unconstitutional the continued racially exclusionary admissions policy of the Country Schoolhouse, which of the following is the STRONGEST argument AGAINST school?

(A) Since education is a public function, Country Schoolhouse may not discriminate on racial grounds.

(B) Since the state is constitutionally obligated to eliminate segregation in all public and private educational institutions, Country Schoolhouse may not discriminate on racial grounds.

(C) Each state is constitutionally obligated to eliminate segregation in all public and private educational institutions.

(D) Teachers who are licensed by a state accreditation entity are forbidden to discriminate on racial grounds.

21. Ben and Sheila Wellness owned a relatively low-income apartment complex in the State of Euphoria. Two months ago, one of the units in the complex became vacant. Ben and Sheila advertised in the local paper for a new tenant. A few days later, Malcolm, a Black man who had become disabled due to a manufacturing accident, telephonically requested to "see" the unit. Sheila recognized the accent and responded, "Sorry, the unit has already been rented." Malcolm sub-

sequently discovered that the unit had, in fact, not been rented at the time he asked to inspect it. Malcolm retained an attorney, whose research disclosed a U.S. statute which prohibited "any denial of housing based solely upon racial or ethnic grounds."

Based upon the foregoing, the *most easily justifiable* basis upon which Congress could have enacted this statute is the:

(A) Thirteenth Amendment.

(B) Fourteenth Amendment.

(C) General Welfare Clause of Article 1, Section 8.

(D) Contracts Clause.

22. During his gubernatorial campaign, Malcolm Duke vociferously promised the citizens of the State of Primera he would "boost the state's sagging economy." True to his word, as soon as Malcolm Duke became the Governor of Primera by garnering 63% of the popular vote, he induced the legislature to enact a statute requiring all business entities selling goods in Primera with annual sales in excess of $1 million in any calendar year to make at least 10% of their purchases each year from companies doing business in Primera. Breed Corporation, whose sales within Primera the prior year were in excess of $1 million, prefers to *not* comply with the new law. It retains an attorney to assert that it is unconstitutional.

Based upon the foregoing, which of the following constitutional provisions probably represents the *strongest* basis for invalidating this statue:

(A) The Commerce Clause.

(B) The Due Process Clause of the Fourteenth Amendment.

(C) The Privileges and Immunities Clause of the Fourteenth Amendment.

(D) The Equal Protection Clause.

23. There had recently been newspaper articles and television shows about the "poaching" of animals from national parks and recreation areas (including Yosemite National Park). The "animal rights" lobby persuaded Congress to pass legislation which made "the taking of any type of live wildlife" by a private citizen from a federal area illegal. In fact, in addition to monetary fines, anyone convicted under this statute could be compelled to spend up to three years in a federal prison. Two days after passage of this legislation and the necessary presidential signature, Charles Winterhead was apprehended attempting to remove a "live" squirrel from a federal preserve. Charles claimed that he had no knowledge of the recent change in law, and asserted that the federal law was unconstitutional.

Based upon the foregoing, which of the following represents the *strongest* basis for sustaining the statute against constitutional attack by Charles?

(A) The Commerce Clause of Article I, Section 8.

(B) The Privileges and Immunities Clause of Article IV.

(C) The Enforcement Clause of the Fourteenth Amendment.

(D) The Property Clause of Article IV, Section 3.

24. A recent federal study entitled "Car Thefts in the United States" con-

cluded that approximately 22% of all stolen vehicles were transported into adjoining states and disposed of in those states. One of the report's recommendations was that Congress enact legislation which would establish a national vehicle registry. This would, according to the report, make it easier for police within a state to determine if a particular vehicle had been stolen from another state.

Anxious to demonstrate their anti-crime fervor to potential voters, Congress quickly passed this legislation. However, the law required each vehicle owner to complete forms containing the required information and send them, along with $18, to a federally established national registry in Oklahoma City. Of course, a few registered drivers contend that the new law infringes upon their "privacy." They commenced an action contending that the law was unconstitutional.

Based upon the foregoing, the statute is probably:

(A) Constitutional, since Congress has the power to regulate property for the general welfare.

(B) Constitutional, since Congress could determine that vehicle thefts affect interstate commerce.

(C) Unconstitutional, since the study found that the vast majority of stolen vehicles remain within the state in which they are stolen.

(D) Unconstitutional, since the registration of vehicles is a matter impliedly reserved to the states by the Tenth Amendment.

25. Medico Enterprises, a major drug manufacturer, has just announced its ability to produce a drug which, when taken by females, avoids pregnancy without any harmful side effects. The FDA approved the drug one week ago. Medico now plans to distribute the drug called "Gogoco" throughout the United States. However, legislators in the State of Butah are 'fearful that Gogoco would have a pernicious moral effect on the young. They pass legislation forbidding the sale or distribution of Gogoco to minors within their jurisdiction. The age of majority in Butah is twenty-one. The ACLU and the largest retail pharmacy (eight stores) within Butah have joined in an action to declare the new law unconstitutional.

Based upon the foregoing, probably the **strongest** constitutional argument which could be asserted for invalidating this statute is that it:

(A) Constitutes an undue burden on interstate commerce.

(B) Denies minors a fundamental right.

(C) Violates a privilege or immunity of national citizenship.

(D) Violates the First Amendment right to freedom of religion because it regulates morals.

26. Daniel Baker owned a substantial real estate development company. He decided to develop a large residential community in Springdale, Euphoria, which would showcase "Family Values; The Way America Was in the Fifties." Accordingly, Daniel's development plan includes covenants and restrictions (CCR's) which mandate that all homeowners (1) paint their houses at least once a year, using white paint only,

and (2) maintain well-manicured lawns in the front of their property. Before borrowing the necessary funds, Daniel consulted an attorney for the purpose of preparing the CCR's which would be incorporated into the deed given to each purchaser. However, she advised Daniel that legislation pending in the Euphoria legislature would make all privately imposed CCR's unenforceable. The Euphoria Land Use Board would (via zoning) have sole, exclusive control in these matters.

Based upon the foregoing, if Daniel decided to challenge the proposed legislation, which of the following constitutional concepts is probably the **least** likely to succeed?

(A) Deprivation of property rights without compensation.

(B) Privileges and immunities (Article IV, Section 2).

(C) Excessive use of police power.

(D) Impairment of contracts.

27. The State of Euphoria places a high value upon computer education, which legislators believe is the "wave of the future." As a consequence, the legislature has enacted a special, state-sponsored loan program for college or graduate students majoring in computer-related studies. However, only residents of Euphoria who are U.S. citizens are eligible for this program.

William Gaung applied for a loan pursuant to this program. His application was about to be granted, when the reviewing officer noticed that he was merely a legal resident alien. As a consequence, the application was rejected. When William inquired as to why the loan program was restricted to U.S. citizens, he

was advised that an 11-year-old federal study had concluded that only 36% of resident legal aliens still remained in the jurisdiction of their collegiate schooling within five years after their education had been concluded.

William promptly commenced an action in federal court, contending that the restriction contained in the Euphoria loan program was unconstitutional.

Based upon the foregoing, it is most likely that the loan program's restriction to U.S. citizens is probably:

(A) Constitutional, since aliens are not a "discrete and insular minority."

(B) Constitutional, since the line drawn by Euphoria was reasonably related to a legitimate state interest.

(C) Unconstitutional, since the justification for this restriction is insufficient to overcome the burden imposed on states for alienage classification.

(D) Unconstitutional, since the Privileges and Immunities Clause of Article IV does not permit such arbitrary classifications.

28. Alison, who works for American Bracks, Inc., is Vice-President of Marketing. She was recently promoted. As part of her promotion, Alison had to relocate from the State of Argon to the corporate headquarters in the State of Mercer. Alison moved to Mercer in September. She planned to vote the "Republican ticket" in the upcoming local and gubernatorial elections in November. However, when Alison

went to the polls in November, she was ***not*** permitted to vote. Alison was informed that a Mercer law provided that persons moving into the jurisdiction could ***not*** vote in any elections, until they had demonstrated their "bona fide intent" to become residents of the state by living there for six months. Since Alison had only been a citizen of Mercer slightly more than two months, she could not vote in ***any*** election.

Based upon the foregoing, the ***strongest*** constitutional argument that Alison could assert to invalidate the Mercer statute is probably that:

(A) It can be legitimately presumed persons moving to a new jurisdiction intend to remain there.

(B) The statute discriminates against interstate commerce.

(C) There are no sufficiently compelling reasons to justify the exclusion from voting of new residents.

(D) Mercer could utilize less restrictive means to assure that only genuine residents voted in its elections.

29. Muffy became addicted to cocaine while attending an exclusive all-girls' prep school. She took the drug to maintain her weight and stay up all night studying or writing papers. When Muffy entered an Ivy League college, she was still addicted to cocaine. To acquire money to support her habit, Muffy sold cocaine. One night, when she was 19 years old, Muffy was arrested, and later convicted for possession and distribution of cocaine (a felony).

Muffy subsequently transferred to another college, where she met Biff. Muffy and Biff fell in love and married after graduation. They settled in Euphoria. Biff never knew of Muffy's past cocaine use or arrest. Unfortunately, Muffy soon again began using cocaine, without Biff's knowledge. Two years after their marriage, Muffy gave birth to twin daughters. However, six months later, Muffy was again arrested for possession of cocaine, and convicted (her second felony).

A State of Euphoria statute requires that any adult who has been twice convicted of a drug abuse-related felony, shall permanently lose custody of a minor child. Euphoria commenced an action under the statute to terminate Muffy's parental rights because of the second felony conviction. Muffy contends in rebuttal that the statute is unconstitutional as applied to her in this situation.

Based on the foregoing, it is most likely that the burden of persuasion in this matter is upon:

(A) Muffy, to show that the statute is ***not*** rationally related to a legitimate state interest.

(B) Euphoria, to show that the statute as applied to Muffy is rationally related to a legitimate state interest.

(C) Euphoria, to show the statute satisfies a compelling state interest.

(D) Muffy, to show that no substantial state interest is furthered by the statute.

30. In the State of Wissola, there has recently been a spate of accidents involving commercial trucks and vans. Apparently, as drivers seek to

impress their employers with the expeditious manner in which their tasks can be accomplished, they occasionally exceed the speed limit or take unnecessary chances. Believing that accidents could be lessened if the drivers of these vehicles wore harness (rather than simply waist-type) seat belts, Wissola enacted a law requiring the former in all "commercially utilized trucks and vans." Private trucks or vans were ***not*** affected.

BUPS, a national entity which delivers packages in Wissola and twenty-two other states, objects to this law. Some of the BUPS trucks which operate in Wissola also deliver packages in adjoining states which do ***not*** require this type of seat belt. BUPS estimates that it would incur substantial costs to equip all of its trucks which constantly or occasionally operate in Wissola with harness-type seat belts. Also, several of its drivers have expressed unhappiness with the new law.

Based upon the foregoing, probably the ***best*** constitutional basis for invalidating the new Wissola law is the:

(A) Due Process Clause.

(B) Equal Protection Clause.

(C) Burden on Interstate Commerce doctrine.

(D) Contracts Clause.

31. The State of Euphoria has recently experienced an increase in violent crime. Local citizens groups are demanding that the government provide additional police to better protect law abiding citizen-taxpayers. The particularly vociferous "Tired of Being Victims" group,

along with local police unions and the Governor of Euphoria, petitioned the federal government for greater police protection.

After much lobbying, Congress passed (and the President signed) a law requiring state and local police department to receive federal funds to hire sufficient patrol officers. The law provides that each city of 50,000 or more residents must have at least two police officers for every 500 citizens. Cities with less than 50,000 inhabitants are not expressly covered by this legislation.

The ***strongest*** constitutional basis for validating the enactment of the statute is the:

(A) War and defense powers.

(B) Tenth Amendment.

(C) Privileges and Immunities Clause of the Fourteenth Amendment.

(D) Power to Tax and Spend for the General Welfare.

32. Martha, a citizen of the State of Spud, is an ardent disciple of Reverend Richquick, who tells his followers that the more money they contribute to his church, the higher will be their places in heaven. Martha is very concerned that her place in heaven is questionable. As a consequence, she takes up Tupperware selling to enhance her contributions to Richquick's church. Martha does not have a commercial license to sell Tupperware, even though "persons engaged in retail sales" are required to have one. However, persons engaged in the retail sale of items for "religious purposes" are exempt from the license requirement.

One day, Martha sells Tupperware to Kathryn, an undercover police officer. When Kathryn asked Martha for a copy of her commercial license for retail sales, Martha admitted she didn't have one. Martha was then arrested, and charged with violating this law. Martha's attorney, hired for her by Reverend Richquick, asserts that her sales were for "religious purposes," and thus exempt from the statute in question.

Based upon the foregoing, it is most likely that, under the statute in question, Martha is:

(A) Not guilty, if Martha's religious beliefs are sincerely held.

(B) Not guilty, since under the First Amendment, a state may not criminalize *bona fide* religious tenets.

(C) Guilty, because a generally applicable criminal prohibition may infringe upon religious activities.

(D) Guilty, if the factfinder concludes that Martha's religious beliefs are clearly erroneous.

33. State X passed a law requiring all single family dwellings whose composition was more than 60% stucco to be reinforced with metal slats within 2 years. This process would ordinarily cost approximately $1,200. The law was passed after a report pertaining to potential damage in the event of an earthquake indicated that loss of life and property would be diminished as a result of such metal reinforcement. However, statistics indicate that 64% of all single family dwellings in State X which have a composition of more than 60% stucco are owned by Hispanic individuals.

Is State X's law unconstitutional?

(A) No, because there is a rational basis for the law.

(B) Yes, because the strict scrutiny standard is not satisfied in this instance.

(C) Yes, because the law has a disproportionately negative racial impact.

(D) Yes, because the $1,200 fee necessary to reinforce the homes violates due process.

34. A state legislative committee wants you to draft legislation to make all restrictions on land use imposed by deeds (now or hereafter recorded) enforceable, so that public planning through zoning will have exclusive control in matters of land-use. Which of the following is LEAST likely to be a consideration in drafting such legislation?

(A) Compensation for property rights taken by public authority.

(B) The impairment of contracts clause; Article I, Section 10, (Clause 1).

(C) The privileges and immunities clause of Article IV, Section 2.

(D) The Tenth Amendment.

35. There has recently been a dramatic increase in gasoline prices. This development has incensed many citizens, and engendered numerous groups whose stated purpose is to "throw out" their present legislators. Fearful of such a voter reaction, Congress hurriedly enacted a statute which allows the Energy Secretary to "set" the retail price of gasoline which is produced in America or brought into the United

States from a foreign country. Numerous large oil companies have asserted that this law is unconstitutional.

Based upon the foregoing, the **strongest** argument for upholding this statute is the power of Congress to:

(A) Enact laws for the general welfare.

(B) Regulate the sale of products or goods which are manufactured or produced in the United States.

(C) Regulate the importation of foreign goods and products brought into the U.S. from abroad.

(D) Regulate interstate and foreign commerce.

Questions 36-37 are based upon the following fact situation:

Legislators in the State of Euphoria were very concerned about its skyrocketing divorce rate. Divorces in this jurisdiction were occurring at almost a 70% rate for marriages which had occurred within the prior ten years. The legislature therefore passed a law which declared that no couple could obtain a marriage license, unless and until they had paid for and received at least fifteen hours of marriage and family counseling from a licensed counselor in that state. The Euphoria State Bar persuaded the legislature to include another provision, which required a couple who had applied for a marriage license to pay for and attend at least ten hours of classes given by an attorney of that state pertaining to community property principles. In Euphoria, a couple could apply for a marriage license if the older person was at least 18 years of age, and the younger

one at least 16 years old.

36. Paul and Mary were 19 and 18 years old, respectively. They intend to attend college, marry, and then go to law school. They were both incensed at the new law and retained Artis Schlimebag, Esq., to represent them in having the legislation declared unconstitutional.

Based upon the foregoing, Mr. Schlimebag commenced an action on their behalf in U.S. District Court. In response, the Euphoria State Attorney General moved for dismissal.

The **strongest** basis for dismissal is probably that:

(A) Paul and Mary are citizens of the same state.

(B) No substantial federal question is presented.

(C) The suit is not ripe.

(D) The suit presents a non-justiciable political question.

37. Assuming Paul and Mary's action was **not** dismissed and that the age of majority (i.e., when one can vote) in Euphoria is twenty-one, it is most likely that the burden of proof is upon:

(A) The plaintiffs, since Euphoria may regulate the conditions for marriage pursuant to the Tenth Amendment.

(B) The plaintiffs, since an enactment by a state legislature is presumed to be constitutional.

(C) The State of Euphoria, since marriage is a fundamental right.

(D) The State of Euphoria, since legislation affecting minors is subject to strict scrutiny.

Questions 38-39 are based on the following fact situation:

A recently enacted State X law forbids legal aliens from owning more than 100 acres of land within the jurisdiction and directs the state attorney general to bring an action in ejectment whenever an alien owns in excess thereof. Zane, a resident legal alien, purchased 200 acres of land in State X after passage of that law. He brings an action in federal court to enjoin the State X Attorney General from enforcing the statute against him. The defendant moved to dismiss the complaint.

38. The STRONGEST argument for Zane is that:

   (A) States are forbidden by the commerce clause from interfering with the rights of aliens to own land.

   (B) The State X statute violates the equal protection clause of the Fourteenth Amendment.

   (C) The State X statute adversely affects Zane's right to travel.

   (D) The State X statute violates the obligation of contracts clause.

39. The federal court should:

   (A) Dismiss the action, because under the U.S. Constitution aliens may not sue in federal court.

   (B) Dismiss the action, because a state has the power to determine the qualifications for landholding within its boundaries.

(C) Hear the action, if the United Nations Charter forbids such discrimination.

(D) Hear the action, because a federal question is presented.

40. James, a practicing Buddhist, had dreamed of working for a governmental agency. He intended to use his Buddhist training to "humanize big bureaucracy." One day, James heard of an opening for a secretary at the State of Yodah Environmental Agency, and immediately applied. Pursuant to agency policy, James was given a standardized test, which he passed. He was then interviewed by an employee of the State Employment Office.

James' application was rejected one week later. There is no statute, regulation, or departmental policy which requires any explanation to rejected applicants. However, in a few instances (5-10% of the time), applicants have received personal or telephonic post-interview discussions by Yodah Employment Office personnel as to why they were unsuccessful. These explanations are permitted by Yodah Employment Agency regulations, but are completely discretionary. Some of the Employment Office personnel occasionally believe that their comments might assist applicants with subsequent job interviews. James specifically asked for a personal post-interview discussion, but was refused.

Based upon the foregoing, if James commenced an action to compel the Employment Officer to provide him with information similar to that supplied to other rejected applicants who had received post-interview feedback, is it most likely that:

(A) He will be unsuccessful, since the employment of individuals is reserved to the states under the Tenth Amendment.

(B) He will be unsuccessful, since there is no protectable "property interest" in employment by a state agency.

(C) He will be successful, since the right to governmental employment is a protected "liberty" interest within the Due Process Clause.

(D) He will be successful, since James' treatment by Yodah contravenes the Equal Protection Clause.

41. At night, Angela works as a part-time singer in local nightclubs. But, during the day, she is employed as a secretary by the City of Trigera (where she has been employed for just over five years). According to a Trigera ordinance, Angela cannot acquire tenure until she has been employed by the municipality for ten consecutive years. Until now, Angela's one-year contract has been renewed in a timely manner. Recently, however, Trigera experienced a recession. As a consequence, there were job cutbacks and Angela was informed that her one-year contract would not be renewed. Although Angela (1) asked for a written statement as to why she was not being rehired, and (2) requested an opportunity for a hearing, she was refused. Trigera officials cited state law and city department rules which do not require either a statement of reasons or a hearing. Angela seeks to compel Trigera to furnish her with a statement of its reasons for failing to rehire her.

Based upon the foregoing, the situation which would probably provide the **strongest** constitutional argument which Angela could assert is:

(A) In the expectation of continued employment based upon renewal of her contract for five years, Angela had just purchased a home in close physical proximity to her job.

(B) The contracts of only a relatively few secretaries were not renewed that year.

(C) Angela had rejected another job offer after being verbally assured of continued re-employment by the State of Trigera officer for whom she worked.

(D) No evidence exists that any of the secretaries retained by the State of Trigera are more qualified than Angela.

42. The State of Euphoria operates a large parking lot near the state capitol building. Within the parking lot structure is a restaurant which has operated in a highly profitable manner for more than three years. Euphoria has entered into a lease for this space with the owner of this facility for ten years. Several persons of Hispanic origin have recently complained that they have been denied service by the restaurant. However, the restaurant owner contends that they were denied service only after they had acted in a loud, overbearing manner. One of the aggrieved persons commenced an action in U.S. District Court, contending that the restaurant's discrimination against him violated the Equal Protection Clause of the Fourteenth Amendment. He alleged that operation of

the restaurant constituted "state action."

Based upon the foregoing, the District Court will most likely:

(A) Hear the case on the merits, since a federal claim is presented.

(B) Hear the case on the merits, since Euphoria is a defendant.

(C) Abstain from jurisdiction, since any alleged constitutional issues should first be heard in a state court.

(D) Dismiss the case for lack of jurisdiction, if the plaintiff and restaurant owner are both citizens of Euphoria.

43. The State of Euphoria accredits both public and private schools, licenses their teachers, and supplies textbooks pertaining to secular subjects to all of its educational institutions. Euphoria also supplies athletic gear to the various varsity teams in its high schools and corresponding grade levels at private schools. The Bastion is a private school in Euphoria which offers secondary education. It has a well established policy of denying admission applications from persons whose parents are registered members of the Republican Party or prominently espouse the views of that entity. The principals of The Bastion sincerely believe that the "ideas" promoted by these organizations are extremely dangerous to society.

In a suit to enjoin as unconstitutional the exclusionary admissions policy of The Bastion, which of the following is most likely the **strongest** argument **against** that school?

(A) Education is a public function, and so The Bastion may not discriminate.

(B) A state is constitutionally obligated to eliminate segregation in public educational institutions.

(C) A state is constitutionally obligated to eliminate discrimination in public and private educational institutions.

(D) Schools which are licensed by a state accreditation entity are forbidden to discriminate.

44. The City of Littletown recently enacted an ordinance which prohibited parades or demonstrations between the hours of 4:00 p.m. and 6:30 p.m. The purpose of the ordinance was to preclude such events during "rush" hour, when traffic might become ensnarled and motorists might become violent if obliged to remain in non-moving vehicles for an extended period of time. However, to avoid any challenges that streets were "public forums," and that such "speech activities" as parades and demonstrations could not be precluded in public forums, exceptions to this prohibition could be made by the Littletown Police Department Commissioner. If the Commissioner were presented with a waiver application at least 72 hours before a planned event, that official could approve it. The Police Commissioner was instructed to give "prompt" attention to such applications, and to determine all applications in an "even-handed manner."

Based upon the foregoing, if the statute is constitutionally challenged, it is most likely that it would be found:

(A) Unconstitutional, since traditional public forums must be made reasonably available for speech activities without condition.

(B) Unconstitutional, since the statute vests too much discretion in the Littletown Police Commissioner.

(C) Constitutional, since the restrictions are narrowly tailored to promote a significant governmental purpose.

(D) Constitutional, since the Littletown Police Commissioner is required to give waiver applications his "prompt" attention and decide them in an "evenhanded manner."

Questions 45-46 are based upon the following fact situation:

Congress recently enacted legislation which provided monetary grants to public schools and integrated religious schools for the purchase of computers. These grants were based solely upon the number of students at each institution. The purpose of this legislation was to make certain that America did not fall behind in the technological arena. This legislation also provided for hiring computer-education teachers, who are expressly prohibited from providing any type of religious instruction at either public or private schools.

45. Based upon the foregoing, if Alex, an avowed atheist and federal taxpayer, challenges the statute, it is most likely that:
    (A) He lacks standing, if he has no children in either a public or private school.

(B) He lacks standing, since the legislation in question is a general funding measure.

(C) He has standing, since the statute arguably contravenes a specific governmental limitation.

(D) He has standing, if the expenditure in question was made pursuant to the "General Welfare" Clause.

46. Assuming Alex has standing, the portion of the statute providing for the funding of computer-education teachers probably is:

    (A) Constitutional, since the statute applies equally to public and private religious schools.

    (B) Constitutional, since (given the prohibition against any type of religious instruction) there is insufficient governmental/religious entanglement.

    (C) Unconstitutional, since this portion of the statute might result in excessive governmental/religious entanglement.

    (D) Unconstitutional, since private, non-religious schools are **not** included within the statute.

47. Clarence had worked as a Federal Public Defender for almost twenty years. He was about to celebrate his sixtieth birthday. There is, however, a U.S. law which requires Federal Public Defenders to retire at age 60. Accordingly, when Clarence returned to his office the day before he became 60, there was a letter on his desk. This letter explained that retirement was mandatory and instructed him to "clean out his desk" by the close of the following day.

Clarence called a friend of his, Melvin, who had worked at the F.B.I. for twelve years. Melvin advised Clarence that F.B.I. agents did not have to retire until they had reached age 70. Clarence, who is currently working on a number of interesting cases, decides to seek a declaratory judgment that would extend his mandatory retirement until age 70.

Based upon the foregoing, the **strongest** argument that Clarence could make to invalidate the present law is probably that this legislation:

(A) Discriminates against him in violation of the Fifth Amendment.

(B) Violates the Fifth Amendment's Due Process Clause, since employment is a "property right."

(C) Violates the "Privileges and Immunity" Clause.

(D) Violates the Equal Protection Clause of the Fourteenth Amendment.

Questions 48-49 are based on the following fact situation:

Congress decided that the application of the Uniform Consumer Credit Code ("UCCC") should be the same throughout the United States. To that end, it enacted the UCCC as a federal law and made it directly applicable to all consumer credit, small loans, and retail installment sales. The law is intended to protect borrowers and buyers against unfair practices by suppliers of consumer credit.

48. Which of the following constitutional provisions may be MOST

EASILY used to justify federal enactment of this statute?

(A) The obligation of contracts clause.

(B) The privileges and immunities clause of the Fourteenth Amendment.

(C) The commerce clause.

(D) The equal protection clause of the Fourteenth Amendment.

49. A particular religious organization, pursuant to the tenets of its faith, makes loans throughout the country for the construction of churches. The federal UCCC would substantially interfere with the organization's objective of expanding religious institutions. The organization seeks to obtain a declaratory judgment that the federal law may not be applied to its lending activities. Which of the following best describes the burden that must be sustained?

(A) The federal government must demonstrate that the governmental interest outweighs the interference with the organization's lending activities.

(B) The federal government must demonstrate that it rationally believed that the UCCC helps to achieve a legitimate national interest when applied to both religious and secular lending activities.

(C) The organization must demonstrate that no reasonable legislator could believe that application of the UCCC to this organization would be helpful in accomplishing a legitimate governmental objective.

(D) The organization must demonstrate a specific congressional purpose to inhibit the accomplishment of the organization's religious objectives.

Questions 50-51 are based upon the following fact situation:

The State of Caldonia is in the midst of a severe recession. As a result, foreign investors have purchased many businesses and a substantial amount of real estate. Mack Winston, the Governor of Caldonia, is running for re-election. As part of his gubernatorial campaign, Mack promises that, if re-elected, he will "prevent foreigners from buying up our state." He is re-elected by a landslide vote, and promptly prevails upon the Caldonia legislature to pass a law which forbids aliens from owning a "controlling" interest in any company incorporated in Caldonia. He directs the State Attorney General to commence a criminal action to vigorously enforce the new enactment.

Misho, a wealthy Taiwanese businessman, who was unaware of the new law, purchased 60% of the shares of Walco, Inc. (a private company incorporated in Caldonia) for $50,000. Misho had reached a verbal agreement for the purchase of the shares before the law was passed, but the transaction was not "closed" until one week after the law became effective. Misho is a legal alien. When the Caldonia Attorney General filed a criminal action against Misho pursuant to the new law, Misho commenced an action in federal court to enjoin enforcement of the statute and dismiss the criminal complaint against him.

50. Based upon the foregoing, it is most likely that the federal court will:

(A) Dismiss the action, because aliens may not sue in federal court.

(B) Dismiss the action, since a state may determine the qualifications for the ownership of assets within its boundaries.

(C) Hear the action, since a state is defendant.

(D) Hear the action, since a federal question is presented.

51. Based upon the foregoing, Misho's **strongest** argument to have the new Caldonia law declared unconstitutional is probably that it:

(A) Violates the Impairment of Contracts Clause.

(B) Violates the Equal Protection Clause.

(C) Violates the Privileges and Immunities Clause.

(D) Violates the Interstate Commerce Clause.

Questions 52-53 are based upon the following fact situation:

State X College ("College") is engaged in an important micro-biological research project under a grant from the U.S. Army. This research requires the use of several hundred monkeys which College has already purchased. Recently, the State X legislature enacted a law which forbids the use of various animals (including monkeys) for research purposes (the "Act"). Utilizing a special procedure whereby its case could be heard by the State X Supreme Court, the College asserted that the Act was unconstitutional. The State X Supreme Court held in favor of College.

52. State X now seeks review in the U.S. Supreme court. The U.S. Supreme Court will probably:

    (A) Refuse to hear the case, since the U.S. Army is the only party with standing to contest the State X law.

    (B) Refuse to hear the case, unless it grants State X's petition for certiorari.

    (C) Hear the case, since State X has an automatic right of appeal.

    (D) Hear the case, since a federal question has been resolved by a state court.

53. Of the following theories, which would probably represent the WEAKEST argument by College for invalidation of the Act?

    (A) The Act is violative of the Fourteenth Amendment's due process clause.

    (B) The Act contravenes the commerce clause.

    (C) The Act is invalid under the supremacy clause.

    (D) The Act contravenes the impairment of contracts clause.

54. Martin and Dorothy lived together in the State of Euphoria, but were unmarried. Dorothy became pregnant with Martin's child. Martin, who had always been very insecure, accused Dorothy of "sleeping around," and told her that he doubted the child belonged to him. The baby girl conceived by Dorothy was, unfortunately, afflicted with Down's syndrome. Dorothy named the baby Patricia. One month after Patricia's birth, Martin ordered Dorothy and the baby "out," and cut off all contact with them.

One year after Patricia's birth, Martin bought a winning $10 million lottery ticket. However, on the way to collect his prize, Martin was struck and killed by a bus. Martin was survived by one sister, one brother, and both of his parents. He had no other living relatives.

When Dorothy read about Martin's death in the newspaper, she filed a claim with the appropriate state court seeking intestacy benefits for Patricia (since Martin, who died intestate, was the father). Euphoria state law, however, prohibited unacknowledged, illegitimate children from inheriting through their father. Intestacy principles, exclusive of the unacknowledged, illegitimate child, were applicable. After Patricia's claim was rejected, Dorothy filed suit in federal court alleging that the Euphoria statute was invalid.

Based upon the foregoing, Patricia's ***strongest*** argument for invalidating the statute upon constitutional grounds is probably that it:

    (A) Denies Patricia procedural due process, since it doesn't give her an opportunity to prove paternity.

    (B) Is not substantially related to an important governmental interest, and therefore violates the Equal Protection Clause.

    (C) Violates the Privileges and Immunities Clause of the Fourteenth Amendment.

    (D) Deprives Patricia of her fundamental right to inherit property.

55. The State of Butah has a statute which requires all public employees to swear or affirm that they will "oppose anyone seeking to overthrow the State or Federal government by force, violence, or any other unlawful means." John Jones passed all of the physical and written tests necessary to become a fireman in the City of Amityville (in the State of Butah). However, he adamantly refused to take the oath described immediately above, and was not hired. Jones retained an attorney, who filed a complaint in the appropriate U.S. District Court. The complaint alleged that the statute was unconstitutional and sought to enjoin its application.

Based upon the foregoing, the **strongest** argument for **sustaining** the statute against constitutional attack is most likely that:

(A) Governmental employment is not a "right," and therefore may be conditioned upon an oath or affirmation.

(B) The Tenth Amendment permits a state to determine the qualifications of those employed by it.

(C) The oath in this situation is merely a commitment to abide by legal procedures.

(D) A state is entitled to refuse employment to potentially disloyal persons.

56. Shahad fled Iran with his family to escape religious and political persecution. In Iran, Shahad had worked at the palace motor pool. Since legally arriving in the United States, he has lived in the State of Trent. Shahad has been learning English, and is able to communicate fairly well. He recently applied for a job as a mechanic at the Trent High-

way Patrol's main garage. However, Shahad was informed that he is prohibited from obtaining the job because of a Trent law which provides that the state may employ only U.S. citizens. Shahad's attorney commenced an action in U.S. District Court challenging the statute's constitutionality.

Based upon the foregoing, which of the following statements concerning the burden of proof is most likely correct:

(A) Trent must prove that the citizenship requirement promotes a compelling state interest which cannot be satisfied by any less burdensome means.

(B) Trent must prove that there is a rational relationship between the citizenship requirement and a legitimate state interest.

(C) Shahad must prove that the citizenship requirement fails to advance an "important" state interest.

(D) Shahad must prove that there is no rational relationship between the citizenship requirement and any legitimate state interest.

Questions 57-58 are based upon the following fact situation:

Marvin was recently transferred by his company from the State of Facia to the State of Libertania. Marvin has one son, age fifteen, who began attending the local public high school. One night, at dinner, Marvin asked his son, Steve, "What did you learn at school today?" Steve excitedly told Marvin that part of his Sex Education course was about "safe sex." To Marvin's horror, Steve told him that at the end of the class, the teacher had distributed free condoms.

Marvin was so outraged that the following day, at 1:00 p.m., he went to the School Superintendent's office. However, the School Superintendent refused to see Marvin. Marvin then spontaneously staged a one-man demonstration. He began yelling and shouting on the steps of the building: "The school administration is run by sex perverts and child molesters, who are utterly destroying our children. I'll kill those SOB's." The School Superintendent eventually appeared and asked Marvin to leave. Marvin refused, continued his diatribe, and advised the School Superintendent that he was a "filthy, SOB pervert," that he (Marvin) should kill "in a slow manner."

There are two pertinent statutes. The first one prohibits "all speeches or demonstrations in front of any public school or government building during usual school or business hours." The second imposes sanctions on any person "who shall, with or without, provocation, use toward another, and in his presence, opprobrious words or abusive language tending to cause a breach of the peace." These ordinances have not yet been the subject of judicial interpretation. Marvin is prosecuted under both statutes, but asserts that they are unconstitutional.

57. With respect to the first statute, the applicable burden of proof is which one of the following?

   (A) Libertania must prove that the statute advanced an important governmental interest and was narrowly tailored to accomplish this objective.

   (B) Libertania must prove that it had a rational basis for enacting the statute.

   (C) Marvin must prove that Libertania failed to have a compelling interest or a less restrictive means by which it could satisfy the statute's purpose.

   (D) Marvin must prove that Libertania did not have a rational basis for the statute.

58. Which of the following is the **strongest** constitutional argument for invalidating the second statute?

   (A) Prior restraints cannot be imposed on speech in public places.

   (B) Regulation of speech or expressive activity may not be unduly vague.

   (C) Regulation of speech may not be content oriented.

   (D) The First Amendment right of speech or expressive activity is assured by the Fourteenth Amendment.

59. The State of Araho wanted to promote its domestic insurance companies. Those companies had recently suffered economic difficulties as a consequence of a state requirement that they offer earthquake insurance. The Araho State Legislature passed a law which taxed the profits of out-of-state insurance companies at a higher rate than local companies. Congress had previously passed the McCarran-Ferguson Act, which insulates state regulation of the insurance industry from the Commerce Clause. Gamco, an out-of-state insurance company doing business in Araho, commenced an action to invalidate the new law.

Based upon the foregoing, it is most likely that the statute would be held to be:

(A) Unconstitutional, as violative of the Equal Protection Clause.

(B) Unconstitutional, since it discriminates against interstate commerce.

(C) Unconstitutional, under the Supremacy Clause.

(D) Constitutional, since it is rationally related to a legitimate state objective.

60. North Carolina and South Carolina have similar meat verification standards, which include inspections at slaughterhouses. The City of Amityville, located in North Carolina, recently had a serious outbreak of meat poisoning. The source of the problem was believed to be improperly butchered meat brought into the city from outside of the area. The Amityville City Council passed an ordinance forbidding any retail concern in that city from purchasing or selling meat which was not killed at a slaughterhouse inspected by the Amityville Department of Sanitation. This entity inspects slaughterhouses within a 50-mile radius of the city, but does not attempt to cross state lines. South Carolina has meat inspection laws somewhat similar (although not identical) to those employed by Amityville within the State of North Carolina.

The owner of a butcher shop in South Carolina sold meat from a slaughterhouse in that state to Owen, a butcher in Amityville. Owen was charged under the above described ordinance.

Based upon the foregoing, if Owen asserts that the charges against

him should be dismissed on the grounds that the ordinance is unconstitutional, it is most likely that he is:

(A) Correct, since the statute violates the Equal Protection Clause.

(B) Correct, since the statute is violative of the dormant Commerce Clause.

(C) Incorrect, because the statute is rationally related to a legitimate governmental objective.

(D) Incorrect, since citizens are presumed to know the law.

61. Littleton is a small midwestern town. Its two largest, most traveled streets are Main Street and Broadway Avenue. Recently, two parades on these streets caused unusually extensive traffic jams. As a consequence, the City Council of Littleton enacted a statute which forbade all parades or demonstrations on either street. The ordinance did *not* affect speech activities on any other street. Citizens Against Big Government ("CABG") believes that the City Council is pro-business, and enacted the new statute simply to make it more difficult for citizens to bring complaints to the public's attention. CABG decided to stage a demonstration on Main Street, but was advised by their legal counsel to first seek to have the law declared unconstitutional.

Based upon the foregoing, if CABG asserts that the Littleton statute is unconstitutional, it is most likely that a court would rule that it is:

(A) Constitutional, since it is content neutral.

(B) Constitutional, since it merely excludes speech from two specific places.

(C) Unconstitutional, since streets are traditional "public forums."

(D) Unconstitutional, since it is insufficiently narrowly tailored to serve a significant governmental interest.

62. The town of Amityville has an ordinance which provides: "No demonstration or parade involving more than 20 persons shall take place on the town's streets without the prior issuance of a permit." The permit was to be issued by the Police Commissioner if he concluded that "the proposed activity would not be detrimental to the overall community, giving due consideration to factors such as the time, place and manner of the parade or demonstration." Tricia, a member of a women's rights organization called WAR ("Women's Amityville Rights") ignored the ordinance and held a demonstration involving 30 of her adherents on an Amityville street without seeking a permit. She was arrested and charged with violating the ordinance.

Based upon the foregoing, if Tricia contends that she cannot be successfully prosecuted under the foregoing statute, it is most likely that:

(A) She is correct, since the statute is overly broad.

(B) She is correct, since the statute attempts to regulate speech activity in a traditional public forum.

(C) She is incorrect, since she failed to obtain a declaratory judgment prior to violating the statute.

(D) She is incorrect, since the statute permits a procedure for obtaining a waiver of the 20-person limit.

63. Two years ago, Hobson was appointed to a tribunal established pursuant to an act of Congress. The tribunal's duties were to review claims made by veterans and to make recommendations on their merits to the Veterans Administration. Congress later abolished the tribunal and established a different format for review of such claims. Hobson was offered a federal administrative position in the same bureau at a lesser salary. He thereupon sued the government on the ground that Congress may not (1) remove a federal judge from office during good behavior, or (2) diminish his compensation during continuance in office. Government attorneys filed a motion to dismiss the action. The court should:

(A) Deny the motion, because the independence of the federal judiciary is constitutionally guaranteed by Article III.

(B) Deny the motion, because Hobson has established a property right to federal employment on the tribunal.

(C) Grant the motion, because Hobson lacked standing to raise the question.

(D) Grant the motion, because Hobson was not a judge under Article III and therefore was not entitled to life tenure.

Questions 64-65 are based on the following fact situation:

Bosco is an importer and distributor of goods from South America. His headquarters (and only place of business) is in State Orange. In June of last year, Bosco received a large shipment of vases from a manufacturer in Peru. The items which Bosco purchases are ordinarily stored in his warehouse until a purchaser is located. In December of last year, Rudy, a citizen of State Blue, called Bosco to inquire about the vases. Bosco sent Bando, one of his employees to show Rudy a sample of the bases and to negotiate a possible agreement. A sale for 1,000 of the vases was negotiated by Bando, subject to Bosco's acceptance. Bando and Rudy then drove to Bosco's headquarters, where Bosco (after insisting upon an additional $1.00 per item) approved the deal. Rudy then presented a check to Bosco for the proper amount. One of Bosco's drivers then delivered the vases to Rudy in State Blue.

State Orange imposes an *ad valorem* tax on all personal property physically located within the jurisdiction on July 31. State Blue imposes a sales tax of 6% on all purchases made by its residents. State Orange has a 3% sales tax.

64. If Bosco contends that the State Orange *ad valorem* tax on the vases is invalid, which of the following statements is probably MOST accurate?

(A) Bosco is correct, because the vases were sold later that same year.

(B) Bosco is correct, because the vases were still "imports."

(C) Bosco is correct, if the tax was simply a means of reimbursing State Orange for its inspection of imported goods.

(D) Bosco is incorrect, because the import-export clause applies only to taxes on goods which are in transit.

65. If State Blue assessed a sales tax upon Bosco with respect to the vases purchased by Rudy, it would probably:

(A) Be constitutional, because the transaction was negotiated in State Blue and Rudy was a State Blue resident when he purchased the items.

(B) Be constitutional, because the items were sold and purchased with the knowledge that Rudy would re-sell them in State Blue.

(C) Be unconstitutional, because the sale was consummated in State Orange.

(D) Be unconstitutional, because the tax would violate the import-export clause.

Questions 66-67 are based upon the following fact situation:

A congressional subcommittee found that the wheat industry has been suffering severe price and supply fluctuations in recent years. In response, Congress enacted the following statute: "No person may cultivate in wheat more than the amount of land she cultivated in wheat in the immediately preceding year. If a farmer cultivates more than the allotted land: (1) she may not sell wheat grown on excess acreage in interstate commerce, and (2) a tax of $3.00 per bushel will be imposed on wheat grown on the excess acreage, whether grown for sale on the open market or for home consumption, seed, or livestock feed." Weedy planted 20 acres, which was 10 acres over his allotment. On these 10 acres he harvested 120 bushels. A tax of $360 was assessed against him and he was enjoined from selling his wheat to a buyer in another state.

66. Weedy challenges the tax on wheat he grew for home consumption on the ground that Congress exceeded its authority under the commerce clause. Which of the following statements is the MOST ACCURATE regarding Weedy's claim?

    (A) Weedy is correct, because the statute regulates the local production and consumption of wheat, and is therefore beyond the reach of Congressional power under the commerce clause.

    (B) Weedy is correct, because wheat planted and harvested for home consumption has only an indirect effect on interstate commerce.

    (C) Weedy is incorrect, because Congress could rationally find that wheat grown for home consumption, in the aggregate, affects the national wheat market.

    (D) Weedy is incorrect, because the statute is a proper regulation of a product after interstate commerce has ended.

67. Assuming, rightly or wrongly, that Congress has no authority under the commerce clause to enact the statute, which statement, if true, is LEAST RELEVANT to Weedy's claim that the tax is unconstitutional?

    (A) The tax provision is enforced and collected by the Department of Agriculture.

    (B) The jurisdiction in which Weedy has his farm also taxes wheat grown in excess of an allotment set by a state statute.

    (C) The $3.00 per bushel tax amounts to 60% of the average selling price of each bushel (an amount which effectively discourages all but a very few farmers, like Weedy, from overproducing).

    (D) All monies collected under the tax provision are to be spent on a grant to one wheat producing company to study how that company could maximize it's profits.

Questions 68-70 are based upon the following fact situation:

Fisheries, Inc. leased from the State of X, for a 5-year period, 200 acres of state-owned natural oyster beds. The lease granted Fisheries "complete rights" to farm the beds and sell all oysters extracted from them. Shortly thereafter, an industrial accident resulted in an unusual accumulation of waste materials in X's offshore waters. This pollution discolored over 70% of the oysters in the natural beds. The discolored oysters could be eaten without physical illness, but the pollution gave them a slightly bitter taste. Fearful that public consumption of the discolored oysters would permanently injure the market for X's oysters, the State of X adopted legislation prohibiting the sale of the discolored oysters. Also, to protect local interests dependent on the oyster market, it prohibited any fishery from selling unaffected oysters to out-of-state entities if local purchasers are willing to purchase the items on terms similar to those of the prospective out-of-state buyers.

After harvesting a large quantity of oysters, Fisheries contracted to sell a quantity of discolored oysters to Aldo, and a quantity of normal oysters to Bart. Both Aldo and Bart are out-of-state purchasers who offered a higher price than any local buyer. State X brought suit under the statute to enjoin both sales.

68. What is the MOST ACCURATE statement regarding Fisheries' claim that the statute violates the obligation of contracts clause of the U.S. Constitution?

 (A) Fisheries is correct, since all of its rights under the contract with State X have been impaired.

 (B) Fisheries is incorrect, because the statute affects only a peripheral part of the contract (i.e., the right to sell normal oysters to local buyers is unaffected).

 (C) Fisheries is incorrect, because the constitutional provision applies only to contracts between individuals, not between a state and an individual.

 (D) Fisheries is correct, because a court will probably find against the validity of the statute.

69. What is the MOST ACCURATE statement regarding Fisheries' claim that the statute constitutes a "taking" of private property without just compensation?

 (A) The statute causes a "taking" because the restriction applies to oysters that are concededly not physically harmful to the public.

 (B) The statute causes a "taking" because it results in a reduction in the value of Fisheries' lease, which is a property interest.

 (C) The statute causes a "taking" because there is no public benefit (i.e., only the oyster industry would benefit from the ban on the sale of discolored oysters).

 (D) The statute probably does **not** constitute a "taking" because the sale of discolored oysters could adversely affect future oyster sales by State X vendors.

70. What is the MOST ACCURATE statement regarding Fisheries' claim that the injunction against the sale of normal oysters to Bart violates the interstate commerce clause of the U.S. Constitution?

 (A) Fisheries is correct, because the statute discriminates against out-of-state buyers.

 (B) Fisheries is incorrect, because out-of-state buyers may make purchases from local oyster sellers when no local buyer is willing to do so.

 (C) Fisheries is incorrect because, although the statute discriminates against out-of-state buyers, it has a valid health, safety and welfare purpose.

 (D) Fisheries is incorrect, because the statute seeks to conserve oysters (a local natural resource).

Questions 71-74 are based upon the following fact situation:

The town of Red Neck is in State X. It has a municipal ordinance that reads: "No parade or public procession shall be held without first obtaining written permission from the town licensing commission." It is a misdemeanor to parade without having obtained a license.

The Southern Socialist League ("SSL") planned a march down Red Neck's main street for July 4. On June 25, the SSL applied to the town licensing commission for a parade permit, but was refused. On June 27, the SSL announced that it would hold its march, despite the denial of the permit. On July 4, when members of the SSL began to march, the police moved in and ordered them to disperse. When they refused, several members of the SSL were arrested.

71. Which is the MOST CORRECT statement regarding whether or not the U.S. Supreme Court would declare the Red Neck ordinance unconstitutional?

    (A) The statute is unconstitutionally vague.

    (B) The statute is unconstitutionally overbroad.

    (C) The statute is both unconstitutionally vague and overbroad.

    (D) The statute is neither vague nor overbroad.

72. Assume that, (1) SSL members were convicted of parading without a permit, and (2) the conviction was affirmed without opinion by the State X Supreme Court. What is the MOST ACCURATE statement regarding the disposition of the case before the U.S. Supreme Court?

    (A) SSL was correct in disobeying the statute, because although it is valid on its face, the denial of the permit by the licensing board was done arbitrarily.

    (B) SSL was correct in disobeying the statute, because it was void on its face.

    (C) SSL was incorrect in disobeying the statute, because it was valid on its face (and therefore the SSL was required to seek redress through proper judicial channels).

    (D) SSL was incorrect in disobeying the statute, because although it is void on its face, the SSL was required to contest the denial of the permit through proper judicial channels.

73. Assume instead that upon affirming the convictions of the SSL members, the State X Supreme Court interpreted the licensing statute as "not vesting unbridled discretion in the commission, but requiring it to give consideration, without unfair discrimination, to time, place, and manner in relation to other proper uses of the streets." Assume further that the U.S. Supreme Court would hold denial of the permit to be arbitrary and without authority. What is the MOST ACCURATE statement regarding the disposition of the case before the U.S. Supreme Court?

    (A) The conviction of SSL members will be affirmed, because the State X Supreme Court subsequently gave the statute a constitutional construction.

    (B) The conviction of SSL members will be reversed, because the statute (though not void on its face) was incorrectly applied.

    (C) The conviction of SSL members will be affirmed, if members of the SSL had reason to anticipate such a curative construction by the State X Supreme Court.

    (D) The conviction of SSL members will be affirmed, because the SSL could have applied for its permit months earlier (and thus had time to make a proper appeal of the denial of the permit).

74. Assume that (1) after the SSL had (on June 27) proclaimed its intention to proceed with the march despite the denial of a permit, the licensing commission sought and obtained an ex-parte injunction prohibiting this activity on July 3, and (2) served it upon SSL members later that day. Assume further that the U.S. Supreme Court would hold denial of the permit to be arbitrary and without authority. Members of the SSL proceeded with the march on July 4, and were held in contempt for violating the injunction.

Which statement is LEAST RELEVANT to the U.S. Supreme Court in deciding whether to affirm or reverse the convictions of the SSL members for contempt because they violated the injunction?

(A) The injunction was granted on July 3, the day before the scheduled march.

(B) The denial of the permit was violative of the constitutional rights of SSL members.

(C) The court which issued the injunction had subject matter jurisdiction over the matter.

(D) The SSL did not attempt to appeal the injunction before attempting the parade.

Questions 75-76 are based upon the following fact situation:

Article 7.6 of the State Z Constitution provides that: "Every person shall have the right to publicly express his views in any manner which does not unreasonably interfere with the privacy or lawful activities of others." On July 4, the Supreme Court of Z held that Article 7.6 "precludes the owner of a shopping center from enforcing a complete ban upon

sign carrying on the premises against persons who pose no threat of actual and substantial disruption of the normal activities of the shopping center."

This ruling was handed down in the case of *Ray v. Orwell*, a suit for injunctive relief brought by a student, Ray, who had been ejected from the Orwell Plaza shopping mall for peaceably walking up and down the interior of the mall carrying a sign saying, "Detente--no! National security--yes!" The security guards had told Ray that all sign-carrying was banned at the mall and that if he returned he would be criminally prosecuted. In affirming the trial court's issuance of an injunction prohibiting enforcement of the ban by Orwell against Ray, the State Z Supreme Court reasoned as follows:

"Article 7.6 imposes an obligation on every person to respect every other person's right to publicly express himself in a reasonable manner. That obligation does not cease to exist merely because a person holds legal title to the premises on which the other chooses to exercise his right to express his views, especially where, as here, the so-called 'private property' is open to the public."

75. Ray, the plaintiff in *Ray v. Orwell*, did **not** base his claim for relief on the U.S. Constitution. Which essential element of a federal claim was missing?

(A) Actual interference with the exercise of his claimed right of free speech.

(B) State action interfering with the exercise of his claimed right of free speech.

(C) An actual controversy had **not** arisen, since no criminal prosecution had occurred.

(D) Sign carrying is not a protected mode of expression.

76. The United States Supreme Court denied the Orwell's petition for certiorari by a vote of 6-3, despite Orwell's claim that his due process rights had been violated. Which of the following statements is the most accurate description of the significance of the action taken by the U.S. Supreme Court?

(A) Six members of the U.S. Supreme Court believed that the decision of the Supreme Court of Z was correct.

(B) Three members of the U.S. Supreme Court believed that the decision of the Supreme Court of Z was not correct.

(C) Six members of the U.S. Supreme Court believed that the case involved no federal question.

(D) Three members of the U.S. Supreme Court believed that the case should be reviewed.

Questions 77-78 are based upon the following fact situation:

California imposed a tax on goods sold by a Nevada company to a California resident. The Nevada company has no office, plant, or place of business within California. Orders are telephoned by the seller's traveling salespersons in California to the home office in Nevada for approval. The goods are then shipped from Nevada. Title passes on delivery of the goods to the carrier in Nevada.

77. What kind of tax can California constitutionally impose on the goods?

(A) Either a sales tax or a use tax.

(B) A sales tax only.

(C) A use tax only.

(D) Neither a sales nor a use tax.

78. Assume, rightly or wrongly, that California can impose a use tax on the goods. Can California collect the tax directly from the Nevada Company?

(A) Yes, because the tax is a sales tax.

(B) Yes, because adequate contacts exist to satisfy the due process clause.

(C) No, because adequate contacts do not exist to satisfy the due process clause.

(D) No, because a use tax may only be collected from the purchaser.

79. A newly-enacted state criminal statute provides, in its entirety, "No person shall utter to another person in a public place any annoying, disturbing or unwelcome language." Smith followed an elderly woman for three blocks down a public street, yelling offensive four-letter words in her ear. The woman repeatedly asked Smith to leave her alone, but he refused. In the subsequent prosecution, the first under this statute, Smith

(A) Can be convicted.

(B) Cannot be convicted, because speech of the sort described in this instance is protected by the First and Fourteenth Amendments.

(C) Cannot be convicted, because, though this type of speech may be punished by the state, the state may not do so under this statute.

(D) Cannot be convicted, because the average user of a public street would think Smith's speech/action was amusing and ridiculous, rather than "annoying".

80. Congress passed a law that makes it a crime for a member of the Communist Party to serve as an officer of a labor union. The purpose of the law is to protect the national economy by minimizing the danger of political strikes. Is the law an unconstitutional bill of attainder?

(A) Yes.

(B) No, because it does not list individuals, but rather defines a class.

(C) No, because the purpose of the law is preventive, rather than retributive.

(D) No, because Congress may make the determination that communists are more likely than other to instigate a political strike.

81. In response to a U.S. District Court order to produce confidential presidential communications, the President invokes the claim of executive privilege. What rule of law is most likely to be applicable?

(A) In the absence of an asserted need to protect military, diplomatic, or national security secrets, the privilege is not absolute.

(B) The presidential privilege is always subordinate to the need for evidence in a criminal trial.

(C) There is no presidential privilege.

(D) The presidential privilege is absolute in all proceedings.

82. Flyright airlines is incorporated and has its principal place of business in New York. Flyright does not own any property in Virginia, but its airplanes regularly stop in Virginia as a part of a system of interstate air commerce. Flyright's airplanes stop at Virginia airports about 20 times per day. However, the same airplane does not land every day and none of its aircraft are continuously in Virginia. Some of Flyright's airplanes are *never* in Virginia. Which state can constitutionally levy a tax on the airplanes as personal property?

(A) New York only.

(B) Virginia only.

(C) New York and Virginia.

(D) Neither.

Questions 83-85 are based on the following fact situation:

A State X law requires that persons who desire to run for municipal offices must (1) have been a resident of that city for at least 6 months, (2) pay a "ballot" fee in the amount of $100.00 to defray the cost involved in adding their name to the ballot, and (3) have taken the SAT and achieved a score which placed them in at least the fiftieth percentile of that particular examination. Recently, Congress enacted a statute which precludes states from requiring a filing fee or literacy test as prerequisites to running for public office. Malcolm wanted to run for mayor of a small town in X. When he applied to place his name on the ballot on June 30, he was informed about the SAT score requirement. Malcolm was a successful businessman, but had never gone to college. As a consequence, he had never taken the SAT examination. The test was not given again until late September, and those results would not be available until the middle of December (well after the election, which was to be held on November 4). Malcolm properly filed suit in the State X Supreme Court, seeking declaratory relief.

83. If the State X Supreme Court ruled that, based upon the Supremacy Clause, the state statute was unconstitutional:

   (A) Review by the U.S. Supreme Court is precluded by the "adequate, independent state grounds" doctrine.

   (B) Review may be sought by a petition for a write of certiorari to the U.S. Supreme Court.

   (C) Review by the U.S. Supreme Court is precluded by the abstention doctrine.

   (D) Review by the U.S. Supreme Court is precluded because there are no unresolved federal issues.

84. If the State X Supreme Court held, on November 8, that the statute was valid, the U.S. Supreme Court would probably:

   (A) Refuse to hear the case, because it is now moot.

   (B) Refuse to hear the case, because Malcolm can take the SAT test and run for mayor at the next election.

   (C) Hear the case, despite the mootness doctrine.

   (D) Hear the case, because First Amendment rights are involved.

85. With respect to the merits of this case, the State X Supreme Court

would probably rule that the State X statute is:

   (A) Valid, as a proper exercise of the Tenth Amendment.

   (B) Valid, because the federal statute was passed subsequent to the State X law.

   (C) Invalid, since the provisions of the State X law are in conflict with a valid federal statute.

   (D) Invalid, as to the ballot fee and SAT score provisions.

Questions 86-87 are based on the following fact situation:

State X has enacted a law which reads: "Any student who engages in demonstrations or activities on a high school or college campus which are detrimental to the U.S. government will forthwith cease to be eligible for state financial aid." Arthur, a student at State X University, was involved in a demonstration to keep the C.I.A. off the campus. The protest was held on the State X University football field and was conducted in a peaceful manner. As a result of his participation, Arthur's state scholarship was withdrawn.

86. If the State X statute was deemed to be facially invalid because it was too vague, Arthur:

   (A) Would be entitled to reinstatement of his scholarship.

   (B) Would not be entitled to reinstatement of his scholarship, because financial aid is not a constitutionally guaranteed right.

   (C) Would not be entitled to reinstatement of his scholarship, since the statute does not pertain to criminal behavior.

(D) Would not be entitled to reinstatement of his scholarship,
since the State X law is rationally related to a legitimate
governmental purpose.

87. Arthur's claim that his First
Amendment rights have been violated by the State X University's
action will probably be:

(A) Successful, because demonstrations in a traditional public
forum cannot serve as the basis
for adverse governmental
action.

(B) Successful, because Arthur was
penalized for engaging in symbolic activity.

(C) Unsuccessful, because State X
University, rather than State
X, withdrew the grant.

(D) Unsuccessful, because the
State X scholarship was merely
a privilege (and so could be
withdrawn at will).

Questions 88-89 are based on the following fact situation:

State X has a statute which awards college scholarships to its residents who
have attained a minimum SAT score and
attend a state university. If a State X
resident desires to major in Geology, the
scholarship is extended to out-of-state
universities. Joe, a State X resident,
applied for a scholarship to attend a
State Y college, even though he was not
majoring in Geology. However, his application was rejected. Mike, another State
X resident, was denied a scholarship
because his SAT test score was one point
below the minimum score requirement.

88. Which of the following statements is
probably MOST correct?

(A) State X's refusal to grant Joe a
scholarship is an unconstitutional infringement of his right
to travel.

(B) State X's refusal to grant Joe a
scholarship constitutes a denial
of equal protection, because the
"in-state, out-of-state" classification is irrational.

(C) State X's refusal to grant Joe's
scholarship will be sustained.

(D) State X's refusal to grant Joe a
scholarship is violative of the
privileges and immunities
clause contained in Article IV.

89. Which of the following statements is
probably MOST correct?

(A) State X's refusal to grant Mike
a scholarship violates the privileges and immunities clause of
the Fourteenth Amendment.

(B) State X's refusal to grant Mike
a scholarship constitutes a deprivation of substantive due process, because students who
achieve low SAT scores may
otherwise be financially
unable to attend college.

(C) State X's refusal to grant Mike
a scholarship violates equal
protection, because SAT test
scores are not rationally
related to the governmental
purpose of helping State X residents to attend college.

(D) State X's refusal to grant Mike
a scholarship is valid.

90. John sought dissolution of his marriage to Mary in a State X Court.
However, because of his indigency,
he could not pay the required court

fee of $75.00. The state court refused to grant him a divorce. If John commenced an action claiming that his constitutional rights were violated, what is the MOST LIKELY result?

(A) The state court's action is constitutional, because it satisfies the traditional equal protection test.

(B) The state court's action is constitutional, because it satisfies the strict scrutiny test.

(C) The state court's action is constitutional, because the discrimination is *de facto*, instead of *de jure*.

(D) The state court's action is unconstitutional, because it does not satisfy the strict scrutiny test.

91. State X passes a law barring the sale of motor vehicles to males under 21 and to females under 18. Which of the following propositions of law is the most likely to be applied in determining if the law violates the equal protection clause of the Fourteenth Amendment?

(A) The law is presumptively valid, because gender is not a suspect class.

(B) Absent a compelling state interest, classifications based on gender are invalid.

(C) Unless substantially related to an important government objective, classifications based on gender are invalid.

(D) Statutes favoring women are valid, as long as there is a rational basis for the classification.

92. Congress passes a law limiting federal welfare benefits to those persons who are U.S. Citizens. Upon appeal to the U.S. Supreme Court, which of the following is the probable result?

(A) The law violates the equal protection clause of the U.S. Constitution, because aliens are a suspect class and there is no compelling governmental interest.

(B) The law violates the due process clause of the U.S. Constitution, because welfare benefits are a fundamental right.

(C) The statute is constitutional, because aliens are not entitled to due process.

(D) The statute is constitutional, because preferring U.S. citizens over aliens in the distribution of limited resources such as welfare benefits is not arbitrary or irrational.

93. *The Daily Times* published an editorial in which they accused Joe Smith, who was running for a seat in the State Senate, with violation of a state law which required seekers of public office to report all campaign contributions. In a lawsuit by *Smith v. The Daily Times* for libel, the MOST ACCURATE statement of the newspaper's defense is:

(A) *The Daily Times* has an absolute privilege, because the First Amendment protects freedom of the press.

(B) Senator Smith must prove falsity and actual malice.

(C) Senator Smith must prove falsity.

(D) Senator Smith must prove falsity and show that *The Daily Times* failed to act reasonably.

94. State X enacted a law (the "Act") which gave "bonus points" in the determination of who should receive jobs offered by State X to persons who had served in the armed forces. The legislative history of the Act indicates that its purpose is to reward patriotism and compensate persons who had voluntarily taken themselves out of the job market to serve their country. The legislative history also suggests that persons who had served in the armed forces had acquired a discipline and an ability to precisely follow instructions, superior to comparable persons in civilian life. However, a women's group has recently produced a methodologically valid study which shows that only 15% of veterans are women. This group has now brought suit, claiming that the Act is unconstitutional. Assuming the standing requisite is satisfied, the Act is constitutional so long as:

(A) It is rationally related to a legitimate governmental interest.

(B) It is substantially related to an important governmental objective.

(C) It satisfies a compelling state interest and there is no less burdensome means of accomplishing that objective.

(D) The plaintiff can show that the legislators actually desired to give a hiring preference to males.

Questions 95-96 are based on the following fact situation:

On January 1, the governor of the State of Anxiety signed into law Penal Code Section 96, popularly referred to as "The Obscene Movie Act." The statute contains the following provisions:

(A) As used in subsections B and C, the term obscene movie means a motion picture which, judged as a whole by an average person, depicts sexual acts in a manner which is patently offensive, appeals to the prurient interest in sex, and utterly lacks redeeming social value.

(B) It shall be unlawful to sell or exhibit an obscene movie to another person in exchange for payment or other consideration.

(C) It shall be unlawful to possess an obscene movie for the purpose of selling or exhibiting such obscene movie to another person in exchange for payment or other consideration.

95. In June, Doug was convicted of violating Section 96 based on evidence that he showed obscene movies at his Eros Movie Theatre and charged a $5 per person admission fee. The appellate court affirmed the conviction, notwithstanding the fact that the trial court refused to permit Doug to introduce evidence concerning various efforts made by him to prevent admission by minors and persons who might not have understood that the movies being shown were sexually explicit. Which of the following decisions supports affirmance of the trial court's exclusion of Doug's evidence?

(A) *California v. La Rue*, (409 U.S. 109 (1972))

(B) *Stanley v. Georgia*, (394 U.S. 557 (1969))

(C) *Paris Adult Theatre I v. Slaton*, (413 U.S. 555 (1973))

(D) *Ernoznik v. City of Jacksonville*, (422 U.S. 105 (1975))

96. In July, Dolly was indicted for violating Section 96C, after police officers, acting pursuant to a valid search warrant, discovered a large cache of obscene movies in her home which she candidly admitted constituted the inventory of a mail order film business that she operated. Prior to trial, Dolly moved to quash the indictment on the ground that *Stanley v. Georgia* (394 U.S. 557 (1969)) precludes prosecution for possession of obscene material in the home." The trial court denied the motion and Dolly appealed. How should the appellate court rule?

(A) Reverse, because of the holding in *United States v. Reidel*, (402 U.S. 351, (1971).

(B) Reverse, because *Stanley* recognized a constitutional right to possess obscene material in the home for any purpose.

(C) Affirm, because *Stanley* recognized a constitutional right to possess obscene material in the home for personal use, but did not recognize a constitutional right to possess obscene material in the home for commercial use.

(D) Affirm, because *Stanley* recognized a constitutional right to possess obscene material in the home for commercial use.

97. In the absence of explicit consent by the applicable jurisdiction, which of the following statements is correct with respect to the Eleventh Amendment?

(A) It prevents a citizen of one state from obtaining a monetary judgment against individuals of another jurisdiction who were acting under color of that state's law.

(B) It prevents a citizen of one state from obtaining a monetary judgment against a county or city of another state.

(C) It prevents a citizen of one state from obtaining a monetary judgment against the state in which she resides.

(D) It prevents a citizen of a state from obtaining injunctive relief against officials of that state, even though the latter have acted in contravention of a federal law or the U.S. Constitution.

Questions 98-99 are based on the following fact situation:

Through a study based on information from the major industries in the jurisdiction, the legislature of State Yellow determined that (1) the incidence of absence during night shifts was higher among women than men, and (2) much productivity was lost as a consequence of female absenteeism. The study showed that the reason for the higher rate of absence among women was their need to be home with their children during periods of illness. Therefore, a bill was passed (the "Act") forbidding employers to hire women for nightshift work, and assessing fines for violation thereof.

Jane Doe was denied employment with the ABC Company because of the Act. She filed suit against the appropriate state administrative officer, alleging that the Act was unconstitutional.

98. State Yellow brought a motion to dismiss the complaint on the grounds that Jane had no standing to sue. The court should rule:

    (A) Jane has no standing, because ABC is not being prosecuted by the State Yellow under the Act.

    (B) Jane has no standing, because she was not terminated from existing employment.

    (C) Jane has standing, because she has suffered pecuniary loss as the result of the Act.

    (D) Jane has standing, only if she can show that similar employment in the area could not be found.

99. Jane claims that the Act violates her right to equal protection under the law. On this claim, the court should rule:

    (A) The Act is constitutional if the state can demonstrate a rational basis for it.

    (B) The Act is unconstitutional, unless the state can demonstrate that the legislation is substantially related to an important governmental objective.

    (C) The Act is unconstitutional, because women are a suspect classification.

    (D) The Act is constitutional, because there is no fundamental right to employment in a desired occupation.

100. John, a State Senator in the State of X, is running for a new term of office. His opponent, James, owns the only local newspaper and radio station in John's home town of Crossroads. The only local newspaper in Crossroads, the *Gazette*, published statements which were extremely derogatory of John's performance. Upon John's request for an opportunity to rebut the assertions contained in the Gazette, James refused. John has now commenced an action in the appropriate federal court, asserting that James' refusal to publish his rebuttal violated John's First Amendment rights. Which of the following statements is probably MOST accurate?

    (A) Where a political issue is involved, mass media entities must offer equal access to opposing points of view.

    (B) Newspapers are not required to give equal access to opposing points of view.

    (C) Newspapers must give equal access to opposing points of view where a personal attack or political editorial has been printed.

    (D) There is no rule requiring equal access with respect to mass media entities.

101. Arthur Klubinski was a Bosnian Croat who visited America to raise money for the people in his country. He obtained a permit to speak at a public park. His speech was attended by about 200 Bosnian Croat immigrants to the U.S. and about 10 Muslim Americans. Klubinski made various derogatory comments, such as "All Muslims are liars" and "Muslims control the U.S. press." Suddenly, four of the Muslims in the crowd began to shake their fists angrily and advance towards Klubinski. There were 15 police officers at this event who had ringed Klubinski and the speaking podium. Sensing a confrontation, the police asked Klubinski to dis-

continue his speech. When he refused, they arrested him pursuant to the local "breach of the peace" ordinance. (You may assume that this law was adequately drafted.) However, Klubinski now contends that his First Amendment rights had been violated, and so no prosecution can occur.

Based upon the foregoing, it is most likely that Klubinski:

(A) Can be successfully convicted, under the "fighting words" doctrine.

(B) Can be successfully convicted, since his words were calculated to engender a violent response.

(C) Cannot be convicted, since Klubinski was merely expressing an opinion (rather than making a statement which was factual in nature).

(D) Cannot be convicted, since there were an adequate number of police present to restrain the persons moving towards the podium.

102. Amityville is normally a quiet, midwestern town. However, about 50 protesters recently picketed the main abortion clinic. Although they have refrained from blocking access to, or egress from, the clinic, members of the group waved "Murderer" and "Baby Killer" signs. A local ordinance forbids "the making of any public statement which is calculated to be offensive to the person addressed." In addition to the "Baby Killer" signs, the protesters also screamed "Killer" and "Murderer" at persons entering or leaving the clinic. Finally, several of the protesters were arrested and prosecuted under the above-mentioned ordi-

nance.

Based upon the foregoing, it is most likely that the arrested protesters:

(A) Cannot be successfully prosecuted, since the term "offensive" is too vague.

(B) Cannot be successfully prosecuted, if they sincerely believed that the statements which they made were factually true.

(C) Can be successfully prosecuted, since their conduct would be offensive to a reasonable person.

(D) Can be successfully prosecuted, if the demonstrators intended their speech to offend the listener.

103. Bob Bilton, a citizen of the State of Euphoria, was fired from his job as a teacher at a public school. He subsequently asserted that his termination violated both Euphoria's constitution and the Due Process Clause. He commenced an action in a Euphoria state court, and requested a non-jury trial. The court ruled that each of Bob's assertions was correct, and that he should be reinstated immediately. The State of Euphoria then appealed the case to the Supreme Court of Euphoria, but Bob's assertions in the lower court were affirmed in all respects.

The State of Euphoria now seeks review of the decision by the U.S. Supreme Court. If it attempts to do so, its writ of certiorari will probably be:

(A) Rejected.

(B) Rejected, because there is no U.S. Supreme Court review of state court decisions.

(C) Heard, if the Supreme Court, in its discretion, decides to hear the case.

(D) Heard, because there was a federal claim.

104. As a consequence of the "litigation explosion," federal district courts have become terribly clogged. In an effort to break this logjam, Congress enacts a law which eliminates diversity of citizensip jurisdiction completely.

Based upon the foregoing, it is most likely that this statute is:

(A) Unconstitutional, since it violates the Equal Protection Clause.

(B) Unconstitutional, since the U.S. Constitution specifically provides for cases between citizens of different states.

(C) Constitutional by virtue of the powers given to Congress in Article III, Section 1.

(D) Constitutional because cases between citizens of different states can be litigated in state courts.

105. Recently, there has been a great deal of litigation concerning breast implants. Many manufacturers have been obliged to seek protection under the bankruptcy laws because of these unforeseen lawsuits. Additionally, there are numerous studies which suggest that, even when successful, the breast implant process may have numerous harmful side effects. In response to this situation, Congress enacted a $3,000 tax on any breast implant procedure, to be paid by the operating surgeon prior to the implantation. The legislative history shows that the principal

purpose of Congress in enacting this law was to discourage such implants, and that a relatively small amount of revenue would be generated from it. In its first year, the legislation produced only about $1 million in collections.

Amy, a woman who seeks a breast implant, commenced an action to have the statute declared unconstitutional.

Based upon the foregoing, it is most likely that the statute is:

(A) Unconstitutional, since it infringes on Amy's right of privacy.

(B) Unconstitutional, since the statute's purpose was regulatory, rather than revenue-raising, in nature.

(C) Constitutional, under Congress' power to "levy and collect taxes...;" Article I, Section 8.

(D) Constitutional, under Congress' power to legislate for the general welfare.

Questions 106-107 are based upon the following fact situation:

Recently, several studies have indicated highway accidents often resulted when drivers spilled liquids which they were drinking onto their lap. As a consequence, Congress enacted a statute requiring all cars to have cup or container holders. The federal statute also gave the minimum dimensions of each cup/container holder. Additionally, the act stated that states which prohibited the drinking of any type of liquid while driving would receive a specific amount of federal funds (based upon the population of that jurisdiction) as a "safe driving" jurisdiction. In response to the federal statute, the State of Drunkaria passed a law which prohibited the drinking of any substance while driving. Ralph, who liked to drink his morning coffee while driving to his place of employment, has asserted that the federal statute is unconstitutional.

106. Based upon the foregoing, the **strongest** basis for upholding the constitutionality of the federal law is that:

(A) The "no drinking" objective promotes highway safety and benefits the public welfare.

(B) Surveys throughout the country indicated that a vast majority of the people favored the "no drinking while driving" law.

(C) When the states accepted federal monies to finance their highways, they ceded authority over these roads to the national government.

(D) Assuming the federal government paid for a portion of the construction costs, it can regulate the use of state highways.

107. Based upon the foregoing, the portion of the federal statute which predicates the disbursement of "bonus" highway funds on a prohibition against driving while drinking is most likely:

(A) Constitutional, only on the basis of the Commerce Clause.

(B) Constitutional, only on the basis of the spending power.

(C) Constitutional, on the basis of both the Commerce Clause and spending power.

(D) Unconstitutional, since it is an infringement on states' rights under the Tenth Amendment.

108. Citizens of the State of Euphoria have recently been complaining that most lawyers practicing in the state are extremely unethical. Several legislators have contended that the Euphoria attorneys who attended out-of-state law schools were exposed to professors who advocated overly liberal ideas and viewpoints, which was the primary cause for the moral deterioration of this group. As a consequence, the Euphoria legislature passed a law restricting admission to the Bar in that jurisdiction to persons who had been educated at an in-state college and law school. Amy, a Euphoria citizen who attended college in that state, but law school in New York City (at Columbia), believes that this statute is unconstitutional.

Based upon the foregoing, it is most likely that the Euphoria statute is:

(A) Unconstitutional, as an undue burden on interstate commerce.

(B) Unconstitutional, as a violation of the Privileges and Immunities Clause of the Fourteenth Amendment.

(C) Constitutional, since a state could reasonably believe that the quality of out-of-state law schools is inferior.

(D) Constitutional, because practicing law is a privilege (not a right) which states may bestow in any manner which they deem reasonable.

109. The State of Goldcoast passed a law requiring all single family dwellings whose composition was more than

60% stucco to be reinforced with metal slats within two years. This process would ordinarily cost approximately $1,200 per dwelling. The law was passed after a report pertaining to potential damage in the event of an earthquake indicated that loss of life and property would be reduced as a result of these metal reinforcements. However, statistics indicate that 64% of all single family dwellings in Goldcoast which have a composition of more than 60% stucco are owned by Hispanic individuals.

Based upon the foregoing, is the Goldcoast law unconstitutional?

(A) No, because there is a rational basis for the statute.

(B) Yes, because the strict scrutiny standard is not satisfied in this instance.

(C) Yes, because the law has a disproportionately negative racial impact.

(D) Yes, because the $1,200 outlay necessary to reinforce the homes violates the due process of Hispanic homeowners.

110. The City of Amityville has recently received numerous complaints about its police department. Many of its citizens contended that the police fail to adequately enforce the laws, often advising lawbreakers to "get out of town," rather than arresting them. A newspaper story concluded that approximately 60% of the Amityville police officers lived outside of the city. In fact, many of the Amityville police officers lived across a nearby river, in the State of Peddle. As a consequence, the Amityville City Council passed a law which required all new police officers to live within the city limits. The

present members of the police force were given a three-year "grace" period to move into Amityville.

Based upon the foregoing, the **strongest** argument that the Amityville law is unconstitutional would be under the:

(A) Privileges and Immunities Clause of the Fourteenth Amendment.

(B) Due Process Clause of the Fourteenth Amendment.

(C) Privileges and Immunities Clause of Article IV, Section 2.

(D) Obligation of Contracts Clause.

111. The U.S. Senate was conducting hearings into organized crime. As part of its investigation, Al "Biggy" Boone was subpoenaed to testify before the appropriate committee. However, although he was duly served, Boone failed to appear. A U.S. statute authorizes the U.S. Attorney General to prosecute contempts of Congress. The Senate directed the U.S. Attorney General to begin criminal contempt proceedings against Boone. However, the U.S. Attorney General refused to commence any type of legal proceedings against him.

Based upon the foregoing, the U.S. Attorney General's non-action is most likely:

(A) Improper, because the U.S. Attorney General must prosecute if directed to do so by the Senate.

(B) Improper, because the U.S. Attorney General's primary function is to prosecute those who violate federal law.

(C) Proper, since the U.S. Attorney General decides, independently, which cases to prosecute or not.

(D) Proper, because the decision to prosecute or not is exclusively an executive one.

112. Robert Anthracite was the U.S. Ambassador to Slumberland. Unfortunately for Mr. Anthracite, he was photographed by a reporter of a local newspaper holding a famous model snugly in an intimate embrace. The picture was reprinted in numerous U.S. newspapers, causing an uproar and demands for his dismissal. Mr. Antracite was subpoenaed by a House Committee to appear before, and testify about, this incident. However, he refused to answer any questions posed to him which directly pertained to this incident. He did ***not***, however, "take the Fifth" (Amendment).

Based upon the foregoing, the ***strongest*** argument which Mr. Anthracite could assert as a defense is that:

(A) The questions were unrelated to matters upon which Congress may legislate.

(B) House Committees may ask only about matters pertaining to the expenditure of funds.

(C) Since it was the body which confirmed his appointment, only the Senate may question Mr. Anthracite about matters that relate to his duties.

(D) Neither members of the U.S. House of Representatives or U.S. Senate may question the performance of duties by an executive officer.

113. The State of Euphoria has a "911" emergency phone line. Mary Smythe is an English citizen who moved to America three years ago. Mary has permanent resident status, but is not yet a U.S. citizen. Euphoria has a Public Utilities Commission ("PUC") rule that only American citizens can be "911" emergency operators. This rule was promulgated to make certain that persons answering the phone would understand and respond to the caller. Mary applied for a position as a "911" operator. Although otherwise completely qualified, her application was rejected because she is not an American citizen. There is no question that Mary flawlessly speaks the "Queen's English."

Based upon the foregoing, if Mary asserts that the Euphoria regulation is unconstitutional as applied to her, it is most likely that she:

(A) Will prevail, since the regulation has a rational basis.

(B) Will prevail, since she is completely qualified to assume the position in question.

(C) Will not prevail, since the regulation is rationally related to a legitimate governmental purpose.

(D) Will not prevail, since the regulation satisfies an important governmental interest and is narrowly tailored to achieve that objective.

114. Shocked by recent studies which disclosed jail overcrowding and the fact that criminals serve only about 25% of their prescribed time, Congress enacted legislation which would establish a nine-member Jail Reform Commission ("JRC"). The purpose of the JRC was to (1) inves-

tigate the reasons for jail overcrowding and early dismissal of
convicts, (2) promulgate rules pertaining to the operation and functioning of jails to make them more
efficient, and (3) establish a quasi-
judicial system to prosecute any
person or entity that failed to follow
the rules which the JRC would
issue. To assure a partisan response
to the JRC, the chairperson was to
be appointed by the Vice-President,
four members were to be selected by
the President Pro Tempore of the
Senate, and four members by the
Speaker of the House. (You may
assume that standing exists.)

Based upon the foregoing, the
strongest argument that could be
made to invalidate the legislation
described above is that:

(A) Legislative functions may not
be delegated by Congress to an
agency without clear, precise
guidelines.

(B) Congress had no constitutional
basis to enact legislation dealing with these issues.

(C) The legislation provides no
opportunity for persons
affected by the rules to contest
them.

(D) The Commission is unlawful
because its members were not
appointed by the President.

115. Recently, there has been a spate of
complaints to local and federal legislators by persons who found that
mortgages had been unknowingly
placed upon their homes as part of a
program to encourage borrowing
for substantial improvements to
their dwellings. These complainants
have contended that, in many
instances, the improvements were
inadequately made. Besides, it took

the homeowners several years to
remove the mortgages, which
impaired their ability to obtain
credit. The actions commenced in
state court to remove the mortgages
often took two or more years to conclude. As a consequence, Congress
enacted a federal law which
required full disclosure by the home
improving entity and allowed for an
action to be brought by a complainant in the U.S. District Court whose
jurisdiction included the site of the
subject home.

Several lending entities objected to
the federal law. They brought an
action contending that the statute
was unconstitutional.

Based upon the foregoing, the
strongest basis for sustaining the
validity of this statute is most likely
the:

(A) Obligation of Contracts Clause.

(B) Commerce Clause.

(C) Equal Protection Clause of the
Fourteenth Amendment.

(D) Privileges and Immunities
Clause of the Fourteenth
Amendment.

116. The U.S. government was extremely
concerned about germ warfare. The
CIA had developed information that
certain foreign subversive groups
might use germ warfare to extort
large amounts of money or punish
nations which they felt were hostile
to their cause. As a consequence,
the CIA entered into a written contract with Tooledoo University in
the State of Euphoria. Under this
agreement, the university was to
document the effects of a large-scale
biological research project. The program was scheduled to last about
three years and involve about 5,000

animals (i.e., dogs, cats, monkeys, etc.). Tooledoo University was to be paid approximately $250,000 for performing this research and presenting the CIA with its written results.

The Save Our Animals Society ("SOAS") asserts that this statute is unconstitutional, and should be invalidated. The SOAS, after an expensive lobbying effort, persuaded the Euphoria legislature to pass an act which prohibited the use of domestic animals and monkeys for biological research purposes.

Based upon the foregoing, which of the following represents the *least likely* basis for invalidating the Euphoria law?

(A) The Due Process Clause of the Fourteenth Amendment.

(B) The Commerce Clause.

(C) The Supremacy Clause.

(D) The Impairment of Contracts Clause.

117. The State of Bootah has a statute which makes it unlawful to make a speech, picket or demonstrate within 200 feet of any governmental building, or within 200 feet of any building in which a Bootah governmental entity has an office. Joseph Brighton, a state legislator who voted against this law five years ago, but who is no longer in office, would like to make a speech in front of the State Welfare Department's main office. The purpose of the speech is to contend that this entity is far too lenient with respect to welfare "cheats." Brighton is planning to run again to become a Bootah legislator in that jurisdiction's Senate.

Based upon the foregoing, which of the following situations represents the *most likely* basis upon which Brighton could obtain a hearing in a federal court challenging the validity of the Bootah statute?

(A) He is intending to run for office at the next election.

(B) He voted against the statute when it was enacted by the Bootah state legislature.

(C) He is a member of an organization which seeks to invalidate welfare funding measures which waste taxpayer monies.

(D) Brighton had been a Bootah state taxpayer for the preceding three years.

118. The U.S. Congress recently enacted a law which expressed support for colleges of all types. Shortly thereafter, the Department of the Interior gifted land which it owned to Armstrong College, a private religious institution. The gift did not, however, specify that no religious instruction take place within classrooms built upon the donated land. Malcolm and Malena Cooper commenced an action in the appropriate U.S. District Court, contending that the gift constituted a violation of the First Amendment requirement of church/state separation. The Coopers are U.S. taxpayers and avowed atheists.

On these facts, it is most likely that:

(A) The gift is unconstitutional, since the college made no commitment that only secular courses would be taught upon the donated land.

(B) The gift is unconstitutional, since only Congress may convey a gift of U.S. property.

(C) The gift is constitutional, since this appears to be merely a one-time conveyance of U.S. property.

(D) The Coopers lack standing to challenge the gift.

119. Recently, the State of Euphoria ended its local welfare system. As a consequence, numerous state legislators received death threats. The Euphoria legislature responded by enacting a statute which made it illegal to "threaten, or to incite another, to commit bodily harm upon any Euphoria public official while in the course of, or as a result of, the performance of his/her duties." Jim Blender wrote to the Euphoria legislator for his district.

His letter stated, "You've hurt me more than you can imagine. You deserve to die for what you've done. You're a callous beast who should rot in Hell. Die, die, you SOB."

Based upon the foregoing, if the Euphoria State Attorney General commences an action against Mr. Blender under the statute described above, it is most likely that:

(A) The statute is unconstitutionally vague.

(B) The statute is unconstitutionally overbroad.

(C) The statute is constitutional, but cannot serve as the basis for punishment in this situation.

(D) The statute is constitutional, and Mr. Blender can be punished pursuant to it.

ANSWERS TO
MULTIPLE CHOICE QUESTIONS

1. **B** A party lacks standing unless he has suffered a direct injury as a consequence of the defendant's conduct. When the plaintiff suffers a diminution of enjoyment in the performance of an activity, that diminution of enjoyment constitutes an adequate "injury" for standing purposes; the harm need not be economic in nature; *Sierra Club v. Morton*, 405 U.S. 727 (1972). Since Kevin has used, and will continue to use, the facility covered by the legislation, he has arguably been injured by the Secretary of the Interior's failure to perform his statutory duties. (*See* ELO Ch.16-III(C)(2)(a).) Choice **A** is incorrect, since there is no *per se* right of U.S. citizens to sue a federal official for failure to perform her duties. There must be a direct injury to the plaintiff. Choice **C** is incorrect, since (while the statement of law is accurate) Kevin has in fact suffered a direct and immediate injury. Finally, Choice **D** is incorrect because the failure to incur economic loss does ***not*** preclude an otherwise "injured" party from maintaining an action.

2. **D** To avoid violating the Establishment Clause, governmental assistance to religious schools (1) must have a secular purpose, (2) must neither advance nor inhibit religion, and (3) must not entangle government with religion. Governmental services may ordinarily be rendered at religious schools where the activity is ***impersonal*** in nature, and the cost of complying with state ordered mandates is ordinarily reimbursable; *Wolman v. Walter,* 433 U.S. 229 (1977). Since (1) the brief testing at the religious school is relatively impersonal in nature (presumably, similar tests are given to all students with possible psychological problems), and (2) the travel expenditures only offset state-ordered counseling held at public schools, the legislation is probably constitutional. (*See* ELO Ch.15-II(L)(8)(c).) Choice **C** is incorrect, since services rendered by public employees at religious institutions are not *per se* valid. The rendition of services which entail more than a brief, impersonal visit, must be provided away from the religious institution; *Meek v. Pettinger*, 421 U.S. 349 (1975). Choice **A** is incorrect, since the fact that governmental services are provided at the religious institution does not make the activity *per se* unconstitutional. The rendering of such services must, however, ordinarily be impersonal and relatively brief. Finally, Choice **B** is incorrect, since reimbursement to religious schools or their students for the cost of complying with state mandated activities is ordinarily valid; *Committee for Public Education v. Regan*, 444 U.S. 646 (1980).

3. **C** Generally applicable criminal statutes whose purpose is not to burden a particular religious belief are constitutional, regardless of the extent to which a religious tenet is burdened by the legislation; *Employment Division v. Smith*, 494 U.S. 872 (1990). In addition, no balancing of the state's interest in its prohibition against the burden on the individual's beliefs need be carried out, as long as the ban is generally applicable, and not motivated by a government desire to affect religion. Since the criminal leg-

islation (1) is generally applicable, and (2) was not intended to hinder the Sikkum religion, it is constitutional. (*See* ELO Ch.15-III(D)(7).) Choice **D** is incorrect, since no judicial "weighing" is required in this situation. Finally, Choices **A** and **B** are incorrect, since it is irrelevant whether the religious tenet involved is a major or minor one. In either event, the law appears to be constitutional in this situation.

4. **C** A "taking" of property occurs where (1) the owner of land is basically deprived of any economically viable use of his/her property, and (2) a legitimate state interest is *not* substantially advanced by the legislation. There must also be a relatively tight fit between the state interest being promoted and the regulation chosen; *Agins v. Tiburon*, 447 U.S. 255 (1980). Bobco is *not* being deprived of *any* viable use of its land, and the present activity is allowed to continue for five more years. In addition, the state interest in providing its residents with pleasant living conditions is directly advanced by the legislation. Thus, no "taking" will be deemed to have occurred. (*See* ELO Ch.11-II(B)(1).) Choice **A** is incorrect, since an owner has no *per se* right to operate land in any manner he/she would like to do so. Finally, Choice **B** is incorrect, since the fact that Bobco's facility preceded the surrounding residential nature of the area does *not* preclude the enactment of legislation limiting Bobco's use of the land. (Note, the Due Process Clause of the Fifth Amendment is applicable to the states via the Fourteenth Amendment.) Choice **D** is incorrect because the taking must substantially advance a legitimate government interest.

5. **A** Under the doctrine of inherent sovereign powers, Congress is empowered to enact legislation pertaining to external affairs. Under the doctrine of inherent sovereign powers, the sovereign (i.e., the federal government) has the inherent power to legislate in those areas traditionally occupied by a central government (whether or not specifically recognized in the U.S. Constitution); *United States v. Curtiss-Wright Export Corp.*, 299 U.S. 304 (1936). Thus, Congress would have the right to make it a crime for any citizen to negotiate with a foreign government. (*See* ELO Ch.8-II(B).) Choice **B** is incorrect because, whatever inherent power the President might have to negotiate for the U.S. with foreign countries, it could *not* serve as a basis for the enactment of federal legislation by Congress. Choice **C** is incorrect because there is no proposition of law that legislation pertaining to foreign relations is exempted from the First Amendment. Finally, Choice **D** is legally incorrect because criminal laws pertaining to international affairs must be as specific as those dealing with domestic matters.

6. **A** Under the U.S. Constitution, states are prohibited from enacting *ex post facto* laws; Article I, Section 10. An *ex post facto* law is one which retroactively (1) makes particular conduct illegal; (2) increases the severity in the definition of criminal conduct; (3) increases the punishment for a crime, or (4) alters the rules of evidence for a particular act; *Collins v. Youngblood*, 497 U.S. 37 (1990). The applicable statute was *not* in effect when the crime was committed. Thus, Dellum's actions were defined more severely retroactively (and the prohibition against *ex post facto* laws violated). (*See* ELO Ch.11-IV(C).) Choice **B** is incorrect, since Dellum's knowledge (or lack of knowledge) of the possible sentence for Aggravated Robbery has no effect

upon his right to assert the *ex post facto* defense. Choice **C** is incorrect, since the moment at which Dellum was actually charged is irrelevant. The severity of punishment for an a criminal act cannot be enhanced retroactively to the date of the act. Finally, Choice **D** is factually incorrect (similar conduct constituted **both** Aggravated Robbery and Armed Robbery). As discussed above, the *ex post facto* prohibition is operative.

7. **C** Commercial speech may be restricted, even though it involves a lawful activity and is not misleading, if (1) the restriction directly promotes a substantial governmental interest, and (2) is no more extensive than necessary to effectuate the governmental interest. The statute is probably constitutional, since there is a substantial governmental interest (i.e., protecting the health of its citizens) which is directly promoted by the legislation in question (i.e., the law would certainly impede sales of a harmful item). (*See* ELO Ch.14-VIII(E)(3).) Choice **D** is incorrect because it does not state the grounds for upholding the statute and because advertising is **not** "misleading" merely because it fails to disclose negative information about the product. Choice **A** is incorrect, since there is no colorable Equal Protection difficulty with the statute. It applies to everyone and is rationally related to a legitimate governmental interest. Finally, Choice **B** is incorrect, since (as discussed above) the legislation does not appear to be violative of the First Amendment; *Posadas de Puerto Rico Associates v. Tourism Co.*, 478 U.S. 328 (1986).

8. **D** An organization has standing if it can show that: (1) the legislation in question causes an injury in fact to its members, who would thereby have a right to sue in their own behalf, (2) the injury is related to the organization's purpose, and (3) the nature of the lawsuit does **not** require the participation of the individual members; *Hunt v. Washington Apple Advertising Comm.*, 432 U.S. 333 (1977). Since presumably most doctors have receptionists at their offices, there has been a measurable injury to the individual members of the APA. (*See* ELO Ch.16-III(C)(3)(d).) Choice **C** is incorrect, since it merely asserts a substantive basis for negating the law without addressing the issue of standing. (This assertion is dubious anyway, since the statute is probably rationally related to a legitimate governmental purpose—enhancing federal revenues from a group capable of absorbing the loss of this deduction.) Choice **A** is incorrect, since the statute's application to all professionals does not destroy standing by the physicians' organization, one of the professional groups affected. Finally, Choice **B** is incorrect because the APA does not lack standing: its individual members are adversely affected by the law.

9. **C** In *Norwood v. Harrison*, 413 U.S. 455 (1973), the U.S. Supreme Court held that a program in which textbooks were purchased by the state and loaned to students in private schools which practiced racial discrimination was unconstitutional. The decision stated that a state could not constitutionally give "…. significant aid to institutions that practice racial or other invidious discrimination." Since in this case the computers are being given to a school which denies admission to Hispanics, the computer program is unconstitutional. Choice **D** is incorrect because, although the Distribution of computers may promote a significant educational function, the distribu-

tion may not be used to favor one group over another. Choice **B** is incorrect because it is overly broad. The Constitution does not forbid private discrimination of any kind. Finally, Choice **A** is incorrect because states may assist private schools, provided the help is secular and does not involve significant government entanglement with religion.

10. **B**   The Establishment Clause of the First Amendment is **not** violated where a governmental activity (1) has a secular purpose, (2) has a secular effect, and (3) does not promote excessive government entanglement with religion. Euphoria's purpose in distributing computers to its students is presumably to enhance the computer literacy of its citizens. In *Board of Education v. Allen*, 392 U.S. 236 (1968), the U.S. Supreme Court held that states may lend secular textbooks to religious schools because this activity does **not** "substantially promote the...religious mission of those schools." Thus, St. Mary's Parochial School could probably successfully contend that the distribution of computers to it causes no state/church entanglement. (*See* ELO Ch.15-II(L)(5).) Choice **A** is incorrect because its proposition is stated too broadly. Not all state-promoted instruction at private schools *is permissible, i.e.,* state promoted instruction at a religious private school is constitutionally **impermissible** if it promotes religious/government entanglement (i.e., if Euphoria sent computer **instructors** to religious schools, this action would probably be unconstitutional). Choice **D** is incorrect because state action may not violate the Establishment Clause, even if the educational function promoted is an important one. Finally, Choice **C** states an incorrect proposition of law. The Free Exercise Clause does **not** mandate similar treatment of public and religious private schools.

11. **B**   Under the free exercise clause of the First Amendment (applicable to the states via the Fourteenth Amendment), if a state statute interferes with the exercise of individual's religious beliefs, a court should balance (1) the state interest sought to be achieved, (2) the severity of the interference with the religious action in question, and (3) the availability of a less burdensome means of satisfying the state interest. If these factors weigh in favor of the religious right asserted, application of the statute in that instance would be constitutional. In determining if the free exercise clause has been violated or not, a court may **not** look into the reasonableness of the religious belief asserted. (*See* ELO Ch.15-III(H)(3).) Choice **C** is incorrect because a court may determine if the conduct asserted by the plaintiff is truly in accord with the tenets and beliefs of the religion to which she allegedly adheres. Choice **D** is incorrect because a court may determine if the party is sincere in the exercise of her religious beliefs; *United States v. Ballard*, 322 U.S. 78 (1944). Finally, Choice **A** is incorrect because the burden of upholding the constitutionality of a statute against a "free exercise" assertion is ordinarily upon the governmental entity, once interference with a religious practice is shown.

12. **D**   Classifications based upon age are ordinarily reviewed under the rational basis test (i.e., the statute is valid if there is a reasonable relationship between a legitimate governmental objective and the legislative means selected to accomplish that purpose). Since the rational relationship test is applicable, Prentis would have to argue that the statute invidiously dis-

criminates against him (i.e., there is no rational relationship between the classification made by the statute and the purpose which it seeks to achieve). (*See* ELO Ch.10-II(F)(2)(a).) Choice **B** is incorrect because, in the absence of a legitimate expectation to the contrary, there is no "property right" to permanent public employment; *Bishop v. Wood*, 426 U.S. 341 (1976). Choice **A** is incorrect because the privileges and immunities clause contained in the Fourteenth Amendment has been construed as precluding a state from impairing "national" rights (i.e., the right to travel from state to state, to petition Congress for grievances, to vote for national officers, to assemble and communicate with respect to national legislation, etc.). Finally, Choice **C** is incorrect because the legislation in question would be within the specific grant of Congressional power to "raise and support armies;" Article I, Section 8.

13. **C** The ability to compete for political office is ordinarily judged by the application of strict scrutiny. The governmental restriction must further "vital state objectives" which could not be accomplished by "significantly less burdensome" means; *American Party of Texas v. White*, 415 U.S. 767 (1974). While a state has a legitimate interest in limiting ballot placement to viable candidates, this could presumably still be accomplished by requiring a lower percentage of voters' signatures and/or an adequate amount of financial assets. An excessive requirement in number of registered voters' signatures arguably keeps potentially viable candidates off of the ballot system. (*See* ELO Ch.10-X(C)(4)(e).) Choice **D** is incorrect because a voters' signature requirement is not, *per se,* unreasonable. The Supreme Court has upheld a "5% of voters in the previous election" requirement. Choice **B** is incorrect because, while it may be the fact that relatively few candidates have succeeded in meeting the voters' signature requirement, that does not justify a system which effectively prevents unpopular candidates from getting on the ballot. Finally, Choice **A** is incorrect because although a state does have an interest in keeping the number of candidates from becoming confusingly large, the requirement for support among 20% of *all* registered voters is probably too difficult.

14. **A** The right to vote has been determined to be a fundamental right. Thus, the statute is constitutional only if it accomplishes a compelling governmental interest and there is no less burdensome means of accomplishing this objective. While there is certainly a governmental interest in requiring voters to be literate, there is probably no "compelling" interest in making certain that they have this ability in the English language only. A voter could arguably be adequately informed about the issues and candidates through reading material in Spanish and through the other media or conversations with other persons. Since the statute imposes a restrictive classification among otherwise equally eligible voters, the statute violates the Equal Protection Clause. (*See* ELO Ch.10-X(B)(3).) Choice **D** is incorrect because Article I, Section 2, of the Constitution does not prevent the states from enforcing the same requirements for voting in Congressional elecions as they do in state elections. Choice **B** is incorrect because, while the right to vote is a fundamental one under the Due Process Clause, the Equal Protection Clause constitutes a stronger argument since this statute imposes a restrictive classification among otherwise equally eligible voters. Finally,

Choice **C** is incorrect because Article I, Section 4, of the Constitution does not give the federal government exclusive control of voters' rights in federal elections. The states may impose the same limitations on voters in federal elections as they do in state elections.

15. **A** The Contracts Clause of the U.S. Constitution prohibits the impairment of contractual rights, unless necessary to achieve a "significant public purpose;" *Energy Reserves Group v. Kansas Power and Light Company*, 459 U.S. 400 (1983). While the improvement of existing highways is a legitimate state function, there are no facts which indicate that the necessity for these repairs had reached emergency proportions. Thus, rescission of the construction contract is probably constitutionally invalid. (*See* ELO Ch.11-III(D)(1).) Choice **D** is incorrect, since the Eleventh Amendment provides only that states may not be sued for ***monetary*** relief in federal court. Bob Pitman's action does not seek monetary damages. Choice **C** is incorrect because there is no general legal proposition that a state legislature may rescind its laws with impunity. Finally, Choice **B** is incorrect because there is no general legal proposition that a state is precluded from rescinding legislation whenever estoppel-type circumstances are present.

16. **D** Pursuant to Article I, Section 8, of the U.S. Constitution, Congress alone has the power to tax and/or spend for the general welfare. The President (whose duty is to execute the laws passed by Congress) is constitutionally required to spend monies allocated by an act of Congress, if ***expressly*** directed to do so. The President may not unilaterally impede implementation of an appropriation passed by Congress. (*See* ELO Ch.3-I(B)(a)(1).) Choice **A** is incorrect because it overstates the powers of the President. Choice **B** is incorrect because the question doesn't deal with the President's control over his subordinates., Choice **C** is incorrect because the question does not deal with issues arising under the Equal Protection Clause.

17. **B** A U.S. taxpayer has standing to challenge a federal spending measure where it is alleged that the expenditure (1) exceeds a specific constitutional limitation on the taxing and spending power, and (2) is part of a federal spending program (as opposed to an incidental expenditure under a regulatory statute); *Flast v. Cohen*, 392 U.S. 83 (1968). Since Allen is contending that the distribution of textbooks to students in a private religious school violates the First Amendment (applicable to the states via the Fourteenth Amendment), he would probably have standing to challenge the statute. (*See* ELO Ch.16-III(B)(2)(3).) Choice **A** is incorrect because, unless the legal standard set forth above is satisfied, the nexus between the payment of taxes and a Congressional expenditure is ordinarily deemed too tenuous to support standing. Choice **C** is incorrect because taxpayer standing with respect to a federal expenditure does exist where (1) the enactment offends a specific constitutional limitation on the spending power, and (2) the expenditure is part of a federal spending program. Finally, Choice **D** is incorrect because Allen is challenging a ***federal*** statute (so the existence, or not, of state action is irrelevant).

18. **D** Governmental action will be deemed to violate the Establishment Clause, unless: (1) it has a secular purpose, (2) the primary effect of the action neither advances nor inhibits religion, and (3) it will not result in excessive entanglement with religion. It has been held that salary supplements for teachers of secular subjects in religious schools involve excessive government entanglement (i.e., the governmental entity would have to constantly monitor the teacher to make certain that he is not injecting religious theories into his subjects); *Lemon v. Kurtzman*, 403 U.S. 602 (1971). (*See* ELO Ch.15-II(L)(6).) Choice **C** is incorrect because a statute which is otherwise valid under the Establishment Clause is not unconstitutional merely because a particular private institution may benefit more than others. Choice **A** is incorrect because it does not address the issue raised. The issue is not whether supplements are paid to teachers of religion, but whether salary supplements may be paid to **all** teachers, public or private, so long as they do not teach religion. Finally, Choice **B** is incorrect because the Establishment Clause is not violated if the tripartite test described above is satisfied.

19. **A** Governmental action will be deemed to violate the Establishment Clause, unless: (1) it has a secular purpose, (2) the primary effect of the action neither advances nor inhibits religion, and (3) it will not result in excessive entanglement with religion. In *Tilton v. Richardson*, 403 U.S. 672 (1971), the U.S. Supreme Court held that a federal construction grant for buildings to be used for strictly secular activities at private colleges (including those operated by religious entities) was constitutional. The Court stated that, while religious education might take place at other facilities at the college, there was no First Amendment infringement. The Court noted that universities are not involved in educating impressionable young people. (*See* ELO Ch.15-II(L)(12).) Choice **B** is incorrect because the construction of buildings could violate the First Amendment if the structures were to be utilized for religious instruction. Choice **C** is legally incorrect (financial aid to a church-operated college does not necessarily "advance" the religious purposes of the institution); *Tilton, supra*. Finally, Choice **D** is incorrect because the U.S. Supreme Court has stated that a one-time disbursement of construction aid for a building in which secular courses are to be taught does not entail substantial governmental surveillance; *Tilton, supra*.

20. **B** Where a governmental entity is involved with a private entity in a significant manner, the latter's conduct may be deemed "state action." The strongest argument **against** Country Schoolhouse is that, as a consequence of the state accrediting, licensing and supplying it with textbooks, the institution has become so intertwined with the governmental authorities that operation of the school could be deemed state action; *Norwood v. Harrison*, 413 U.S. 455 (1973). (*See* ELO Ch.12-III(E)(4).) Choice **A** is incorrect because operation of a private school has been deemed to **not** constitute a public function; *Rendell-Baker v. Kohn*, 457 U.S. 830 (1982). Since education has never been exclusively reserved to the government, it is unlikely that an institution which offers elementary and secondary education would constitute a public function. Choice **C** is legally incorrect (a state is **not** constitutionally obligated to eliminate segregation in private educational institutions). Finally, Choice **D** is incorrect because licensing, while a factor

in determining if a state is significantly involved with a private entity, is insufficient, in itself, to make the latter's activities state action; *Moose Lodge No. 107 v. Irvis*, 407 U.S. 163 (1972).

21. **A** Under the Thirteenth Amendment, slavery and involuntary servitude are forbidden. Section 2 of the Thirteenth Amendment empowers Congress to enact appropriate legislation to accomplish this purpose, including the regulation of conduct undertaken by private individuals. The purpose sought to be achieved by the Thirteenth Amendment was to erase the "badges and incidents" of slavery, including racial discrimination in real estate transactions. Since the statute in question lessens discrimination against Black persons, it probably provides the "most easily justifiable" constitutional basis for the law. (*See* ELO Ch.13-II(G).) Choice **B** is incorrect because the Fourteenth Amendment prohibits discriminatory actions by the states. The statute in question addresses the conduct of private individuals. Choice **C** is incorrect because the general welfare clause is limited to the congressional power to *tax* and *spend* for the general welfare, not to legislate in the name of general welfare; *United States v. Butler*, 297 U.S. 1 (1936). Finally, Choice **D** is incorrect because the Contracts Clause is a restriction upon a state's power to repudiate outstanding agreements. It is ***not*** a basis for enactment of federal legislation.

22. **A** State action or legislation which discriminates against interstate commerce is ordinarily unconstitutional. A state statute which requires a business entity to make purchases within that state is ordinarily viewed as discriminating against interstate commerce. (There are exceptions to this rule, such as where the government is acting as a market participant, etc.) Since the Primera statute requires local entities, at least to some extent, to eschew interstate commerce, the legislation is arguably unconstitutional. While Primera has an interest in improving its economy, it probably ***cannot*** show that requiring certain businesses to purchase a percentage of their goods within that state will have a significant impact on the economy. The fact pattern is somewhat similar to the facts in a U.S. Supreme Court decision which struck down a state statute requiring a utility company to sell locally produced hydroelectric energy solely within that state; *New England Power Co. v. New Hampshire*, 455 U.S. 331 (1982). (*See* ELO Ch.6-I(I)(1).) Choice **D** is incorrect because, while there is a plausible argument that the Equal Protection Clause is violated by the fact that Primera businesses grossing ***less*** than $1 million are not required to purchase goods within that state, economic legislation is ordinarily judged only by the "rational relationship" test. Since improving the Primera economy is a legitimate state purpose and a legitimate objective can be accomplished "one step at a time," the rational relationship test is satisfied. Choice **C** is incorrect because the Privileges and Immunities Clause of the Fourteenth Amendment prevents states from impairing rights of national citizenship (i.e., the right to move from state to state, to petition Congress, to vote for national officers, etc.) and is not applicable to these facts. Finally, Choice **B** is incorrect because the due process clause is not violated if a state pursues a legitimate state objective by rational means.

23. **D** Article IV, Section 3 of the U.S. Constitution provides that Congress shall have the power to "make all needful rules and regulations respecting the territory or other property belonging to the United States." (*See* ELO Ch.3-I(C)(2).) Since the act in question pertains to "national" parks and recreation areas, Choice **D** represents the "strongest" means of sustaining this law. Choice **A** is incorrect because, while the legislation *might* be sustainable under the Commerce Clause (i.e., interstate commerce would arguably be diminished by a law which prevents the removal of wildlife from federally owned land), it is a less direct means of sustaining the statute than a specific enumerated power which pertains to the subject matter of the enactment. Choice **C** is incorrect because the Enforcement Clause of the Fourteenth Amendment only empowers Congress to implement the constraints upon state action described in that provision. Finally, Choice **B** is incorrect because the Privileges and Immunities Clause of Article IV, Section 2, precludes states from discriminating against U.S. citizens from other jurisdictions. It does not constitute a basis upon which federal legislation can be enacted.

24. **B** Any activity (even though primarily intrastate) which, in the aggregate, could have a significant impact upon the movement of persons, information or items across state lines is regulable by Congress under the Commerce Clause. Since motor vehicles can be moved easily across state lines and obviously are instruments of interstate commerce, the legislation could be premised upon the Commerce Clause. (*See* ELO Ch.4-IV(A).) Choice **A** is incorrect because Congress' power to regulate for the general welfare applies only to matters of taxation and spending. Choice **C** is incorrect because, even if most vehicles remained within the particular state in which they were stolen, Congress could have reasonably concluded that the movement of stolen cars across state lines would adversely affect interstate commerece (i.e., if her car is stolen, the owner cannot travel to another state to purchase items or work). Finally, Choice **D** is incorrect because the Tenth Amendment merely reserves to the states whatever powers cannot be exercised by Congress under the U.S. Constitution. It is not a basis for nullifying Congress' right to legislate.

25. **B** Governmental action which infringes upon a fundamental right violates substantive due process, unless there is a compelling interest involved and there is no less burdensome means of accomplishing that objective. The right to utilize contraceptive devices has been held to be a fundamental right; *Griswold v. Connecticut*, 381 U.S. 479 (1965); and has been extended to apply to unmarried persons; *Eisenstadt v. Baird,* 405 U.S. 438 (1972). Thus, the law in question arguably violates the Due Process Clause of the 14th Amendment. (*See* ELO Ch.9-IV(D)(3).) Choice **A** is incorrect because there is no indication that the statute in question constitutes an undue burden upon interstate commerce; the impact of the legislation upon interstate commerce is minimal compared to the state objective sought to be achieved by the act. In fact, the legislation would probably have a rather minor effect upon interstate commerce. Choice **C** is incorrect because the Fourteenth Amendment has been interpreted to protect only a very limited number of *national citizenship* rights (i.e., moving freely from state to state, petitioning Congress, voting for national officers, advocating

national legislation, etc.), which do not include the right to contraceptives. Finally, Choice **D** is incorrect because a law which arguably regulates moral conduct is *not*, *ipso facto*, a violation of the freedom of religion.

26. **B** The Privileges and Immunities Clause contained in Article IV, Section 2 of the U.S. Constitution, precludes a state from discriminating against the citizens of other states with respect to the exercise of rights that are "fundamental to national unity," such as the right to be employed, the right to practice one's profession, and the right to engage in business. Since the legislation in question applies to all persons within or without Euphoria and to all property in Euphoria (i.e., parcels owned by citizens of Euphoria, as well as those owned by persons residing outside of the state), the Privileges and Immunities Clause is probably the *least* applicable doctrine mentioned. (*See* ELO Ch.7-IB(B)(1).) Choice **C** is incorrect because the constitutional basis for this legislation is the police power (reserved to the states in the Tenth Amendment). Choice **A** is incorrect because the proposed legislation might arguably constitute an unconstitutional deprivation of property under the Fourteenth Amendment. This is because restrictions placed in deeds can often increase the value of real property. Finally, Choice **D** is incorrect because the CCR's in deeds are typically a significant part of a land sale transaction and the legislation in question might impair existing and prospective contractual relationships.

27. **C** Under the Equal Protection Clause of the Fourteenth Amendment, state legislation pertaining to legal aliens is ordinarily subject to strict scrutiny (i.e., there must be a compelling state interest and no less burdensome means of accomplishing that objective). However, where the classification affects an area which involves the "execution of broad public policy," such as a law preventing aliens from becoming state troopers, the "mere rationality" test is utilized; *Foley v. Connelie*, 435 U.S. 291 (1978). Since the Euphoria legislation impairs the general rights of legal aliens, it must meet the strict scrutiny test. Euphoria's objective in enacting this legislation was probably to extend the disbursement of funds only to persons who would remain in their jurisdiction and thus strengthen the state's technology base. However, there is probably no compelling state interest in limiting computer training to U.S. citizens, and there are less burdensome means of accomplishing this objective (*e.g.*, require students to become U.S. citizens during their training period). Thus, the alienage restriction is probably unconstitutional. (*See* ELO Ch.10-VI(B) & (C)(3).) Choice **D** is incorrect because the Privileges and Immunities Clause of Article IV, Section 2, does *not* apply to aliens. They are not "citizens of a state" within the meaning of that provision. Choice **B** is incorrect because, even if the line drawn by the state was reasonably related to a legitimate governmental interest, the strict scrutiny standard, which is stricter, is not satisfied. Finally, Choice **A** is incorrect because legal aliens *are* viewed as a "discrete and insular minority."

28. **D** Requirements that voters have resided within the state for more than a certain time prior to Election Day are strictly scrutinized; *Dunn v. Blumstein*, 405 U.S. 330 (1972). Such requirements have been struck down on the grounds that they interfere with the fundamental right to vote and the

right to travel. While a state might have a compelling interest in verifying that only *bona fide* residents (i.e., those living and intending to remain within the jurisdiction) can vote, the legislation in question precludes new residents from voting, even if they intend to remain in the state. A less strict means of assuring that only *bona fide* residents vote would be to require an affidavit from them, stating that they intend to continue residing in the jurisdiction. (*See* ELO Ch.10-X(B)(6).) Choice **C** is incorrect because a state may limit the franchise to *bona fide* residents. Thus, non-residents may be precluded from voting in local elections. Choice **A** is incorrect because persons moving into a new jurisdiction can constitutionally be precluded from voting for officials in that area, if they did *not* intend to remain there and there is no legal presumption that persons residing in a state at a given moment intend to remain there. Finally, Choice **B** is incorrect because the statute arguably does not costittute an undue burden upon interstate commerce (i.e., persons would probably *not* be dissuaded from moving to another state simply because they could not vote in the next local election).

29. **C**   The Supreme Court has held that each person has a fundamental right to live with members of her family; *Moore v. City of East Cleveland*, 431 U.S. 494 (1977). Thus, the governmental entity has the burden of proving that any action affecting this right is necessary to achieve a compelling government interest, and that there are no less burdensome means available. (*See* ELO Ch.9-IV(N)(2).) Choice **B** is incorrect because it is less than the burden of proof imposed on a state. Again, where a fundamental right is infringed, a state must show that a *compelling* governmental interest is advanced, not merely a *legitimate* one. Choice **D** incorrectly places the burden of persuasion upon Muffy. Once it's established that a fundamental right is involved, the burden of proof is upon the governmental entity. Finally, Choice **A** is incorrect because it (1) places the burden of persuasion upon Muffy, and (2) understates the measure of proof required. When a fundamental right is infringed upon, the governmental entity must show that a "compelling" interest is involved.

30. **C**   A state law is invalid where it results in an undue burden upon interstate commerce (i.e., the local interest sought to be protected by the legislation is outweighed by the burden which it places upon the movement of persons, things or information across state lines). If BUPS can show that (1) other jurisdictions in which it operates do not require the seat belts in question, and (2) substantial cost and inconvenience will be incurred by it in complying with the law, the statute will probably be declared unconstitutional; *Bibb v. Navajo Freight Lines, Inc.*, 359 U.S. 520 (1959). (*See* ELO Ch.6-I(H)(4)(a).) Choice **B** is incorrect because, under these facts, all common carriers are equally affected. The fact that not all vehicles are covered by the statute is immaterial. A governmental entity may address a health or safety problem "one step at a time," and, since the evil complained of is confined to commercial vehicles, the line of demarcation is not unreasonable. Choice **A** is incorrect because no fundamental right is involved and the statute would be tested by the rational relationship test. Since the seat belts prescribed by the statute probably enhance the safety of persons on

highways within Wissola, this test is satisfied. Finally, Choice **D** is incorrect because the facts do not give rise to a contracts clause issue.

31.	**D**	Under Article I, Section 8, of the U.S. Constitution, Congress has the power to tax and spend for the general welfare. The general welfare is arguably served by providing federal funds for the hiring of police officers by the states and cities. While Congress may not exercise the spending power in violation of specific constitutional provisions (i.e., the Establishment Clause), restricting federal aid to cities of a presribed size would not run afoul of this principle. (*See* ELO Ch.3-I(B)(a)(1).) Choice **B** is incorrect because the Tenth Amendment is the basis of the states' police power (rather than a source of *federal* spending authority). Choice **A** is incorrect because the relationship of the power to make war and provide for the national defense and the statute in question, is more tenuous than the relationship of the taxing and spending power. Finally, Choice **C** is incorrect because the Privileges and Immunities Clause of the Fourteenth Amendment does not confer any power upon Congress. Rather, it precludes the states from hindering the exercise of rights inherent in national citizenship (i.e., to travel from state to state, petition representatives of Congress, etc.).

32.	**A**	A generally applicable criminal law is enforceable, regardless of the burden which it imposes upon an individual's religious beliefs; *Employment Division v. Smith*, 494 U.S. 872 (1990). The state need not balance its interests its against the burden on the individual's beliefs, as long as the law is generally applicable and not motivated by a government desire to affect religion. In this case however, the statute specifically exempts sales activities undertaken for a "religious purpose." As long as Martha sincerely believed that her sales were for a "religious purpose," she would (under the applicable statute) be exempt from the licensing requirement. (*See* ELO Ch.15-III(E)(7).) Choice **B** is incorrect because the statute is not attempting to criminalize religious beliefs. Choice **C** is incorrect because (while the legal proposition is correctly stated) persons engaging in sales for a "religious purpose" are exempted under the applicable statute. Finally, Choice **D** is incorrect, since the factfinder's conclusion that the religious belief in question is erroneous is irrelevant. As long as Martha's beliefs were sincerely held, she is exempt from the statute.

33.	**A**	Where there is a lack of purposeful discrimination, state laws are ordinarily reviewed under the rational relationship test (i.e., the legislation in question must be rationally related to a legitimate state objective). Although there is a disproportionately adverse effect upon Hispanics, there is no indication that the State X legislature sought to discriminate against this group. In fact, their actions appear to be taken in response to a report indicating that life and property could be saved by the integration of metal slats into the homes in question. (*See* ELO Ch.10-III(C).) Choice **B** is incorrect because strict scrutiny is *not* applicable (i.e., the law was not a deliberate attempt to disadvantage a particular minority). Choice **C** is incorrect because the fact that a law has a disproportionately adverse impact upon a particular group does not automatically trigger the strict scrutiny review. The discrimination must be purposeful in nature. Finally, Choice **D** is incorrect because the $1,200 fee necessary to comply with the law would probably ***not*** constitute such an undue burden as to be violative of due process (especially since homeowners have 2 years to complete the improvement).

34. **C** The privileges and immunities clause contained in Article IV, Section 2, of the U.S. Constitution precludes a state from discriminating against the citizens of other states with respect to the exercise of national rights. Since the legislation in question pertains to ***all*** deeds within the state (i.e., those parcels owned by citizens of the jurisdiction and those which are owned by persons residing outside of the state), the privileges and immunities clause of Article IV, Section 2, of the U.S. Constitution would probably be the ***least*** important doctrine mentioned. (*See* ELO Ch.7-IV(B)(1).) Choice **D** is incorrect because the constitutional basis for the legislation requested is the police power (reserved to the states in the Tenth Amendment). Choice **A** is incorrect because the proposed legislation might constitute an unconstitutional deprivation of property under the Fourteenth Amendment. This result would occur because, if the restrictions previously placed in deeds ceased to be effective, land owned by an individual would often become less valuable (i.e., if subdivision restrictions ceased to exist, each landowner's parcel would probably be less valuable). Finally, Choice **B** is incorrect because deeds are frequently made pursuant to a contract. Thus, the legislation in question would impair existing contractual relationships (i.e., persons buying a lot within a subdivision ordinarily do so upon the vendor's promise that other parcels will be subject to similar restrictions); Article I, Section 10 (Clause 1).

35. **D** Any activity (even though primarily intrastate) which, in the aggregate, could have a significant impact upon the movement of persons, information or items across state lines is regulable under the Commerce Clause. Since the price of oil certainly has an impact upon interstate and foreign commerce (i.e., the more or less expensive it is, the greater or lesser is the likelihood that it will be purchased), the statute in question is constitutional under the Commerce Clause. (*See* ELO Ch.4-IV(A).) Choice **B** is incorrect because it is too broad. Purchases and sales which have no effect upon interstate commerce cannot be regulated by Congress. Also, the Choice does not deal with the regulation of imported products. Choice **C** is incorrect because the fact that Congress has the authority to regulate the importation of goods from abroad is not a basis for regulating items produced within the United States. Finally, Choice **A** is incorrect because Congress has no power to enact general legislation for the "general welfare." The "general welfare" clause has been interpreted as applying only to the taxing and spending power.

36. **C** Federal courts will not hear a matter until it is "ripe" (i.e., there is an actual dispute between parties having adverse legal interests); *Poe v. Ullman*, 367 U.S. 497 (1961). Since Paul has apparently not yet even proposed to Mary, nor have they applied for a marriage license, a federal court would probably conclude that the "ripeness" prerequisite has ***not*** been satisfied. (*See* ELO Ch.16-V(C).) Choice **B** is incorrect because a substantial federal question is presented (i.e., may a state attach the condition of prior coun-

seling to a fundamental right such as marriage?). Choice **A** is incorrect because residence is immaterial in a case involving subject matter jurisdiction over a federal question (i.e., a claim arising under the U.S. Constitution). Finally, Choice **D** is incorrect because no political question (i.e., one involving the inter-relationship of co-equal branches of government) is presented by this fact pattern.

37. **C** Governmental action which infringes upon a fundamental right violates the Due Process Clause of the 14th Amendment, unless a compelling interest is involved and there is no less burdensome means of accomplishing that objective. The right to marry is a fundamental one; *Zablocki v. Redhail*, 434 U.S. 374 (1978). Thus, the "strict scrutiny" standard applies in this instance, and the state has the burden of proof. (*See* ELO Ch.9-IV(N)(4).) Choice **D** is incorrect because there is no legal principle which mandates strict scrutiny with respect to any legislation affecting minors. Choice **B** is incorrect because, while there is an initial presumption that legislation is valid, this is overcome by evidence that a "fundamental right" is involved (the determination that a fundamental right is involved is made by the court). Finally, Choice **A** is incorrect because, although the statement is true, action under the Tenth Amendment is subject to the Due Process Clause of the Fourteenth Amendment.

38. **B** Under the equal protection clause of the Fourteenth Amendment, state legislation pertaining to legal aliens is subject to strict scrutiny (i.e., there must be a compelling state interest and no less burdensome means of accomplishing that objective); unless the classification affects a position which is governmental ("bound up with the operation of the state as a governmental entity") or political in nature (in which event, the legislation in question is tested by the rational relationship standard). Since there does not appear to be a compelling reason to preclude aliens from owning more than one hundred acres of land within the state, Zane could probably successfully contend that the legislation violates the equal protection clause of the Fourteenth Amendment. (*See* ELO Ch.10-VI(B) & (C)(3).) Choice **A** is incorrect because while there would arguably be an affect upon interstate commerce (i.e., legal aliens would probably make less trips to, and purchase less land in, State X as a consequence of the enactment), the undue burden upon interstate commerce necessary to invalidate state legislation would probably **not** exist. Choice **C** is incorrect because the law does not preclude Zane from coming into, or egressing from, State X. Finally, Choice **D** is incorrect because Zane purchased the land in question **after** the passage of the pertinent statute. Thus, the legislation did not impair an outstanding contractual obligation.

39. **D** Pursuant to Article III, Section 1, of the U.S. Constitution, Congress has empowered U.S. District Courts to hear federal questions (i.e., those involving a claim arising under the U.S. Constitution, a congressional act or a federal treaty). Since Zane could claim that the statute violates the equal protection clause of the Fourteenth Amendment, a federal claim is involved. Thus, a U.S. District Court should hear the action. (*See* ELO Ch.3-I(C)(2).) Choice **C** is incorrect because federal courts are empowered to hear Zane's action based upon the U.S. Constitution, rather than the

United Nations Charter. Choice **B** is legally incorrect (state qualifications for landholding within the jurisdiction are subject to constitutional limitations). Finally, Choice **A** is legally incorrect (the U.S. Constitution does not prohibit aliens from commencing an action in federal court).

40. **B** Generally, there is no due process "right" to public employment. Thus, it is unlikely that James can successfully compel the Euphoria Employment Office to furnish him with an explanation as to why his application for employment was unsuccessful. (*See* ELO Ch.9-V(B) & (C).) Choice **A** is incorrect because it simply restates the principle that the Tenth Amendment reserves to the states all powers not specifically assigned to the federal government. It does **not**, however, empower states to ignore the other provisions of the Constitution (i.e., the Due Process and Equal Protection Clauses, etc.). Choice **C** is incorrect because, as explained above, there is no Due Process Clause right to public employment. Finally, Choice **D** is incorrect. Although the Equal Protection Clause guarantees that people who are similarly situated will be treated similarly, it is reasonable to permit state employment officers discretion whether or not to confer with unsuccessful applicants (i.e., granting all applicants post-rejection interviews might become too time-consuming).

41. **C** There is ordinarily no Due Process Clause "property" interest in a governmental job. However, procedural Due Process protections of notice and a timely hearing may attach when a governmental employee is given reason to believe that her employment is not simply "at will;" *Perry v. Sinderman*, 408 U.S. 593 (1972). If the state officer for whom Angela worked had assured her that she would be rehired, Angela's procedural due process right to a statement of reasons and a timely hearing would arguably attach. (*See* ELO Ch.9-V(E)(2).) Choice **A** is incorrect because a state employee is not entitled to rely on the expectation of continued employment. Choice **B** is incorrect because the fact pattern fails to suggest that Angela's termination was based upon her status in a protected classification (i.e., race, sex, religion, etc.). Finally, Choice **D** is incorrect because there is no constitutional right to employment purely on the basis of merit.

42. **A** The Supreme Court and such inferior federal courts as are established by Congress are empowered to hear cases arising under the U.S Constitution; Article III, Section 2. Since the plaintiff is claiming that the restaurant's conduct violates the Equal Protection Clause of the Fourteenth Amendment, a federal claim (i.e., one arising under the U.S. Constitution) is involved. However, to support his claim, he must show that the State of Euphoria is involved because Article III, Section 2, applies to actions by the states, not by private citizens. His claim is supported by *Burton v. Wilmington Parking Authority*, 365 U.S. 715 (1961), on the basis of the "symbiotic" relationship between the state and the restaurant owner. Since the extensive contact between the state and the restaurant owner results in each party's benefitting from the other's conduct, the requisite state action may be found. Therefore, a federal district court has subject matter jurisdiction. (*See* ELO Ch.3-I(C)(2) and Ch.12-III(D).) Choice **B** is incorrect because there is no federal court jurisdiction based simply on the presence of a state as a party. Choice **C** is incorrect because a federal court will

abstain only when (1) a state statute is claimed to be unconstitutional, and (2) there is a possibility that a curative interpretation might be rendered by a state court. In this instance, no state legislation is at issue. Finally, Choice **D** is incorrect because citizens of the same state can sue each other in a U.S. District Court, if a federal claim is asserted.

43. **B** Where a state is involved with a private entity in a significant manner, the latter's conduct may be deemed "state action." The strongest argument against The Bastion is that, as a consequence of its extensive dealings with Euphoria—accreditation, licensing and supplying textbooks—the institution has become so intertwined with the state that the school's operation has become state action; *Norwood v. Harrison*, 413 U.S. 455 (1973). Thus, under the Equal Protection Clause, it cannot discriminate on the basis of party affiliation or political viewpoint. (*See* ELO Ch.12-III(E)(4).) Choice **A** is incorrect because operation of a private school is *not* ordinarily a public function; *Rendell-Baker v. Kohn*, 457 U.S. 830 (1982). Choice **C** is legally incorrect (a state is *not* constitutionally obligated to take action to eliminate segregation in *private* educational institutions). Finally, Choice **D** is incorrect because licensing—while one factor in determining if a state is so significantly involved with a private entity as to constitute "state action"— is insufficient, in itself; *Moose Lodge No. 107 v. Irvis*, 407 U.S. 163 (1972).

44. **B** A statute is overly broad on its face (and therefore invalid) when the governmental agency empowered to enforce it has virtually unlimited discretion. Although the Littletown Police Commissioner is instructed to enforce the waiver provision in an "even-handed" manner, the statute permits too much discretion in the Commissioner without any checks on his decisions. The statute cannot be a constitutional basis for prosecution. (*See* ELO Ch.14-III(A)(1) & IV(E)(2).) Choice **A** is incorrect because speech activities in traditional public forums can be conditioned and circumscribed. Choice **C** is incorrect because, although the restrictions are narrowly tailored, no governmental interest, however significant, can justify unconstitutional limits on free speech. Finally, Choice **D** is incorrect because, despite the instruction to grant waiver permits in an "even-handed manner," the statute is still overly broad.

45. **C** A U.S. taxpayer has standing to challenge a federal spending measure if he alleges that the expenditure (1) exceeds a specific constitutional limitation on the taxing and spending power of Congress, and (2) is part of a federal spending program (as opposed to an incidental expenditure under a regulatory statute); *Flast v. Cohen*, 392 U.S. 83 (1968). Since Alex is apparently contending that monetary grants for the distribution of computers to students in private religious schools violate the First Amendment which operates as a specific limitation on Congress' Taxing and Spending powers, he probably has standing to challenge the statute. (*See* ELO Ch.16-III(B)(2)-(3).) Choices **A** and **B** are incorrect because, as explained above, Alex has "taxpayer standing" in this particular situation. Finally, Choice **D** is incorrect because it is too narrow. It is not a condition of "standing" that the citizen rely on the General Welfare clause for his claim.

46. **C**   Governmental action which benefits religion is deemed to violate the Establishment Clause, unless: (1) it has a secular purpose, (2) the primary effect of the action neither advances nor inhibits religion, and (3) it will not result in excessive entanglement with religion. It has been held that salary supplements for teachers of secular subjects in religious schools involves excessive government entanglement (i.e., the governmental entity would have to constantly monitor the teachers to make certain that they did not interject religious instruction into their subjects); *Lemon v. Kurtzman*, 403 U.S. 602 (1971). The statute here would come within that decision. (*See* ELO Ch.15-II(L)(6).) Choice **D** is incorrect because there is not necessarily an Equal Protection violation. Congress could presumably decide that private non-religious schools as a class ordinarily have the means to purchase their own computers. Finally, Choice **A** is incorrect because the equal treatment of public and private religious schools is immaterial to the issue of excessive entanglement by Congress. Choice **B** is incorrect because there is excessive governmental entanglement by virtue of the use of governmental funds to retain computer teachers.

47. **A**   Classifications based upon age are ordinarily viewed under the rational basis test (i.e., there must be a reasonable relationship between a legitimate governmental objective and the legislative means selected to accomplish that purpose). Clarence's strongest argument from the choices offered appears to be that the statute pertaining to mandatory retirement of Federal Public Defenders is invalid under the Fifth Amendment, which applies the requirements of due process to the federal government. The "Equal Protection" concept has been found to exist under the Fifth Amendment's Due Process Clause. (However, Clarence probably will ***not*** prevail because the Courts are loath to apply the clause to economic rights.) (*See* ELO Ch.10-II(F)(2)(a).) Choice **B** is incorrect because, in the absence of a legitimate expectation to the contrary, there is no "property right" to permanent public employment; *Bishop v. Wood*, 426 U.S. 341 (1976). Choice **C** is incorrect because the Fourteenth Amendment applies only to state action and the Privileges and Immunities Clause contained in the Fourteenth Amendment has been limited to precluding a state from impairing "national" rights (i.e., the right to travel from state to state, to petition Congress for grievances, etc.). Finally, Choice **D** is incorrect because the Fourteenth Amendment applies only to the states, not the federal government.

48. **C**   Any activity (even though primarily intrastate) which, in the aggregate, could have a significant impact upon the movement of persons, information or items across state lines is regulable under the commerce clause. Since legislation pertaining to consumer credit arguably has an affect upon the interstate movement of monies, it is valid under the commerce clause. In fact, the act is somewhat similar to that which was specifically approved by the Supreme Court, as a proper assertion of the commerce clause in *Perez v. United States*, 402 U.S. 146 (1971). (*See* ELO Ch.4-IV(F)(3).) Choice **D** is incorrect because the equal protection clause of the Fourteenth Amendment is a restriction upon state action (not a basis for federal legislation). Choice **A** is incorrect because the impairment of contracts clause is a restriction upon state conduct (i.e., it precludes states from impairing obligations created under outstanding agreements), rather than a basis for the

enactment of federal legislation. Finally, Choice **B** is incorrect because the privileges and immunities clause of the Fourteenth Amendment precludes states from impairing the exercise of rights of national citizenship (i.e., the right to travel from state to state, the right to petition representatives of the U.S. government, etc.). It is ***not*** a source of federal legislative power.

49.   **A**   Under the free exercise clause of the First Amendment (applicable to the states via the Fourteenth Amendment), if a state statute interferes with the exercise of an individual's religious beliefs, a court should balance (1) the state interest sought to be achieved, (2) the severity of the interference with the religious action, and (3) whether the state could satisfy its interest by a less burdensome means. If these factors weigh in favor of the religious right asserted, application of the statute in that instance would be unconstitutional. (*See* ELO Ch.15-III(A)(3).) The statement embodied in Choice **A** most nearly replicates the applicable rule of law. Choice **B** is incorrect because, where a significant interference with religious practices occurs, the governmental entity must ordinarily demonstrate that the interest which it seeks to achieve outweighs the religious practice which is impaired by the legislation. Choice **D** is legally incorrect (an organization need not establish a specific congressional intent to inhibit a religious organization's objectives for First Amendment protections to be operative). Finally, Choice **C** is legally incorrect because, where a significant aspect of a religious organization's practices have been impaired, the burden is on the governmental entity to demonstrate that its objective outweighs that interference.

50.   **D**   Pursuant to Article III, Section 1, of the U.S. Constitution, Congress has empowered U.S. District Courts to hear cases involving federal questions (i.e., those involving a claim under the U.S. Constitution, a Congressional act, or a federal treaty). Since Misho will probably assert that the Equal Protection Clause of the Fourteenth Amendment has been violated by the Caldonia statute, a federal claim is involved. Thus, the U.S. District Court should hear the matter. (*See* ELO Ch.3-I(C)(2).) Choice **A** is legally incorrect (the U.S. Constitution does ***not*** preclude aliens from commencing an action in federal court). Choice **C** is incorrect because the presence of a state as a party is not by itself a basis for federal court jurisdiction. Finally, Choice **B** is incorrect because, although the states may legislate with respect to the ownership of property, the legislation is subject to the U.S. Constitution.

51.   **B**   Under the Equal Protection Clause of the Fourteenth Amendment, state legislation pertaining to aliens is ordinarily adjudged by the strict scrutiny standard (i.e., there must be a compelling state interest and no less burdensome means of accomplishing that objective). There does not appear to be a compelling reason to preclude aliens—especially legal aliens—from owning a controlling interest in corporations located within Caldonia. While this group might arguably not have the civic ardor possessed by a U.S. citizen, this fact would hardly be "compelling." (*See* ELO Ch.10-VI(B).) Choice **A** is incorrect because it is not the *strongest argument*. The Attorney General would argue that the oral contract to purchase could be avoided by Misho under the Statute of Frauds (i.e., the contract was unenforceable

until reduced to a writing signed by Misho, since the aggregate value of the stock was "$500 or more;" U.C.C. § 2-201) and that Misho could have avoided the agreement, since one can legally avoid a contract which is contrary to law. Choice **D** is incorrect because, while there would arguably be an effect upon interstate commerce (i.e., legal aliens would presumably make fewer trips to, and purchase fewer businesses in, Caldonia), the effect would not be "unduly burdensome", the required standard for judicial intervention. Finally, Choice **C** is incorrect because the Privileges and Immunities Clause applies only to U.S. citizens.

52. **B**   A decision may be appealed as of right to the U.S. Supreme Court where (1) a state court has held a federal statute or treaty invalid, (2) a state court has upheld a state statute against the claim that it is unconstitutional or invalid under the supremacy clause, or (3) a federal court of appeal has held a state statute (a) unconstitutional, or (b) contrary to a federal statute or treaty. A petition for certiorari (a discretionary form of review) may be granted where a (1) state court has held a state statute (a) unconstitutional, or (b) contrary to a federal statute or treaty, or (2) federal court of appeal has decided a novel, but significant, federal question (a claim arising under the Constitution, a federal statute or a U.S. treaty), and there is no appeal as of right. Since the State X Supreme Court invalidated a state statute as being contrary to the Constitution, review by the U.S. Supreme Court could only occur by means of certiorari. (*See* ELO Ch.2-IV(B)(1)(a).) Choice **A** is incorrect because (1) State X, being the party which lost below, is the only entity which is now capable of appealing the case, and (2) State X College, being a party to the grant, had standing to raise the constitutional issue below. Finally, Choices **C** and **D** are incorrect because no automatic right of appeal existed in these circumstances.

53. **B**   Where state legislation places an undue burden upon interstate commerce (i.e., the local interest sought to be protected is outweighed by the hindrance to interstate commerce resulting from the law), the law is unconstitutional. Except for the possible consequence of fewer monkeys (if needed) being imported into State X for the purpose of completing the research, the Act would have virtually no effect upon interstate commerce. (*See* ELO Ch.6-I(F).) Choice **A** is incorrect because, as a consequence of the law, College has a number of animals which have suddenly become valueless to it. Thus, a taking without due process of law has arguably occurred. Choice **D** is incorrect because a grant does constitute a contract, which (as a consequence of the Act) significantly hinders the workings of the federal government and is invalid under the Supremacy Clause. Since the U.S. Army has contracted with College for the research in question, the Act is arguably unconstitutional as applied to the grant. Choice **C** is incorrect because it may be possible to argue that the state's action is impeding a federal interest in the research.

54. **B**   Under the Fourteenth Amendment's Equal Protection Clause, classifications based upon illegitimacy must be substantially related to an important state interest (middle level scrutiny; *Clark v. Jeter*, 486 U.S. 456 (1988). While Euphoria may have an interest in discouraging out-of-wedlock births and avoiding fraudulent claims, the state cannot simply bar all

unacknowledged, illegitimate children from having any chance to inherit. These children must be given at least some reasonable opportunity to obtain a judicial detrermination of paternity. Therefore, it is unlikely that the statute would withstand middle level scrutiny. A statute which prevented acknowledged illegitimate children from inheriting from their fathers was rejected in *Trimble v. Gordon*, 430 U.S. 762 (1977). A six-year statute of limitations on paternity suits was invalidated in *Clark v. Jeter supra*). (*See* ELO Ch.10-VII(C)(1).) Choice **D** is incorrect because there is no "fundamental right" to inherit property. Choice **C** is incorrect because the Privileges and Immunities Clause of the Fourteenth Amendment prevents the states from impeding the rights of *national* citizenship (i.e., the right to travel from state to state, to petition federal officials, etc.); the right to inherit from one's father is not a national right. Finally, Choice **A** is incorrect because, to this point, U.S. Supreme Court decisions pertaining to the rights of illegitimate children have been predicated upon the Equal Protection Clause. Additionally, Patricia's rights are substantive rights, not procedural rights. No notice or hearing can enlarge her rights as limited by this statute.

55. **C**   Although governmental oath requirements must be narrowly tailored to avoid infringement of First Amendment rights, a state may condition public employment upon a positive oath to abide by constitutional, lawful processes; *Cole v. Richardson*, 405 U.S. 676 (1972). Butah's strongest argument for sustaining the statute would be that it merely requires individuals to pledge to avoid illegal conduct. (*See* ELO Ch.14-X(C)(6).) Choice **A** is incorrect because, while government employment is a privilege (rather than a right), it may not be conditioned upon an affirmation or oath to refrain from activities protected by the First Amendment. Choice **B** is incorrect because the Tenth Amendment is merly a recitation of the states' right to exercise powers not delegated to the federal government. It does not empower the states to affix conditions upon employment which are constitutionally improper. Finally, Choice **D** is incorrect because, while a state is justified in keeping disloyal persons out of governmental positions, it cannot cannot condition public employment upon so loose a standard as "potential disloyalty" or upon any oath or affirmation which violates the First Amendment rights of job applicants.

56. **A**   Under the Equal Protection Clause of the Fourteenth Amendment, state or local regulations which facially discriminate against aliens (persons without US citizenship) must ordinarily satisfy the strict scrutiny test (i.e., there must be a compelling governmental interest which is promoted by the statute and no less burdensome means of accomplishing that objective). However, where an alien is applying for a position which has *political,* as ooposed to solely *economic,* functions, a state need only satisfy the rational relationship test. Under these facts, since Shahad seeks a job as a mechanic in a garage motor pool, a job with no poltitical elements, the strict scrutiny standard is applicable. (*See* ELO Ch.10-VI(C).) Choice **B** is incorrect because an alien applicant for a non-political job is entitled to the application of strict scuriny of a statute which bars him from the job. Finally, Choices **C** and **D** are incorrect because, as discussed above, the

burden of proof is upon the State of Trent to demonstrate that the statute withstands a strict scrutiny analysis.

57. **A** When a statute affecting speech pertains to time, place, or the manner of expression (as opposed to content), the governmental entity has the burden of showing that the statute supports an "important" social objective and is narrowly tailored to accomplish that result. Additionally, the governmental entity must "leave open alternative channels" for communicating the information sought to be expressed; *Clark v. Community for Creative Non-Violence*, 468 U.S. 288 (1984), *Alternative Channels, Metromedia, Inc. v. San Diego*, 453 U.S. 490 (1981). Since the first statute is a content-neutral, "time, place, manner of expression" law, Libertania must satisfy the standard stated in Choice **A**. (*See* ELO Ch.14-IV(A)(5).) Choice **B** is incorrect because, as described above, Libertania must satisfy a higher standard under these circumstances. Finally, Choices **C** and **D** are incorrect because the burden of proof is upon the state.

58. **B** A statute is unduly vague (and therefore invalid under the Due Process Clause of the Fourteenth Amendment) when a person of ordinary intelligence would be unable to determine if actions which are being contemplated are proscribed by the language. The words "opprobrious" and "abusive" are probably too subjective to apprise a person of average intelligence what words would subject him to criminal culpability. (*See* ELO Ch.14-III(B).) Choice **A** is legally incorrect (even public forums are subject to limitations upon time, place and manner of communication). Choice **C** is also legally incorrect (some speech content, such as "fighting words," may be regulated in certain situations). Finally, Choice **D** is incorrect because, although it expresses a general constitutional principle, a governmental entity may promulgate limitations as to time, place and manner of communication (even with respect to public forums).

59. **A** Where state regulation promotes domestic businesses by penalizing out-of-state interests, it violates the Equal Protection Clause of the Fourteenth Amendment; *Metropolitan Life Ins. Co. v. Ward*, 470 U.S. 869 (1985). Although the statute involves insurance companies (which are exempted from attack under the Commerce Clause), the U.S. Supreme Court has held that such legislation is violative of the Equal Protection Clause (*supra*). The only purpose of the statute was to promote the business of its domestic insurers by penalizing foreign insurers who seek to do business in Araho; this is not a legitimate state purpose. (*See* ELO Ch.10-II(B)(3).) Choice **B** is incorrect because the McCarran-Ferguson Act exempts state insurance regulation from attack under the Commerce Clause, not the Equal Protection Clause. Choice **C** is incorrect because the Supremacy Clause comes imto play only when Congress has *preempted* an area of legislation; that was not the case in the *Metropolitan* case. Finally, Choice **D** is incorrect because the Equal Protection Clause may not be circumscribed or avoided even by leglislation related to a legitimate state objective.

60. **B** The dormant Commerce Clause prevents a state or local government from placing an undue burden upon interstate commerce if the national interest in promoting interstate commerce overrides the local interest in regulating

its own affairs. In determining if a regulation is invalid, the court will consider whether a less burdensome alternative is available. Since Amityville could presumably inspect the incoming meat when it arrived at a local destination, its ordinance is probably unreasonable; *Dean Milk Co. v. City of Madison*, 340 U.S. 349 (1951). (*See* ELO Ch.6-I(G)(3)(a)(i).) Choice **A** is incorrect because no clearly improper classification is drawn by the statute. It applies to everyone bring meat into Amityville. Of course, a local entity is not authorized to assert its authority beyond state lines. Choice **C** is incorrect because the dormant Commerce Clause is not satisfied by a mere showing of a rational relationship to a legitimate governmental objective. Finally, Choice **D** is incorrect because it is a statement of an obvious truth which is immaterial to the issue at hand; the fact that citizens are presumed to know the law does not mean that they have to accept a law which is constitutional.

61. **D**   While streets are a traditional public forum, speech on streets can be circumscribed if the regulation is: (1) content neutral, (2) narrowly tailored to satisfy a significant governmental interest, and (3) leaves open alternative channels for communication. The inconvenience caused by traffic on two occasions is probably an insufficient governmental interest. Also, the means chosen here are not "narrowly tailored." Presumably, the parades or demonstrations could be permitted at times other than peak traffic periods (i.e., in the early afternoon, on Sundays, etc.). A complete exclusion from the two most public areas is probably too broad. (*See* ELO Ch.14-VI(M)(2)(d).) Choice **C** is incorrect, since some speech activity in streets can be restricted (although the limitations must be narrowly tailored). Choice **A** is incorrect because, as discussed above, although the statute is content neutral, it imposes unreasonable restrictions on the exercise of speech in a public place. Finally, Choice **B** is incorrect because, as discussed above, the restrictions are too broad.

62. **A**   A statute which attempts to control speech but which is overly broad *on its face* cannot serve as the basis for criminal prosecution. Since the determination whether to issue a waiver of the 20-person limitation is left to the sole discretion of the Police Commissioner pursuant to a vague standard of application ("not...detrimental to the overall community"), the Amityville statute is overly broad and therefore unconstitutional on its face. Thus, it cannot be utilized to prosecute Tricia. (*See* ELO Ch.14-III(A).) Choice **B** is incorrect because speech activities in traditional public forums can be circumscribed, provided the restrictions are narrowly tailored and promote a significant governmental objective. Choice **C** is incorrect because a defendant charged with commission of a crime is not obliged to seek a declaratory judgment but may challenge the statute in her direct defense. Choice **D** is incorrect because the procedure under which a waiver could be obtained was itself overly broad and left to the sole discretion of the Police Commissioner.

63. **D**   Federal judges hold their offices during good behavior and are protected from diminution of salary. Pursuant to Article I, Congress may establish administrative courts for the purpose of adjudicating "public rights" or "obligations" with respect to the U.S. Government (rather than amongst

private parties). The tenure and salary of judges of administrative tribunals is dependent upon the legislation which established the tribunal. Since Hobson's position was not established pursuant to Article III of the U.S. Constitution, Hobson is not entitled to hold office during good behavior and avoid any diminution in salary. Choice **A** is incorrect because administrative agencies are established by Congress pursuant to Article I of the U.S. Constitution. Thus, while the independence of the federal judiciary is constitutionally guaranteed by Article III, Hobson was **not** a member of that group. Choice **B** is incorrect because property rights to governmental employment must arise from a source independent of the U.S. Constitution (i.e., rules or understandings indicating that employment would not be withdrawn). Since the facts fail to indicate that any such rules or understandings existed, Hobson could not claim a "property" right to continuation of his position. Finally, Choice **C** is incorrect because Hobson did suffer a direct and immediate injury as a consequence of Congress' action. The law does not, however, permit recovery by Hobson in this instance.

64. **D**   States are not, without the consent of Congress, allowed to tax imports or exports, except where necessary for reimbursement with respect to the execution of its inspection laws; Article I, Section 10 (Clause 2). Since the goods in question were not "in transit", they were subject to a non-discriminatory *ad valorem* tax; *Michelin Tire Corp. v. Wages, Tax Commissioner*, 423 U.S. 276 (1976). Choice **C** is incorrect because, if the tax were necessary to reimburse State Orange for its inspection of imported items, it would be valid. Choice **B** is incorrect because the vases had lost their character as imports (i.e., they had been purchased by Bosco and would be held, indefinitely, until a purchaser for them was found). Finally, Choice **A** is incorrect because the fact that the vases were sold that year does not preclude an *ad valorem* tax on items owned by, and in, Bosco's possession on the date (July 31) that the tax was applied.

65. **C**   Under the due process and commerce clauses, a state may **not** ordinarily impose a sales tax on the out-of-state seller of an item where the transaction is consummated outside of that jurisdiction; *McCleod v. J.E. Dilworth Co.*, 322 U.S. 327 (1944). Although the transaction was arguably initiated in State Blue, it was subject to Bosco's acceptance. This did not occur until the contract was reviewed and re-negotiated by Bosco in State Orange. Thus, the transaction was consummated in State Orange and only that jurisdiction could assess a **sales** tax. Choice **D** is incorrect because, as discussed in the answer to the preceding question, the vases were not "in transit" when delivered to Bosco. Choices **A** and **B** are incorrect because the transaction was consummated in State Orange and Bosco has no meaningful contacts with State Blue. Thus, both the commerce and due process clauses would preclude the levy of a sales tax on Bosco by State Blue. State Blue might, however, be able to impose a 3% **use** tax upon Rudy with respect to the vases.

66. **C**   Any activity (even though primarily intrastate) which, in the aggregate, could have a significant impact upon the movement of persons, information or items across state lines is regulable under the commerce clause. While

the wheat in question was specifically grown for home consumption, this activity (in the aggregate) arguably has a negative impact upon the movement of wheat across state lines (i.e., there would be a decreased need for persons in that jurisdiction to purchase out-of-state wheat). (*See* ELO Ch.6-I(F).) Choice **A** is incorrect because the fact that an activity is performed intrastate does not preclude it from having a significant impact upon interstate commerce. Choice **B** is incorrect because the fact that a local activity has only an indirect effect upon interstate commerce does not detract from the applicability of the interstate commerce clause (as long as the activity has, in the aggregate, a significant effect upon interstate commerce). Finally, Choice **D** is incorrect because the wheat in question has not been shipped or transported across state lines.

67. **B**   Congress has the power to assess and collect taxes for the general welfare (but may not assess and collect taxes, however, to accomplish a regulatory purpose). The fact that the state in which Weedy is located also taxes the particular wheat involved has no relevance in determining the constitutionality of the federal statute. (*See* ELO Ch.3-I(B)(1)(a)(i).) Choice **A** is incorrect because the fact that the tax is collected by the Department of Agriculture (as opposed to the Treasury Department) arguably indicates that the tax has a regulatory purpose. Choice **C** is incorrect because the fact that a tax has the obvious effect of greatly enhancing the cost of an item tends to show that the purpose of the enactment was primarily regulatory in nature. Finally, Choice **D** is incorrect because it indicates that the income producing portion of the statute was aimed at benefiting a particular entity (rather than the general welfare).

68. **D**   States may not ordinarily impair obligations created by outstanding contracts; Article I, Section 10. An impairment of contractual obligations between a state and a private entity is constitutional only if it is reasonable and necessary to accomplish an important public purpose; *U.S. Trust Co. v. New Jersey*, 431 U.S. 1 (1977). Pursuant to the Tenth Amendment, a state may legislate for the safety, health and general welfare of its citizens. The contract places no constraints upon the right to sell oysters. The statute, however, precludes sales (1) of all discolored oysters, and (2) to out-of-state purchasers where local buyers are willing to purchase the items. While the legislation's purpose appears to be legitimate (i.e., to prevent injury to the oyster market), the legislature's fear that a diminishment of the oyster market will occur as a consequence of a slightly bitter taste probably does not constitute a sufficient "necessity" to alter the agreement. (*See* ELO Ch.11-III(B)(2)(b)(i).) Choice **B** is incorrect, because the right to sell all of the oysters harvested was presumably a central part of the agreement. Choice **C** is incorrect because the impairment of contracts clause applies to agreements amongst private entities. Finally, Choice **A** is factually incorrect because the legislation has not affected "all" of Fisheries' rights. It may still farm the oyster beds and sell non-discolored items to (1) local entities for any price, and (2) out-of-state buyers if local entities are unwilling to meet the price to be paid by the former group.

69. **D** Under the Fourteenth Amendment, states may not appropriate private property for public use without providing just compensation to the owner. Since (1) no physical property of Fisheries has been appropriated by State X, and (2) the statute in question is arguably a regulation aimed at protecting the general public (the economy of State X), it is unlikely that a "taking" would be deemed to have occurred in this instance. (*See* ELO Ch.11-II(B)(3).) Choice **A** is incorrect because, while the items in question are not physically harmful, a general economic harm to the public welfare could result if out-of-state purchasers cease buying State X oysters. Choice **B** is incorrect because public welfare legislation which incidentally affects property interests does not result in a "taking" under the Fourteenth Amendment; *Goldblatt v. Hempstead*, 369 U.S. 590 (1962). Finally, Choice **C** is incorrect because the entire State X citizenry would arguably be financially injured if there was a significant decline in the demand for oysters originating in that state.

70. **A** Where a state law discriminates against interstate commerce in favor of local interests, the state must justify the legislation by showing an overriding local benefit and the absence of any non-discriminatory alternatives; *Hughes v. Oklahoma*, 441 U.S. 322 (1979). While the preservation of an important local source of income is a legitimate state purpose, that interest could arguably be protected by requiring (1) a warning to out-of-state purchasers that the particular oysters being sold might have a slightly bitter taste, or (2) potential buyers to sample the product, so that a decision could be made if their customers would be satisfied with the item. (*See* ELO Ch.6-I(J)(3)(b).) Choice **B** is incorrect because out-of-state buyers are being discriminated against (i.e., they can only purchase oysters if local buyers are unwilling to do so on similar terms). Choice **C** is incorrect because, while legitimate state interests are being served (the protection of the local economy), no overriding purpose is served in that the absence of oysters from local restaurants would probably not justify the second class status conferred upon out-of-state purchasers; *City of Philadelphia v. New Jersey*, 437 U.S. 617 (1978). Finally, Choice **D** is incorrect because there is no *per se* right of states to protect natural resources. Where legislation places out-of-state commerce at a disadvantage, the state must show that a substantial benefit will be derived and there is no non-discriminatory means of achieving that goal.

71. **B** A statute is unduly vague (and therefore invalid) when a person of ordinary intelligence would be unable to determine if the actions which he is contemplating are proscribed. A statute is overly broad on its face (and therefore invalid) when the governmental entity empowered to enforce the law has virtually unlimited discretion in its determination of whether the law has been violated. Since the applicable statute appears to vest total discretion in the town licensing committee (i.e., no guidelines are provided with respect to the circumstances or conditions pursuant to which a license is to be granted), the statute is probably overly broad. (*See* ELO Ch.14-III(A), (B) and IV(E)(2).) Choice **A** is incorrect because the statute is ***not*** ambiguous (i.e., it clearly states that a permit must be obtained from the licensing commission). Choice **C** is incorrect because the statute in ques-

tion is overly broad, but not constitutionally infirm due to vagueness. Finally, Choice **D** is incorrect because the statute is overly broad.

72. **B** A statute which is overly broad on its face cannot ordinarily serve as the basis for governmental action; *Lovell v. Griffin*, 303 U.S. 444 (1938). Since the statute appears to be overly broad on its face, the U.S. Supreme Court would reverse the misdemeanor conviction of SSL members. (*See* ELO Ch.14-III(A).) Choice **A** is incorrect because the statute was *not* valid on its face (i.e., absolutely no standards pursuant to which a determination as to whether a license should be granted have been provided). Choice **C** is incorrect because, the statute being invalid on its face, SSL members were *not* required to seek redress through appropriate judicial channels. Finally, Choice **D** is incorrect because a statute which is overly broad *on its face* may not ordinarily serve as the basis for governmental action.

73. **C** Where persons violating a statute which is facially overbroad should have anticipated a constitutionally curative construction, the law may serve as the basis for a criminal conviction; *Shuttlesworth v. Birmingham*, 394 U.S. 147 (1969). If the SSL members who were convicted had reason to believe that a proper narrowing construction of the statute in question would be made by the Dixie Supreme Court, their conviction should be affirmed. (*See* ELO Ch.14-IV(E)(5)(c).) Choice **B** is incorrect because, if the statute in question was *not* facially overbroad (i.e., it was merely overly broad as applied), it could serve as the basis for a criminal prosecution (unless it was unconstitutionally applied). In such instance, the party affected by the statute would be obliged to seek redress through proper judicial channels. Choice **A** is incorrect because, despite the subsequent curative interpretation by the Dixie Supreme court, a statute which is facially overbroad cannot serve as the basis for a criminal prosecution (assuming the defendants had no reason to anticipate a curative construction). Finally, Choice **D** is incorrect because it is not necessary to obtain a judicial determination of the unconstitutionality of a facially overbroad statute prior to disobeying the enactment.

74. **B** Unless patently void on its face (i.e., issued by a court which lacked subject matter jurisdiction), a contempt conviction for disobeying a *judicial* order is ordinarily valid (even if such order was improperly issued); *Walker v. City of Birmingham*, 388 U.S. 307 (1967). However, where, for the purpose of frustrating the defendant's First Amendment rights, an injunction is not sought until the last possible moment, a conviction for failing to obey the injunction might be unconstitutional. The fact that the permit was unconstitutionally denied would be irrelevant, since the contempt of court conviction is predicated upon the defendants' refusal to abide by a court order (not the violation of the licensing ordinance). Even if the licensing ordinance was invalid, adherence to the court order would still ordinarily be required. (*See* ELO Ch.14-IV(E)(5)(d).) Choice **C** is relevant because, if the court clearly lacked subject matter jurisdiction, its order could be disregarded. Choice **D** is relevant because a court order (even if erroneously issued) must ordinarily be challenged by appeal. It ordinarily *cannot* simply be disregarded with impunity. Finally, Choice **A** is relevant because, if the commission deliberately waited until the last moment to obtain an

injunction against the march (i.e., the SSL announced that it would proceed with its march despite the absence of a license on June 27, yet an injunction was not sought until July 3), a conviction for disregarding the injunction might not withstand constitutional scrutiny.

75. **B** There is no First Amendment right to express one's views on another's private property; *Hudgens v. National Labor Relations Board*, 424 U.S. 507 (1976). States may, however, require a private property owner to permit others to express their views on commercial private property, provided such expression poses no threat of actual and substantial disruption to the activities ordinarily conducted on such private property and does not result in a deprivation of the landowner's due process rights; *Pruneyard Shopping Center v. Robins*, 447 U.S. 74 (1980). State action was not involved in the earlier lawsuit (*Ray v. Orwell*). In that case, a private shopping center owner had ejected the plaintiff from the grounds. Thus, a claim based upon the U.S. Constitution did not exist. (*See* ELO Ch.14-IV(N)(3)(c).) Choice **A** is factually incorrect because there was an actual interference with Ray's exercise of his purported right of free speech (i.e., he had been ejected from the shopping center). Choice **C** is incorrect because it is not necessary that a criminal prosecution be imminent for the "actual controversy" requisite of federal court jurisdiction to be operative. This condition is satisfied by an actual, outstanding dispute. Finally, Choice **D** is legally incorrect because sign-carrying is a protected form of First Amendment protection.

76. **D** A decision may be appealed as a right to the U.S. Supreme Court where (1) a state court has held a federal statute or treaty invalid, (2) a state court has upheld a state statute against the claim that it is (a) unconstitutional, or (b) invalid under the supremacy clause, or (3) a federal court of appeal has held a state statute (a) unconstitutional, or (b) contrary to a federal statute or treaty. A petition for certiorari (a discretionary form of review) may be granted where a (1) State Court has held a state statute (a) unconstitutional, or (b) contrary to a federal statute or treaty, or (2) Federal Court of Appeal has decided a novel, but significant, federal question (a claim arising under the Constitution, a federal statute, or a U.S. treaty), and there is no appeal as of right. The denial of Orwell's petition for certiorari indicates only that three members of the U.S. Supreme Court believed that the lower court opinion should be reviewed. (*See* ELO Ch.2-IV(B)(1)(a).) Choice **A** is incorrect because a refusal to grant certiorari has no precedential value, whatsoever. Choice **B** is incorrect because the mere fact that a justice votes to grant certiorari does not necessarily indicate that he believed the lower court was incorrect. Rather, it suggests only that the justice believed the lower court decision should be reviewed by the U.S. Supreme Court. Finally, Choice **C** is incorrect because a refusal to grant certiorari indicates only that the members of the court voting against the petition did ***not*** believe that the action merited review by the U.S. Supreme Court at that time. A refusal to grant certiorari is not indicative of any opinion with respect to the case's merits.

77. **C** Under the due process and commerce clauses, a state may ***not*** ordinarily impose a sales tax on the out-of-state seller of an item where the transaction is consummated outside of that jurisdiction; *McCleod v. J.E. Dilworth*

Co., 322 U.S. 327 (1944). A use tax may be imposed upon the purchaser/user of an item where the good will be used within the state assessing the tax. A use tax may not, however, exceed the difference between (a) the sales tax imposed on such items by the state in which the good will be utilized, and (b) any sales tax assessed against the seller by the state in which the sale was consummated; *Henneford v. Silas Mason Co.*, 300 U.S. 577 (1937). Since the transaction was consummated in Nevada, California cannot impose a sales tax on it. However, California can impose a use tax upon the buyer if the item will be utilized in that state. (*See* ELO Ch.6-I(I)(4).) Thus, Choices **A**, **B** and **D** are incorrect.

78. **B**   Under the due process clause, a state may require an out-of-state seller to collect a use tax pertaining to the purchase of an item by a resident of the taxing state, if the seller physically entered the state in which the buyer is located to solicit the orders in question; *Nelson v. Sears Roebuck & Co.*, 312 U.S. 359 (1941). Since salesmen of the Nevada entity actually entered California to solicit orders for the goods in question, contacts consistent with due process would exist to require the Nevada seller to collect the use tax for California on the item. (*See* ELO Ch.6-I(I)(4).) Choice **A** is incorrect because a sales tax cannot be assessed against the Nevada seller (i.e., the sale was completed in Nevada and the vendor has no permanent employees or agents in California). Choice **C** is incorrect because contacts necessary to satisfy due process do exist by reason of the fact that the order was actually solicited by the vendor's sales personnel in California. (Note, however, that if the purchase had been solicited by telephone or the mail, contacts necessary to satisfy due process would *not* exist; *National Bellas Hess, Inc. v. Illinois Department of Revenue*, 386 U.S. 753 (1967)). Finally, Choice **D** is legally incorrect (a use tax may, in appropriate circumstances, be collected directly from the seller).

79. **C**   A statute is unconstitutionally vague when a person of ordinary intelligence would, even with actual knowledge of the law in question, be uncertain as to whether contemplated conduct was proscribed or not. Expression which is made by the speaker with the intention or likelihood of provoking a violent response (i.e., "fighting words") is punishable pursuant to a properly drawn statute; *Chaplinsky v. New Hampshire*, 315 U.S. 568 (1942). While "fighting words" may be punished, the statute in question is probably too vague (i.e., the words "annoying," "disturbing" and "unwelcome" are too subjective in nature for an average person to determine if particular language is punishable or not). (*See* ELO Ch.14-III(B) & IV(H).) Choice **B** is incorrect because the use of "fighting words" is constitutionally punishable. Choice **A** is incorrect because the statute, as presently drawn, is probably too vague to be the basis of a criminal conviction. Finally, Choice **D** is factually incorrect (i.e., the average person would probably be offended by Smith's language).

80. **A**   Congress is prohibited from passing a bill of attainder (i.e., a law which inflicts punishment upon particular individuals or an identifiable group of persons without a trial); Article I, Section 9. The law in question punishes persons who are members of the Communist Party, simply because such individuals are members of that group; *United States v. Brown*, 381 U.S.

437 (1965). There is no requirement that such persons have the specific intent to further the illegal objectives of that organization. (*See* ELO Ch.11-V(C)(1).) Choice **B** is incorrect because a definable class of individuals is within the proscription of a bill of attainder. Choice **C** is incorrect because, while Congress may have intended to protect the national economy, its classification is too over-inclusive (i.e., the effect of the statute would be to punish persons who did not specifically intend to overthrow the government by illegal means). Finally, Choice **D** is incorrect because Congress may not enact a law which is in conflict with the U.S. Constitution.

81. **A** In the absence of an asserted need to protect military, diplomatic or national security secrets, in criminal cases the privilege pertaining to executive communications is qualified in nature; *U.S. v. Nixon*, 418 U.S. 683 (1974). The executive privilege is ordinarily qualified in nature (i.e., a court, in camera, must weigh the interest being protected against the need for the information which is sought). In the above cited case, the U.S. Supreme Court held that the importance of a pending criminal proceeding outweighed a general claim of executive privilege. (*See* ELO Ch.8-IV(D)(2)(c).) Choice **B** is incorrect because there might be situations where communications would be deemed to be privileged (i.e., they related to a matter of national security), even though the information was sought for a criminal proceeding. Choice **C** is incorrect because there is at least a qualified presidential privilege pertaining to information sought in a criminal trial. Finally, Choice **D** is legally incorrect (i.e., the presidential privilege is qualified, rather than absolute, in nature).

82. **C** Under due process, personal property which is used in interstate commerce may be taxed by the jurisdiction which constitutes the taxpayer's principal place of business and by states in which the items have a taxable situs. Since Flyright's airplanes land in Virginia on a regular basis (about 20 times per day), that jurisdiction can probably place a personal property tax upon the taxpayer's flight equipment; *Braniff Airways v. Nebraska Board of Equalization*, 347 U.S. 590 (1954). While goods within the stream of interstate commerce may not ordinarily be taxed by a state, that rule does not apply to equipment which is regularly utilized in the transportation process. It should be noted, however, that New York and Virginia would be obliged to apportion the aggregate personal property tax upon Flyright's aircraft in an equitable manner. (*See* ELO Ch.6-II(C).) Choices **A**, **B** and **D** are incorrect because ***both*** Virginia and New York may assess a personal property tax against Flyright's airplanes.

83. **B** Where a State Court has invalidated a state statute based upon the ground that it is in conflict with a Federal Law, review by the U.S. Supreme Court can be accomplished only by a writ of certiorari. Since the State X Supreme Court struck down the local ordinance upon the ground that it conflicted with a federal law, review could be obtained only by a favorable response to a petition for writ of certiorari. (*See* ELO Ch.2-IV(B)(1)(a).) Choice **D** is incorrect because a federal issue still exists (i.e., is the State X statute unconstitutional under the Supremacy Clause?). Choice **A** is incorrect because (under the given facts) the State X Supreme Court premised its decision upon the Supremacy Clause. Finally, Choice **C** is incorrect because

the abstention doctrine is primarily applicable to situations where the language contained in a state law might be cured by a narrowing interpretation rendered by a state court. In such event, the constitutional issue would be precluded. In this instance, however, (1) there is nothing vague about the state statute in question, and (2) the constitutional issue has already been decided by a state court. Thus, the abstention doctrine is inapplicable.

84.   **C**   A constitutional issue which would otherwise be rendered moot will ordinarily be heard when it is capable of repetition, yet evading review; *Roe v. Wade*, 410 U.S. 113 (1973). Since other persons might not learn about the SAT requirement until it was too late to take the examination, the constitutional question could continually evade review. (*See* ELO Ch.16-IV(B)(1).) Choice **A** is incorrect because the constitutional issue involved in this instance could continuously recur, if not settled at this time. Choice **D** is factually incorrect (a First Amendment claim has not been asserted by Malcolm). Additionally, case law has not given First Amendment concerns any special consideration with respect to the mootness doctrine. Finally, Choice **B** is incorrect because, while Malcolm could take the SAT examination in time for the next election, there is a possibility that he might subsequently decide to not run for mayor. In such event, the SAT requirement might avoid constitutional scrutiny until it was utilized again by State X to prevent someone else from running for public office. Thus, the mootness doctrine would probably ***not*** be applied in this instance.

85.   **D**   Congress has been empowered to enforce the provisions of the Thirteenth and Fourteenth Amendments by appropriate legislation; Thirteenth Amendment, Section 2, and Fourteenth Amendment, Section 5. Since Congress could have reasonably determined that filing fees and/or literacy tests promote racial discrimination or deny persons equal protection, the federal statute is valid. As a consequence, state legislation which is in conflict with the federal law would be unconstitutional under the Supremacy Clause. (*See* ELO Ch.6-III(B).) Choice **C** is incorrect because the federal statute did not invalidate residency requirements. As a consequence, ***all*** of the provisions of the State X law would not be unconstitutional. Choice **A** is incorrect because the Tenth Amendment only reserves to the states those powers which have not been specifically delegated to the federal government. Finally, Choice **B** is incorrect because application of the Supremacy Clause is not dependent upon the federal statute being in existence ***prior*** to any state law.

86.   **A**   A statute which is unconstitutionally vague cannot serve as the basis of governmental action. If the statute was unconstitutionally vague (i.e., a person of ordinary intelligence could not determine whether contemplated conduct was proscribed), the provision in question would be stricken from the enactment. (*See* ELO Ch.14-III(B).) Choice **B** is incorrect because, while there is no constitutionally guaranteed right to tuition assistance, unconstitutional laws cannot be utilized to affect an existing governmental benefit. Choice **C** is incorrect because statutes which are unconstitutionally vague on their face cannot serve as the basis for governmental action. Finally, Choice **D** is incorrect because the fact that a law is rationally related to a legitimate governmental purpose (i.e., in this instance, protec-

tion of the national government) does not insulate it from attack on constitutional grounds.

87. **B**   A governmental limitation upon symbolic speech (conduct which is intended to communicate a message, and which the viewing audience would understand as such) is permissible if (1) it furthers a substantial interest, (2) it is unrelated to the content of the expression, and (3) the restriction upon First Amendment activity is closely tailored to satisfy the governmental objective; *United States v. O'Brien*, 391 U.S. 367 (1968). In this instance, (1) the conduct in question is related to the content of the speech (i.e., activity detrimental to the federal government), and (2) there probably is no substantial governmental interest in precluding demonstrations critical of recruitment by the C.I.A. on a college campus. Therefore, withdrawal of the scholarship as a result of Arthur's participation in the demonstration is probably invalid. (*See* ELO Ch.14-V(A)(3).) Choice **A** is incorrect because even peaceful demonstrations are subject to reasonable limitations pertaining to time, place and manner. Thus, under proper circumstances, such demonstrations can be the basis of civil or criminal sanctions. Choice **C** is incorrect because the actions of State X University, being a state institution, would constitute governmental action. Finally, Choice **D** is incorrect because constitutionally valid conduct (i.e., in this instance, engaging in an activity protected by the First Amendment) cannot serve as the basis for adverse governmental action.

88. **C**   State legislation pertaining to the health, morals or welfare of its citizens is usually valid if rationally related to a legitimate governmental objective. Joe could contend that the State X statute is irrational because (1) State X residents can obtain scholarships for out-of-state study if Geology courses are taken in another jurisdiction, but (2) no scholarship is extended to State X residents desiring to attend college outside of the jurisdiction for any other reason. If the purpose of the statute was to ease the economic burden upon State X residents who desire to attend college, it is irrational to discriminate against them on the basis of where the institution is located or their course of study. However, the State X statute is rationally related to a valid governmental purpose (i.e., to assist State X residents in obtaining an education). The fact that the State X legislature has chosen not to extend this benefit to residents who choose to attend an out-of-state university would probably ***not*** cause the act to be constitutionally impermissible. The State X legislature might have legitimately decided to assist students who study at colleges in State X because those persons undoubtedly purchase more local products (i.e., food, books, etc.) than persons attending out-of-state universities. An exception for Geology majors might be rationally based upon the determination that persons with a background in that area would benefit the State X economy in a special manner. (*See* ELO Ch.10-II(A)(1).) Choice **A** is incorrect because no significant limitation has been imposed upon Joe's Fourteenth Amendment right to travel (he is merely being denied a particular potential benefit if he elects to attend college in another state). Choice **D** is incorrect because the privileges and immunities clause of Article IV, Section 2, precludes a state from discriminating against the citizens of other jurisdictions. In this instance, State X is merely refusing to extend a particular benefit to one of its own

residents. Finally, Choice **B** is incorrect because, as discussed above, the classifications drawn by the statute are not irrational.

89. **D** State legislation pertaining to the health, morals or welfare of its citizens is usually valid if rationally related to a legitimate governmental objective. The State X legislature could have rationally determined that a specified SAT score was necessary to qualify for scholarship (i.e., those persons who have a greater probability of completing their college education successfully). (*See* ELO Ch.10-II(A)(1).) Choice **A** is incorrect because the privileges and immunities clause of the Fourteenth Amendment precludes a state from discriminating against out-of-state residents with respect to "fundamental" or "important" rights. It does not prevent a jurisdiction from denying privileges to its own citizens if certain pre-conditions are not satisfied. Choice **B** is incorrect because there is no fundamental right to a college education. Finally, Choice **C** is incorrect because, as discussed above, there is a rational basis for requiring a minimum SAT score to obtain a scholarship.

90. **D** Where a fundamental or basic right is involved, statutes must satisfy the strict scrutiny test (i.e., there must be a compelling state interest and no less burdensome means of accomplishing that objective). It has been held that the right to marry and divorce occupies a fundamental position in our society. Thus, a similar statute was determined to be invalid under the due process clause of the Fourteenth Amendment in *Boddie v. Connecticut*, 401 U.S. 371 (1971). The state's desire to defray a part of the expense inherent in the divorce procedure did not rise to the level of a "compelling" interest. (*See* ELO Ch.10-X(D)(9)(a).) Choice **B** is incorrect because the strict scrutiny test, albeit applicable, is **not** met in this instance. Choice **A** is incorrect because (1) the strict scrutiny test would be applicable to a situation involving marital status, and (2) the requisite "compelling" state interest is **not** satisfied. Finally, Choice **C** is incorrect because, although the discrimination resulting from the statute is *de facto* (rather than *de jure*) in nature, this fact alone would not save the law from being unconstitutional upon due process grounds.

91. **C** Under the equal protection clause, classifications which are purposefully based upon gender must (1) serve an important governmental interest, and (2) be substantially related to the achievement of those interests. It replicates the applicable principle of law; *Craig v. Boren*, 429 U.S. 190 (1976). (*See* ELO Ch.10-V(C)(3).) Choice **A** is incorrect because, while laws are ordinarily presumed to be valid, middle level scrutiny is applied to statutes which facially embody gender based classifications. Choice **B** is incorrect because the state interest must merely be "important" (rather than "compelling"). Finally, Choice **D** is incorrect because even legislation which is favorable to women must satisfy middle level scrutiny; *Mississippi University for Women v. Hogan*, 458 U.S. 718 (1982). It might be noted that where the legislation favoring a particular gender is basically remedial in nature (i.e., it attempts to correct prior deliberate unfavorable treatment), it is likely to be upheld; *Califano v. Webster*, 430 U.S. 313 (1977).

92. **D** *Congressional* laws pertaining to aliens are ordinarily reviewed under the rational relationship standard (i.e., the legislation must be rationally related to a legitimate governmental objective); *Mathews v. Diaz*, 426 U.S. 67 (1976). Since the act in question has been passed by Congress (rather than a state legislature), it is *not* subject to a strict scrutiny analysis. Therefore, a law which prefers U.S. citizens over aliens with respect to welfare monies is probably constitutional (for the reason set forth in Choice D). (*See* ELO Ch.10-VI(D).) Choice **A** is incorrect because no equal protection clause is applicable to the federal government (i.e., the Fifth Amendment refers only to due process). Choice **B** is incorrect because there is no case law establishing welfare as a fundamental right; *Dandridge v. Williams*, 397 U.S. 471 (1970). Finally, Choice **C** is incorrect because aliens do have due process rights (i.e., the Fifth Amendment applies to all "persons" within the U.S.). However, the statute in question is valid because citizens of the U.S. may probably be preferred over non-citizens with respect to the receipt of federal monies.

93. **B** Where the plaintiff in a defamation action is a public figure, he must prove that the defendant's statements were (1) false, and (2) made with actual malice (i.e., knowing the statements were incorrect or under circumstances which should have caused the defendant to entertain a serious doubt as to their accuracy). One is a public figure when he voluntarily interjects himself into a public controversy; *Gertz v. Robert Welch, Inc.*, 418 U.S. 323 (1984). Since Smith is probably a "public figure" by reason of his decision to run for a seat in the state senate, he would have to prove that the newspaper's statement was (1) false, and (2) made with actual malice. (*See* ELO Ch.14-VI(C).) Choice **A** is legally incorrect (there is no *absolute* privilege pertaining to mass media entities). Choice **C** is incorrect because, where the plaintiff is a public figure, he must prove that the defendant's statement was made with actual malice. Finally, Choice **D** is incorrect because the plaintiff, as a public figure, must prove that *The Daily Times* acted with actual malice (not simply unreasonably). Also note that the U.S. Supreme Court has stated that where the (1) plaintiff is *not* a public figure, and (2) defendant is a mass media entity, the latter must have acted at least negligently under the circumstances for a defamation action to be successfully asserted; *Gertz, supra*.

94. **A** Under the equal protection clause, classifications which are purposefully based upon gender must (1) serve an important governmental interest, and (2) be substantially related to the achievement of those interests. Since the facts fail to indicate that the State X legislature intentionally sought to discriminate against women, the Act would be upheld as long as the "rational basis" test was satisfied. (*See* ELO Ch.10-V(C)(3).) Choices **B** and **C** are incorrect because they embody more difficult standards than are necessary to validate the State X law. Finally, Choice **D** is incorrect because a showing by the plaintiffs that the legislature intended to discriminate against women is *not* a requisite for validation of the Act. In fact, if such a situation were proven the Act would be more susceptible to attack, since an intermediate level of review would be applicable.

95. **C** Obscene material may be proscribed by a state, even though it is viewed by consenting adults only. In *Paris Adult Theatre I v. Slaton*, 413 U.S. 49 (1973), the U.S. Supreme Court specifically held that obscene materials exhibited only to consenting adults could be regulated. Thus, evidence that minors or non-consenting adults were purposefully excluded from Doug's theatre would be irrelevant. (*See* ELO Ch.14-III(B)(5).) Choice **A** is incorrect because *California v. La Rue*, 409 U.S. 109 (1972), held that states have broad power under the Twenty-First Amendment to prohibit sexually-oriented entertainment in establishments where alcoholic beverages are being sold. It therefore has little pertinence to the evidence excluded by the trial court in this instance. Choice **D** is incorrect because *Ernoznik v. City of Jacksonville*, 422 U.S. 205 (1975), held only that an ordinance prohibiting drive-in movies from showing pictures with nude scenes which were not constitutionally obscene was invalid. Finally, Choice **B** is incorrect because *Stanley v. Georgia*, 394 U.S. 557 (1969), recognized the right to possess obscene material for personal use only. Mailing or importing obscene materials, even for personal use, can be constitutionally constrained; *U.S. v. Reidel*, 402 U.S. 351 (1971); *U.S. v. Twelve 200-Foot Reels*, 413 U.S. 123 (1973), respectively.

96. **C** The mailing of obscene material may be regulated. The *Stanley* case recognized only the right to possess obscene material in one's home for personal use. Mailing or importing obscene materials, even for the recipient's personal use, can be constitutionally constrained; *U.S. v. Twelve 200-Foot Reels*, 413 U.S. 123 (1973). (*See* ELO Ch.14-VII(C)(4)(b).) Choice **D** is incorrect because the *Stanley* case did **not** pertain to the **commercial** sale of obscene material. Choice **A** is incorrect because the *Reidel* case constitutes a basis for upholding, rather than reversing, the trial court's decision. Finally, Choice **B** is incorrect because the *Stanley* decision did **not** recognize a right to possess obscene materials in one's home "for any reason" (i.e., commercial distribution).

97. **C** The Eleventh Amendment bars non-consented to lawsuits in Federal Court by a citizen against a state which could result in a retroactive charge against the general revenues of that jurisdiction; *Edelman v. Jordan*, 415 U.S. 651 (1974). Although the Eleventh Amendment explicitly pertains only to suits by citizens of a state against a different state, the bar contained in this provision has been judicially extended to suits by citizens of a state against their own jurisdiction; *Hans v. Louisiana*, 134 U.S. 1 (1889). (*See* ELO Ch.16-VI(A)(5).) Choices A and B are incorrect because the Eleventh Amendment does not preclude suits against individuals (personally) or subdivisions (i.e., counties, cities, school board, etc.) of a state. Finally, Choice **D** is incorrect because the Eleventh Amendment does not preclude injunctive suits against state officials to require them to act in accordance (1) with a federal law, or (2) in a constitutional manner; *Ex parte Young*, 209 U.S. 123 (1908). It should be noted, however, that if a federal law or the U.S. Constitution were not the basis of the plaintiff's claim, the Eleventh Amendment would preclude a suit for even injunctive relief in federal court; *Pennhurst State School & Hospital v. Halderman*, 104 S.Ct. 900 (1984).

98. **C** A plaintiff must be able to show a direct and immediate personal injury or loss as a consequence of the defendant's action to have standing in a Federal Court. Since Jane has been denied employment at the ABC Company, she has suffered a direct injury as a consequence of the allegedly unconstitutional law. (*See* ELO Ch.16-III(C)(1).) Choice **D** is incorrect because, even if she could obtain similar employment nearby, she has still sustained an immediate injury by being refused employment at the ABC Company. The fact that a plaintiff's injury can be mitigated does not detract from the fact that injury has occurred. Choice **A** is incorrect because the fact that the ABC Company is not being prosecuted has no bearing upon the fact that Jane has been wronged. Finally, Choice **B** is incorrect because Jane suffered a direct injury by reason of the denial of employment at the ABC Company.

99. **B** Under the equal protection clause, classifications which are purposefully based upon gender must (1) serve an important governmental interest, and (2) be substantially related to the achievement of those interests. Since the classification is deliberately gender based, State Yellow must prove that the legislation is substantially related to an important governmental objective. It is unlikely that the desire to reduce absenteeism at night jobs would constitute a sufficiently "important" state interest. It is also unlikely that the statute is narrowly drawn (i.e., only women with young children should be proscribed from working during the evening). (*See* ELO Ch.10-V(C)(3).) Choice **A** is incorrect because, where a purposeful gender based classification exists, a state must prove more than a mere rational basis for the enactment. Choice **C** is incorrect because there is no case law supporting the proposition that women are a suspect classification. Finally, Choice **D** is incorrect because, while factually true (i.e., there is no fundamental right to obtain a particular type of employment), the legislation in question probably does ***not*** satisfy the middle level scrutiny to which it would be held.

100. **B** There is no First Amendment right of access to the print media; *Miami Herald Pub. Co. v. Tornillo*, 418 U.S. 241 (1974). In the above cited case, the U.S. Supreme Court struck down a state statute which required newspapers to print the replies of political candidates whom it had attacked. (*See* ELO Ch.14-IV(N)(5).) Choice **D** is incorrect because broadcasting entities are required to grant individuals the right to reply to personal attacks and concerned parties the right to reply to the station's political editorials; *Red Lion Broadcasting Co. v. FCC*, 395 U.S. 367 (1969). Choice **C** is incorrect because it wrongly applies the rule for broadcasting entities to newspapers. Finally, Choice **A** is incorrect because newspapers are ***not*** required to give access to opposing points of view.

101. **D** "Fighting words" are a general exception to protected categories of speech and are therefore defined very tightly. The term "fighting words" has been defined as speech which contains words which "by their very utterance...tend to incite an immediate breach of the peace;" However, it is not enough that the words used make the audience angry. *Chaplinsky v. New Hampshire*, 315 U.S. 568 (1942); *Terminiello v. Chicago,* 337 U.S. 1 (1949). In any event, the police have the duty to control the crowd, if they can,

rather than arrest the speaker. Assuming that the words in this question can be construed as fighting words, the police apparently had the physical capability to control the crowd and should have done so instead of arresting Kublinski;" *Cox v. Louisiana*, 379 U.S. 536 (1965). Since 15 police officers could presumably have restrained the four Muslims who advanced towards the podium, Klubinski's arrest was inappropriate. (*See* ELO Ch.14-IV(H)(2)(a).) Choice **C** is incorrect because mere opinion can constitute "fighting words" if the opinions are sufficiently incendiary. Choice **A** is incorrect because whether or not Kuplinki's words were "fighting words", there were enough police on hand to restrain the crowd and they had a duty to do so. Finally, Choice **B** is incorrect because, even if the words were calculated to evoke a violent response, the police had an obligation to restrain the crowd before arresting the speaker.

102. **A**   A statute attempting to control speech is unconstitutionally vague when a reasonable person who becomes aware of its terms would have to guess at its meaning and application and would not know whether his conduct was prohibited or not; *Connally v. General Construction Co.*, 269 U.S. 385 (1926*)*. Additionally, speech may not be prohibited simply because it may be "offensive" to the hearer; the speech must be obscene or classified as "fighting words"; *Cohen v. California*, 403 U.S. 15 (1971). The term "offensive" is too vague to support a criminal prosecution. (*See* ELO Ch.14-III(B) & IV(I)(4).) Choice **B** is incorrect because the decision whether speech is protected or not does not depend on the speaker's opinion as to the truth or falsity of his statements. Choice **C** is incorrect because the fact that a "reasonable" person might be offended is too vague a standard by which to judge speech. Finally, Choice **D** is incorrect because intent to offend is not a standard by which the right to speak is judged; it is too vague.

103. **A**   The U.S. Supreme Court has held that it will not review a state court decision otherwise falling within its appellate jurisdiction, if that decision can be supported by an "independent and adequate" state ground. Since the facts tell us that Bob was successful on his Euphoria constitution arguments, the U.S. Supreme Court review could not alter the outcome of the case even if it considered the Due Process argument. (*See* ELO Ch.2-II(D)(2).) Choice **C** is incorrect because the Supreme Court would not exercise its discretion to grant a writ of certiorari under these circumstances. Choice **D** is incorrect because there is no automatic review when a state court decision involves a federal claim, if the state court's decision can stand on other grounds. Finally, Choice **B** is factually incorrect (there can be U.S. Supreme Court review of a state court decision).

104. **C**   Article III, Section 1, of the U.S. Constitution vests the federal judicial power in the Supreme Court and in "such inferior courts as Congress may from time to time ordain and establish." Section 2 extends federal judicial power to "Controversies.....between Citizens of different States,....and between a State, or the Citizens thereof and foreign States, Citizens or Subjects.". This language has been interpreted to mean that Congress may define and restrict those diversity of citizenship cases which may be heard by lower federal courts; for example, Congress has imposed an amount in controversy floor of $50,000 in diversity cases. Congress has the constitu-

tional power to end federal diversity of citzenship jurisdiction completely. (*See* ELO Ch.2-III(A)(1).) Choice **D** is incorrect because, while factually accurate, it is not as good a basis for validating the statute under analysis as Choice **C**. Choice **A** is incorrect because there is no Equal Protection issue under these facts. The impact of the statute would be felt equally by all citizens. Finally, Choice **B** is incorrect because, while diversity cases are referred to in Article 1, Section 2, the Section has been construed to give Congress the authority to limit diversity cases.

105. **C**   In construing the tax power, we look at the conflict between taxation and regulation. As long as a tax produces reasonable revenue and and is not intended solely as disguised regulation, it is ordinarily valid; Article I, Section 8. Thus, even though the principal purpose of this tax is regulatory in nature, it is constitutional. (*See* ELO Ch.5-I(C)(1).) Choice **D** is incorrect because Congress has no specific power to legislate for the general welfare. Choice **A** is incorrect because a woman's right to undergo breast implants has not been held to be a fundamental privacy right entitled to Due Process protection. Finally, Choice **B** is incorrect because, as discussed above, the fact that the tax had a regulatory purpose does **not** *ipso facto* cause it to be unconstitutional.

106. **A**   Under its power to tax to "provide for the general welfare" (Article I, Section 8 (Clause 1), Congress has the inherent power both to disburse and not to disburse the funds it collects. The legislation in question relies on this inherent power. The legislation utilizes the taxing power to provide the general-welfare benefit of reducing traffic accidents. (*See* ELO Ch.5-I(A)(1).) Choice **C** states an incorrect conclusion; the states did ***not*** cede their authority over highways to the national government by accepting federal grants to finance the construction of their roadways. Choice **D** is incorrect because the advance of federal moneys to the states does not carry with it the broad and unconditional right to regulate state highways. The federal right to regulate derives from the Commerce Clause. Finally, Choice **B** is incorrect because surveys do not constitute a constitutionally recognized basis to support federal (or state) legislation.

107. **C**   Any activity (even though primarily intrastate) which, in the aggregate, could have a significant impact upon the movement of persons, information or items across state lines is regulable under the Commerce Clause. A "no drinking while driving" rule would clearly affect interstate commerce (i.e., the reduced threat of highway accidents would induce people to drive more often and longer distances and would enable goods and people to get to their destinations more quickly). As described in the preceding answer, the taxing and spending power also constitutes a constitutional basis for the legislation in question. (*See* ELO Ch.6-I(F).) Choices **A** and **B** are incorrect because, as described immediately above, ***both*** the spending and Commerce Clause support the legislation in question. Finally, Choice **D** is incorrect because the Tenth Amendment provides for the general reservation of powers in the states; the powers of Congress to regulate interstate commerce and to tax and spend for the general welfare override the general reservation.

108. **A**   If a state statute facially discriminates against out-of-state commerce or persons, it is invalid unless the jurisdiction can show (1) that an overriding benefit will accrue to it from the legislation, and (2) there is no less discriminatory alternative to achieve that interest; *Hughes v. Oklahoma*, 441 U.S. 322 (1979). The requirement that lawyers be graduates of Euphoria colleges and law schools burdens interstate commerce by discouraging out-of-state college and law school graduates from relocating to Euphoria. The governmental objective apparently sought to be accomplished by the statute could be accomplished in a less burdensome manner (i.e., by requiring all persons desiring to practice law to pass an appropriate Ethics examination and character analyis). (*See* ELO Ch.6-I(J)(3)(b).) Choice **B** is incorrect because the Privileges and Immunities Clause of the Fourteenth Amendment has been construed to pertain only to rights of national citizenship (i.e., the right to travel from state to state, to petition the federal government, etc.). The Privileges and Immunities Clause contained in Article IV, Section 2, of the U.S. Constitution would probably afford an additional basis for invalidating the Euphoria statute; *Hicklin v. Orbeck*, 437 U.S. 518 (1978) because the right to practice one's calling is a fundamental civil right which the states cannot infringe; however, that option is not raised by the choices offered. Choice **C** is incorrect because, while factually possible (the quality of out-of-state law schools could be inferior and the legislature might reasonably believe this), there are other ways to deal with the skill and integrity of out-of-state lawyers then to bar them altogether. Finally, Choice **D** is incorrect because the right to practice one's calling is a fundamental right protected by the Privileges and Immunities Clause of Article IV, Section 2.

109. **A**   Where there is a lack of purposeful discrimination or *animus* or hostility to a particular group, laws pertaining to social and economic matters are ordinarily reviewed under the *mere rationality* test (i.e., the legislation in question must be rationally related to a legitimate state objective). Although there is a disproportionately adverse effect upon Hispanics, there is no indication that the Goldcoast legislators sought to discriminate against this group. In fact, their actions were taken in response to a report indicating that life and property could be saved by the integration of metal slats into the homes in question. (*See* ELO Ch.10-II(A)(1) & III(C)(1).) Choice **B** is incorrect because strict scrutiny is ***not*** applicable (i.e., the law was not a deliberate act of hostility to, or an attempt to disadvantage, a particular minority). Choice **C** is incorrect because the fact that a law has a disproportionately adverse impact upon a particular group does not, *per se*, trigger a strict scrutiny review. The discrimination must be motivated by hostility or *animus*. Finally, Choice **D** is incorrect because the $1,200 cost necessary to comply with the law would probably ***not*** constitute an undue burden when measured against the anticipated benefit to life and property.

110. **C**   The Privileges and Immunities Clause contained in Article IV, Section 2, of the U.S. Constitution has been interpreted by the Supreme Court to preclude a state from discriminating against the citizens of other states with respect to the exercise of rights "fundamental to national unity." Among these are the right to be employed, to practice one's profession, and to engage in business. By requiring members of the Amityville Police Depart-

ment to live within that city, the Council has prevented the citizens of Peddle from working as police officers in Amityville. On these facts, there is no showing that residents of Peddle are peculiarly responsible for the complaints against the Amityville Police or that there is a "substantial relationship" between Amitville's problem and the proposed solution. (*See* ELO Ch.7-IV(B)(3)(a).) Choice **A** is incorrect because the Privileges and Immunities Clause of the Fourteenth Amendment applies only when a state attempts to curb a right of national citizenship (i.e., the right to travel from state to state, to petition federal officials, etc.). Choice **B** is incorrect because the U.S. Supreme Court has never held that there is a substantive due process right to practice a particular profession or trade. Finally, Choice **D** is essentially correct because the Contract Clause in Article I, Section 10, has been narrowly applied to require that a contract can be impaired only if the impairment is "reasonable and necessary to support an important public purpose" There is no showing that that test is met on these facts. However, Choice **C** is still the better choice because a court might hold that the three-year grace period was a justifiable concession to the contract rights of the Pebble residents.

111. **D** The determination whether to prosecute a case or not falls exclusively within the prerogatives of the executive branch. The U.S. Attorney General is appointed by the President and is entrusted with the President's authority to "take care that the Laws be faithfully executed;" Article II, Section 3. In the exercise of his descretion, he can determine that a particular case should not be prosecuted. (*See* ELO Ch.8-I(B) & (D).) Choice **C** is incorrect because the Attorney General is not entirely independent; he is subject to direction and removal by the President. Choice **A** is incorrect because the determination whether to prosecute particular conduct is exclusively executive in nature. The Senate cannot direct him to prosecute a particular case. Finally, Choice **B** is incorrect because, although it states in general terms one of the Attorney General's prime functions, it ignores the fact that he has discretion in particular cases.

112. **A** Under the "Necessary and Proper" Clause of the U.S. Constitution, Congress has the power to conduct investigations into matters with respect to which it may legislate; *McGrain v. Daugherty*, 276 U.S. 135 (1927). If Mr. Anthracite was questioned about matters which were clearly unrelated to an area in which Congress could legislate, he could refuse to answer. The nature of the inquiry here suggests that Congress was not interested in legislation. (*See* ELO Ch.3-II(B).) Choice **B** is legally incorrect (the House Committee could question Mr. Anthracite about any matter which could be the subject of legislation, not just with regard to the expenditure of funds). The powers of Congress extend beyond the expenditure of funds. Choice **C** is legally incorrect; the power of confirmation is immaterial to the right to conduct investigations (both chambers of the U.S. Congress have the right to conduct investigations into areas which might be the subject of legislation). Finally, Choice **D** is incorrect because Congress may ordinarily question executive officers about the performance of their duties. Such information could be helpful in determining if additional laws should be enacted. While there is a limited executive privilege to refuse to disclose

information which is confidential in nature, this privilege does not extend to all executive communications; *U.S. v. Nixon*, 418 U.S. 683 (1974).

113. **C**   At issue in this question is the impact of the Equal Protection Clause of the Fourteenth Amendment. The PUC rule has imposed an employment classification which must meet the requirements of the Clause. Although the Supreme Court's strict scrutiny standard is usually applicable where the job involved is one which is "bound up with the operation of the state as a governmental entity," the rule in this instance need only satisfy the "rational relationship" test; *Ambach v. Norwick*, 441 U.S. 68 (1979). Responding to emergency calls from the citizenry is a function which could rationally be construed as requiring the special knowledge of an American citizen who would typically be more able to understand and respond to the problem described by the caller. (*See* ELO) Ch.10-VI(C)(7).) Choice **B** is incorrect because the fact that Mary could respond adequately is irrelevant. The test is applied to the general classification, which is a reasonable one, not to the application of the classification to any individual. Choice **A** is intentionally deceptive: it constitutes a basis for validating the statute, not nullifying it. Finally, Choice **D** is incorrect because it states the standards required for strict scrutiny, not mere rationality; as discussed above, the rationality relationship test is applicable in this instance.

114. **D**   Article II, Section 2, of the U.S. Constitution assigns to the President, not the Congress, the power to appoint executive officials. Congress may, however, appoint persons to perform investigatory functions; *Buckley v. Valeo*, 424 U.S. 1 (1976). The authority given to the proposed Commission is essentially executive in nature and Congress cannot usurp the power to appoint its members. (*See* ELO Ch.8-III(B).) Choice **B** is legally incorrect. The scope of this legislation suggests an area that could properly be dealt with by Congress under the Commerce Clause (i.e., the more rationally crime in general is controlled, the greater the ability of people and goods to move freely from state to state). Choice **A** is incorrect because the Supreme Court has permitted Congress to delegate broad regulatory and quasi-legislative powers to an administrative agency under relatively imprecise standards. Finally, Choice **C** is incorrect because the facts as stated do not indicate that Congress intends to preclude citizens from attacking the proposed rules in the courts or in rule-making administrative proceedings.

115. **B**   Any activity (even though primarily intrastate) which, in the aggregate, could have a significant impact upon the movement of persons, information or goods across state lines, may be the subject of legislation under the Commerce Clause. Since transactions between lenders and borrowers have an effect upon the interstate movement of monies (i.e., loans are often made to home borrowers by banks in other states and construction materials often move across state lines), this legislation is valid under the Commerce Clause. The act in question is similar to one which was approved by the Supreme Court as a proper exercise under the Commerce Clause in *Perez v. United States*, 402 U.S. 146 (1971). (*See* ELO Ch.4-IV(G)(1).) Choice **C** is incorrect because the Equal Protection Clause of the Fourteenth Amendment contains restrictions upon state action and is not a basis for federal legislation. Choice **A** is incorrect because the Impairment of Contracts

Clause of Article I, Section 10 is also a restriction upon state action (i.e., it prevents the states from impairing obligations created under outstanding agreements), rather than a basis for the enactment of federal legislation. Finally, Choice **D** is incorrect because the Privileges and Immunities Clause of the Fourteenth Amendment prevents the states from impairing the rights of national citizenship (i.e., the right to travel from state to state, the right to petition representatives of the U.S. government, etc.). It is a limitation on state power, ***not*** a source of federal legislative power.

116. **B**   If state legislation places an undue burden upon interstate commerce (i.e., the local interest sought to be protected is outweighed by the federal interest in protecting interstate commerce from unnecessary local impediments), the legislation is unconstitutional. Except for the possibility that fewer domestic animals and monkeys will be imported into Euphoria for research purposes, the Euphoria enactment has virtually no effect upon interstate commerce. (*See* ELO Ch.6-I(F).) Choice **A** is incorrect because, as a consequence of the law, Tooledoo University has a number of animals which have suddenly become valueless to it, its interest in potentially valuable research has been terminated, and its contracts have been affected. It can be argued that its property has been taken without due process. Choice **D** is incorrect because the parties have executed a written contract, the object of which has been frustrated by the new law. Since the CIA had contracted with Tooledoo for the research in question, the Euphoria statute would appear to be unconstitutional under the Contract Clause of Article I, Section 10. Finally, Choice **C** is incorrect because it is reasonable to argue that Euphoria's new law is impeding a federal interest in the research project and is therefore violating the principles of federal supremacy.

117. **C**   A plaintiff must be able to show a direct and immediate personal injury or loss as a consequence of the state's action in order to have standing to challenge the action or its application in a federal court; *Allen v. Wright*, 468 U.S. 737 (1984). Or he must show that the statute in question is a "specific constitutional limitation" upon taxing and spending policies. His standing to challenge the application of this statute to his proposed speech is greatest as a member of the organization described. (*See* ELO Ch.16-III(C)(2) & (3)(d).) Choice **A** is incorrect because a politician must establish more than *an intent to run* before he has any standing as a candidate. Choice **B** is incorrect because the fact that Brighton had voted against the statute is irrelevant. No one is precluded from exercising his right to change or express his opinions. Finally, Choice **D** is incorrect because the status of taxpayer does not in and of itself confer standing to challenge the constitutionality of legislation.

118. **D**   Federal taxpayers have standing to contest spending measures made pursuant to the Taxing and Spending Clause which infringe upon specific constitutional provisions. However, in this situation: (1) the facts cited do not establish that the gift of land resulted directly from the statute or from any disbursement by Congress, and (2) the gift is justified under the Property Clause (Article IV, Section 3), rather than the Taxing and Spending Clause; *Valley Forge College v. American United*, 454 U.S. 464 (1982). (*See* ELO Ch.16-III(B)(2).) Choice **C** is not a likely result because the fact that federal

property is conveyed on a one-time basis does not shield the transaction from constitutional scrutiny. Choice **A** is not a likely result because the school's commitment could not be required as a condition of the gift; to impose such requirements would be to give the federal government the power to curb all religion. The issue of constitutionality would turn on other questions. Finally, Choice **B** is factually incorrect because federal agencies have the power to transfer property pursuant to the Property Clause cited above, even in the absence of a specific statutory authorization by Congress.

119.   **C**   A defendant may be punished for threatening violence against public officials *if* his threat is real, imminent and unconditional, rather than an expression of political hostility, impatience or resentment; *Watts v. U.S.*, 394 U.S. 705 (1969). While the statute appears constitutional on its face (a person can be punished for threatening real and imminent physical injury to a public official), it probably cannot be constitutionally applied to Mr. Blender in this instance. His remarks appear to suggest that he was simply venting his great frustration and displeasure with the legislation in question and had no immediate intent of inflicting harm upon his representative. (*See* ELO Ch.14-II(F)(5)(b).) Choice **A** is incorrect because the statute is probably not excessively vague. Choice **B** is incorrect for the same basic reason. Finally, Choice **D** is incorrect because, while the statute may be constitutional, it cannot be applied to Mr. Blender because there was no genuine threat of imminent injury to the legislator.

TABLE OF CASES

INDEX

References are to the number of the question raising the issue.
"E" indicates an Essay Question; "M" indicates a Multiple-Choice Question

Products for 1998-99 Academic Year

emanuel®

Emanuel Law Outlines

Steve Emanuel's Outlines have been the most popular in the country for years. Over twenty years of graduates swear by them. In the 1997–98 school year, law students bought an average of 3.0 Emanuels each – that's 130,000 Emanuels.

Civil Procedure ◆	$18.95
Constitutional Law	23.95
Contracts ◆	17.95
Corporations	18.95
Criminal Law ◆	14.95
Criminal Procedure	15.95
Evidence	17.95
Property ◆	17.95
Secured Transactions	14.95
Torts (General Ed.) ◆	17.95
Torts (Prosser Casebook Ed.)	17.95
Keyed to '94 Ed. Prosser, Wade & Schwartz	

Special Offer…First Year Set

All outlines marked ◆ *plus* Steve Emanuel's 1st Year Q & A's *plus* Strategies & Tactics for the First Year Law Student. Everything you need to make it through your first year. $97.50

Lazar Emanuel's *Latin for Lawyers*

A complete glossary and dictionary to help you wade through the complex terminology of the law.

New title   *$15.95*

The Professor Series

All titles in these series are written by leading law professors. Each follows the Emanuel style and format. Each has big, easy-to-read type; extensive citations and notes; and clear, crisp writing. Most have capsule summaries and sample exam Q & A's.

Agency & Partnership	$15.95
Bankruptcy	15.95
Environmental Law	15.95
Family Law	15.95
Federal Income Taxation	15.95
Intellectual Property	17.95
International Law	16.95
Labor Law	15.95
Negotiable Instruments & Payment Systems	14.95
Products Liability	13.95
Professional Responsibility (*new title*)	17.95
Property (*new title*)	17.95
Torts	13.95
Wills & Trusts	15.95

Question & Answer Collections

Siegel's Essay & Multiple–Choice Q & A's

Each book contains 20 to 25 essay questions with model answers, plus 90 to 110 Multistate-style multiple-choice Q & A's. The objective is to acquaint the student with the techniques needed to handle law school exams successfully. Titles are:

Civil Procedure ◆	Evidence
Constitutional Law	Professional Responsibility
Contracts ◆	Property ◆
Corporations	Torts ◆
Criminal Law ◆	Wills & Trusts
Criminal Procedure	

Each title   *$15.95*

The Finz Multistate Method

967 MBE (Multistate Bar Exam)–style multiple choice questions and answers for all six Multistate subjects, each with detailed answers – *plus* a complete 200 question practice exam modeled on the MBE. Perfect for law school and *bar exam* review.

$33.95

Steve Emanuel's First Year Q&A's

1,144 objective–style short-answer questions with detailed answers, in first year subjects. A single volume covers Civil Procedure, Contracts, Criminal Law, Criminal Procedure, Property, and Torts.

$18.95

Siegel's First Year Set - All titles marked ◆, at a discounted price.

$79.95 if purchased separately   *$59.95*

For any titles not available at your local bookstore, call us at 1-800-EMANUEL or order on-line at **http://www.emanuel.com**. Visa, MasterCard, American Express, and Discover accepted.

Law In A Flash Flashcards

Flashcards

Civil Procedure 1 ◆	$16.95
Civil Procedure 2 ◆	16.95
Constitutional Law ▲	16.95
Contracts ◆▲	16.95
Corporations	16.95
Criminal Law ◆▲	16.95
Criminal Procedure ▲	16.95
Evidence ▲	16.95
Future Interests ▲	16.95
Professional Responsibility (953 cards)	32.95
Real Property ◆▲	16.95
Sales (UCC Article 2) ▲	16.95
Torts ◆▲	16.95
Wills & Trusts	16.95

Flashcard Sets

First Year Law Set	95.00

(includes all sets marked ◆ *plus* the book
Strategies & Tactics for First Year Law.)

Multistate Bar Review Set	165.00

(includes all sets marked ▲ *plus* the book
Strategies & Tactics for MBE)

Law In A Flash Software

(for Windows® 3.1 and Windows® 95 only)

- Contains the complete text of the corresponding *Law In A Flash* printed flashcards
- Side-by-side comparison of your own answer to the card's preformulated answer
- Fully customizable, savable sessions – pick which topics to review and in what order
- Mark cards for further review or printing

Every *Law In A Flash* title and set is available as software.

Requirements: 386, 486, or Pentium-based computer running Windows® 3.1, Windows® 95, or Windows® 98; 16 megabytes RAM; 3.5" high-density floppy drive; 3MB free space per title

Individual titles	$19.95
Professional Responsibility (covers 953 cards)	34.95
First Year Law Set*	115.00
Multistate Bar Review Set*	195.00

* These software sets contain the same titles as printed card sets *plus* the corresponding *Strategies & Tactics* books (see below).

Law In A Flash Combo Packs

Flashcards + software, together at a substantial saving.

Individual titles in combo packs	$29.95
Professional Responsibility combo pack	46.95

(Sorry, LIAF Combo packs are not available in sets.)

Strategies & Tactics Series

Strategies & Tactics for the MBE

Packed with the most valuable advice you can find on how to successfully attack the MBE. Each MBE subject is covered, including Criminal Procedure (part of Criminal Law), Future Interests (part of Real Property), and Sales (part of Contracts). The book contains 350 actual past MBE questions broken down by subject, plus a full-length 200-question practice MBE. Each question has a *fully-detailed answer* which describes in detail not only why the correct answer is correct, but why each of the wrong answer choices is wrong. Covers the MBE specifications tested on and after July, 1997.

$34.95

Strategies & Tactics for the First Year Law Student

A complete guide to your first year of law school, from the first day of class to studying for exams. Packed with the inside information that will help you survive what most consider the worst year of law school and come out on top.

$12.95

Strategies & Tactics for the MPRE

Packed with exam tactics that help lead you to the right answers and expert advice on spotting and avoiding the traps set by the Bar Examiners. Contains actual questions from past MPRE's, with detailed answers.

$19.95

simplicity

LEXIS-NEXIS

Is Now

www.lexis-nexis.com/lawschool

- No software to load!
- Access from anywhere – at any time!
- An easier-to-use graphical interface!

Bookmark us today.